The Languages of
Political Islam

# THE LANGUAGES OF POLITICAL ISLAM

## India 1200–1800

MUZAFFAR ALAM

The University of Chicago Press

Muzaffar Alam is professor in the departments of South Asian Languages and Civilizations and History at the University of Chicago. Previously he taught for three decades at Jawaharlal Nehru University in New Delhi. His publications include *The Crisis of Empire in Mughal North India, 1707–1748*; *The Mughal State, 1526–1750*; and most recently, with Seema Alavi, *A European Experience of the Mughal Orient.*

The University of Chicago Press, Chicago 60637
C. Hurst & Co., Ltd., London WC2E 8JZ
Permanent Black, Delhi 110092



13 12 11 10 09 08 07 06 05 04     1 2 3 4 5

ISBN: 0-226-01100-3 (cloth)
ISBN: 0-226-01101-1 (paper)

**Library of Congress Cataloging-in-Publication Data**

Alam, Muzaffar, 1947–
The languages of political Islam : India 1200–1800 / Muzaffar Alam.
p. cm.
Originally published: Delhi : Permanent Black, 2004.
Includes bibliographical references and index.
ISBN 0-226-01100-3 (cloth : alk. paper)—ISBN 0-226-01101-1 (pbk. : alk. paper)
1. Islam—India—History. 2. Islam and politics—India—History. 3. Persian language—Political aspects—India. 4. India—Politics and government—997–1765. 5. India—Politics and government—18th century. 6. Sufism—India—History. 7. Islamic law—India—History. I. Title.

BP63.I4A64 2004
297.2'72'0954—dc22     2004047979

♾ The paper used in this publication meets the minimum requirements of the American National Standard for Information Sciences—Permanence of Paper for Printed Library Materials, ANSI Z39.48-1992.

For
Rizwana, Adnan and Asiya

# Contents

# Preface

This book has germinated out of the S.G. Deuskar Memorial Lectures which I delivered at the Centre for Studies in Social Sciences, Kolkata, in December 1996. When invited by the Centre's Director, Professor Amiya Bagchi, to deliver those lectures, I was engaged in research concerning the nature of a putative 'composite culture' in medieval India which would avoid excessive emphasis on subjects such as Sufism, which are normally treated as central to any such discussion. I had in fact, in certain earlier works, attempted to show that the role of the medieval state, rather than that of the Sufi orders, was crucial in bringing together some of medieval India's major communities. By this means I had tried to nuance the standard understanding of the place of Sufis within areas such as eighteenth-century Awadh.

From this point of departure, it seemed logical to go beyond questions about administrative intervention by the state and to look more closely at the constitution of ideology in medieval north India's Muslim states, with a view to understanding their relations with the wider world of Iran and Central Asia. I therefore began to look at the rich but, in the Indian context somewhat under-studied, textual tradition of treatises on political ethics and political culture within this broad area. I quickly realized that a very radical change had come about in this tradition, within the worlds of eastern Islam, during the course of the move from the use of Arabic to the use of Persian.

The present work is made up, thus, of two related reflections, both located in the context of Islam in the Indian subcontinent. One centres largely on the issue of political thought and ethical treatises (sometimes assimilated in the so-called 'Mirror of Princes' tradition). The second is mainly preoccupied with understanding the role played by the Persian language in defining the political culture of the Mughals. In this way, if one part of this book is focused on the language of politics, the other complements it by looking at the politics of language.

To expand a little on the above: I have tried to discuss the ways in which political Islam adjusted itself to Indian traditions, from the time of its first establishment to the decline of Muslim power in the subcontinent. I suggest that the idea and meaning of political Islam changed alongside the process and experience of rulers of this persuasion actually finding themselves wielding power in north India. Many of the rulers as well as a large number of the political theorists of these centuries clearly suggest the view that, for successful Islamic rule within a region predominantly non-Muslim, the originary language and traditions of Islam cannot escape modification. Theory, orthodoxy and fundamentalist positions are thus questioned by actual practice in new contexts, and it is in fact common knowledge that Muslim political power in India developed forms of governance that were all its own. As importantly, the vocabulary of this new governance underwent significant transformation. Deploying a variety of medieval sources—normative treatises, Sufi texts, collections of *belles-lettres*—I have attempted here to illustrate how the Indian experience of political Islam maintains continuities as well as differences with Islamic power elsewhere.

No singular tradition emerges from these texts, nor from the cultural practices of the subcontinent's Muslims. We see, rather, a series of efforts to contest cultural and political traditions within the internal framework of Muslim power and social practice. Many scholars have contributed to our present understanding of the economic, political, and cultural facets of this period, but I believe few have attempted to integrate them in order to provide an understanding of the connection between the ideals and actual practices of Muslim politics. This book is an attempt in that direction: it seeks to pull into one narrative aspects of the subcontinent's medieval Islamic politics and language, its ideals and multiple realities, which have hitherto been treated as discrete. The book thus also seeks to contribute to contemporary debates concerning the relationship between, on the one hand, normative and textual Islam, and, on the other, changing social and political practices.

In the end, I remain acutely aware of the limitations of my work. I believe its purpose will be more than served if scholars younger than myself use it as a springboard to examine with greater depth and scholarship the issues I have attempted to raise within it.

Some parts of this book have appeared earlier, in varying forms and formats, some as independent essays deriving from my participation in various seminars within India and elsewhere. That patchwork has yielded this new form, a book which, I believe, reveals that the issues treated within it have an internal logic and coherence which goes well beyond the sum of its many, and sometimes fragmented, parts. I had, initially, hoped to add another chapter to this book—on the place of Sufism (particularly with reference to the sixteenth, seventeenth and eighteenth centuries), but was eventually persuaded that that perhaps merits a book in its own right. Areas of this book will be visible in one form or the other in *Tradition, Dissent and Ideology*, ed. R. Champakalakshmi and S. Gopal (Delhi: Oxford University Press, 1996); *Modern Asian Studies*, 32, 1998; *The Making of the Indo-Persian Culture*, ed. M. Alam, F. Delvoye, and M. Gaborieau (Delhi: Manohar, 2000); *Beyond Turk and Hindu*, ed. David Gilmartin and Bruce Lawrence (Gainesville: University Press of Florida, 2000); *Literary Cultures in History*, ed. Sheldon Pollock (Berkeley: University of California Press, 2003).

As regards the spelling and translation of Perso-Arabic words, I have generally followed the system adopted by F. Steingass in his *Comprehensive Persian–English Dictionary*. I have, however, diverged from Steingass when transliterating word combinations and compounds. I have preferred to put a hyphen (-) between the first word and the letter 'i', indicating its combination with the second word. In Perso-Arabic combinations, the Arabic definite article has been consistently written as 'al'. I have thus written *sulh-i kull*, Nizam al-Din and Abd al-Rahman, while Steingass would have transcribed them as *sulhi kull*, Nizamu'd din and Abdu'r rahman.

It is difficult to properly acknowledge the many debts I owe a large number of friends and colleagues who have helped me in the making of this book. It is with pleasure that I thank Professor Amiya Bagchi, who first invited me to deliver the Deuskar Memorial Lectures, which allowed the first formulation of my thoughts. Partha Chatterjee, the Centre's present Director, encouraged me to remedy my excessive immersion in the oral tradition and transcribe the spoken words I regularly inflicted on him into their present, written form.

I must acknowledge in particular the institutions which have supported my ongoing research: work on this book began in 1994 with readings in some materials available in the Bibliothèque Nationale, Paris. It developed further in the spring of that year when I visited the Centre of Non-European Studies, University of Leiden, at the invitation of the Director of the Centre, D.H.A. Kolff. A Charles Wallace funding in the same year enabled me to consult some unpublished Persian materials in England. Wissenschaftskolleg zu Berlin (Institute of Advanced Study, Berlin) provided me with the occasion to work on the relevant Persian manuscripts in the Staatsbibliothek, Berlin, and to rethink and discuss the subject of this book with a diverse group of colleagues: I am particularly grateful for comments to Sanjay Subrahmanyam, who read the entire manuscript, was generous with his time whenever I needed to discuss matters, and made valuable suggestions which resulted in more cogent rearticulations of many of my positions. David Shulman and Velcheru Narayana Rao provided an intellectually stimulating environment in Berlin and urged me to connect my thoughts with developments in the wider Islamic world.

After arriving at the University of Chicago in 2001, my conversations with colleagues: Dipesh Chakrabarty, Cornell Fleischer,

C.M. Naim, Sheldon Pollock and John Woods, as well as students: Alyssa Ayres and Rajeev Kinra, contributed to the expansion and further refinement of this work. I am also grateful for comments by participants in seminars at the Franke Institute for the Humanities, Chicago; St Antony's College, Oxford; the Department of Asian Studies, University of Texas at Austin; and the Department of History, Yale University.

Closer home, Seema Alavi, Neeladri Bhattacharya, Kunal Chakrabarti, Sunil Kumar, Romila Thapar and Ishtiyaq Ahmad Zilli were, as ever, generous with help and advice. Ishtiyaq Sahib was also kind in facilitating my access to some valuable manuscripts in Aligarh. I am obliged to my colleagues and students at the Centre for Historical Studies, Jawaharlal Nehru University, for their cooperation and for several illuminating discussions on medieval Indian politics and culture. Several other friends have been helpful in many ways. I must mention, among them, Raziuddin Aquil, C.A. Bayly, Gautam Bhadra, Meena Bhargava, Barun De, Simon Digby, Mike Fisher, Marc Gaborieau, Jos Gommans, Pankaj Jha, Sudipta Kaviraj, Meenakshi Khanna, Rajeev Kinra, Bruce Lawrence, Harbans Mukhia, Fozail A. Qadri, Francis Richard, John Richards, Francis Robinson, Nilanjan Sarkar, Sunil Sharma, Yogesh Sharma, Dilbagh Singh, Mohamad Tavakoli-Targhi, T. Robert Traverse and Madhu and Kirti Trivedi. I recall with thanks the help I received from Dr W.H. Siddiqi and his colleagues for my research in the Raza Library, Rampur. Dr Siddiqi was kind enough to allow me to use a painting from the library for the book jacket.

As regards my editors and publishers, I must thank Rukun Advani of Permanent Black, David Brent of The University of Chicago Press, and Michael Dwyer of C. Hurst & Co. for their support and encouragement. I appreciate, in particular, the meticulousness and patience with which Rukun edited this book.

I have no appropriate words to express my debt to Rizwana, Adnan and Asiya. Their love and affection have been the mainstay of this work, and much more, over the years. It is to them that this book is lovingly dedicated.

CHAPTER 1

# Introduction

What is the political culture of Islam? Has it been static throughout history? Have Muslims always ruled by the sword, or did they also evolve strategies of cultural accommodation in the lands where they spread their faith and established their power? If we assume the latter, then were these strategies simply the result of a banal pragmatism, or can we also find evidence of an intellectual—even moral—transformation resulting from such accommodation? In other words, is there historical evidence of a *political* Islam quite different from that projected by today's Islamist radicals?

This book is an attempt to understand these questions in the context of Islam in northern India from the thirteenth to the eighteenth centuries, the peak of Islamic power in the region. Islam entered the Indian subcontinent soon after its appearance in Arabia, as attested by seventh-century interactions between Arab traders—then newly converted to Islam—with their Indian business partners and wives across the Indian Ocean, along the Malabar coast. The eighth century, with the Arab invasion of Sindh, brought political Islam to the northern part of the subcontinent. From the eleventh century, following changes in Islam in the Perso-Turkic world and the expansions of the Ghaznavids, a significant part of northern India was incorporated into the Ghaznavid empire. Islamic power grew further with the establishment of the Delhi Sultanate in the twelfth century, and reached its zenith with the Mughals from the sixteenth century through the middle of the eighteenth century, until the Mughals began to be unseated by regional powers and the British. Yet Muslim power and culture continued to flourish in several regions for a long time to come. In the history of political Islam, the Indian subcontinent thus occupies a major position—in terms of geographic spread as well as duration.

My study focuses in particular on a body of materials produced in India and elsewhere in the Perso-Islamic world. This is a deliberate choice, my view being that, in order to better understand developments in the political vocabulary and syntax of this period, it is necessary to look at such materials not in isolation but in their wider context of circulation, which in this case was not Arabia as much as Iran and Central Asia.

The word 'vocabulary' has been used here in a very broad sense. I analyse certain key words connected with the politics of Islamic rule in India, but I do not propose to delineate in detail the philological meanings and significations of these words. Muslim writers used certain terms to denote, for instance, authority, power, state, governance, obedience, resistance, ruler, ruled, victory, defeat, war, and peace. These terms are important, and have been so noted, in considerable depth, by Bernard Lewis in the context of the larger Islamic world.[1] In this book, however, I argue that even in the usages of these key terms there was no continuity or singularity of meaning from medieval times to the present. The word '*sulṭān*', for instance, referred specifically to the ruler and denoted royal power in the larger Islamic world, as well as in India in the pre-Mughal context. And yet this word had become so common in eighteenth-century Mughal India that its meaning had expanded, or rather degenerated into denoting even cousins, distant cousins, and nephews of the reigning monarch—that is to say, even those with no plausible pretensions to power. The word was no longer used, on the other hand, to refer even to the direct descendant of the ruler, who was instead known as the *shāh-ẕāda* or *pādshāh-ẕāda*.

Or, for that matter, take Lahore. Though Lahore was only the capital of a Mughal province, it has almost invariably been mentioned

[1] Bernard Lewis, *The Political Language of Islam*, Chicago, 1988.

in Mughal chronicles as *dār al salṭanat* (abode of the Sultanate). Yet the governor of this province would never go so far as to assume the title of '*sulṭān*', not even in the days when he had acquired a measure of autonomy.[2]

My general argument thus centres on the idea that the deeper meaning and content of the political and religious vocabulary in use changed significantly in the Indian context; further, these changes are, in this region's context, often best understood as part of a longer-term evolution which entails understanding the pre-history of their usages outside South Asia. I shall also try to indicate the extent to which the rhythms of change in the long run were affected by the South Asian context: in other words, with what rapidity did a Perso-Islamic polity become Indianized in its conceptions, and, if there were indeed limits to this process, from where did these limits spring?

It goes more or less without saying that it is futile to speak in the north Indian context of a 'pure' Islam which became 'alloyed' simply by its contact with Indian religious practices and notions. Even before arriving in India, Islam was already in good measure an alloy, so to speak, both at the popular and even at the higher (say, theological) level, having incorporated major elements of pre-Islamic Persian concepts into itself.[3] In fact, the situation in India is a little paradoxical in this respect, for while popular Islam saw tremendous changes and adaptations, such does not seem to have been the case with élite Islam: the latter, in many instances, kept very considerable continuities with its Perso-Turkic precedents. There is, however, a

[2] Cf. Mirza Zahir al-Din Ali Bakht Azfari, *Wāqi'āt-i Azfarī*, ed. T. Chandreshekharan and Saiyid Hamza Husain Umari, Madras, 1957; Muhammad Qasim 'Ibrat Lahori, *'Ibrat-nāma*, ed. Zuhuruddin Ahmad, Lahore, 1977, for instance pp. 8, 9, 10, 15, 23.

[3] For a recent discussion on this issue, see Ehsan Yarshater, 'Persian Presence in the Islamic World', in *The Persian Presence in the Islamic World*, eds Richard G. Hovannisian and Georges Sabagh, Cambridge, 1998, pp. 4–125. See also Robert L. Canfield, ed., *Turko-Persia in Historic Perspective*, Cambridge, 1991.

fruitful space to be explored between a process characterized as 'alloying' (or structural modification), and a more limited process that we can term 'accommodation', for the sake of convenience. This may be on account of the dynamism and resilience of the Perso-Turkic tradition, a tradition that had by no means exhausted its creative energies before entering the Indian sphere. It is significant that many Turko-Persian institutions were adopted even by those 'Hindu' states that came up as a result of resistance against the Muslim rulers.[4] We can see here, perhaps, the work of a section of Indian elites who may have preferred a non-confrontational attitude implied by processes of 'accommodation'. These changes also reflected the dynamism of plural traditions that evolved together in the wake of changing socio-economic conditions in Central and Western Asia, as well as in India.

The book addresses, primarily, issues pertaining to élite Islam in north India. It must be admitted that an examination of changes in popular Islam would have been of enormous value for our purposes. There is need for much more research on changes in popular Islam, specially in relation to Islam's interaction with local non-Islamic religious and cultural traditions.[5] What is suggested here, then, is a history of ideas anchored firmly in social history, and within which

[4] Cf. for instance Phillip B. Wagoner, 'Harihar, Bukka, and the Sultan: The Delhi Sultanate in the Imagination of Vijayanagar', in David Gilmartin and Bruce B. Lawrence, eds, *Beyond Turk and Hindu: Rethinking Religious Identities in Islamicate South Asia*, Gainesville, Florida, 2000, pp. 300–26; Stewart Gordon, *The Marathas 1600–1818*, Cambridge, 1993.

[5] For some recent works in this direction, see Tony K. Stewart, 'Alternative Structures of Authority: Satya Pir on the Frontiers of Bengal', Christopher Shackle, 'Beyond Turk and Hindu: Crossing the Boundaries in Indo-Muslim Romance', and Vasudha Narayan, 'Religious Vocabulary and Religious Identity: A Study of the Tamil *Cirappuranam*', in David Gilmartin and Bruce B. Lawrence, eds, *Beyond Turk and Hindu*, pp. 21–97; David Shulman and Sanjay Subrahmanyam, 'Prince of Poets and Ports: Citakkati, the Maraikkayars and Ramnad, *ca.* 1690–1710', in A.L. Dallapiccola and S. Zingel-Ave Lallemant, eds, *Islam and Indian Religions*, vol. 1, Stuttgart, 1992, pp. 497–535. See also Aditya Behl, 'Rasa and Romance: The *Madhumalati* of Shaikh Manjhan Shattari', Ph.D. thesis, University of Chicago, 1995; Shantanu Phukan, 'Through a Persian

the different intellectual positions that are set out correspond to various tensions provoked by the clash of interests within society—though I do not mean to imply that each ideological position corresponds simply to the expression of a given social interest. On the contrary, it is particularly rewarding to see how the expression of various, and often conflicting, group identities allows the existence of a notion of a sort of 'body politic' in which different groups participate as a collective.

Since these questions are very large ones, it seemed necessary to me to limit the corpus of texts from which they would be treated within a relatively modest history, such as the present one. I have therefore chosen here to focus in particular on the three areas within which the multiple idioms of Indo-Islamic politics between the thirteenth and the eighteenth centuries become clear: namely, law (that is *sharī'a*, but defined—as we shall see—rather broadly); *taṣawwuf* (that is, Sufi ideology and practice); and language.

By law, what is meant here is not the quotidian use of legal arguments in urban or rural contexts (an important issue in its own right), but rather a notion of law as *norms*, such norms being also seen as constituting and governing the political and social field. In the vocabulary of the period, this requires us to focus on the term *sharī'a*, which has also been much discussed in other historical contexts. The Muslim sultans of India attempted, in their own limited ways, to resolve problems that related to the compatibility of the *sharī'a* with their political actions. But the ambivalence continued, and even regional sultans during the fifteenth century had to turn to the *sharī'a* to legitimate their political acts. For a politically amenable interpretation of the *sharī'a* in 1579, even Akbar sought the approval of the *'ulamā'*. Towards the last phase of Akbar's reign, however—and in the seventeenth and eighteenth centuries under the Mughal regime—the *sharī'a* no longer occupied a central place in political discourse.

---

Prism: Hindi and *Padmavat* in the Mughal Imagination', Ph.D. thesis, University of Chicago, 2000; Romila Thapar, *Somanatha: The Many Voices of History*, Delhi, 2004, pp. 145–67.

What explains this shift? I would suggest that three different pressures were at work. First, the mythic code of normative behaviour among the Mughals—the *Tūra-i Chengīzī* or *Yāsā-i Chengīzī*[6]—weakened the determining role of the *sharī'a*. This customary code, whose lineage the Timurids traced to Chengiz Khan, was often invoked to legitimate the political practices of rulers and the everyday life of people. Second, the imperatives of nomadic life made strict adherence to the *sharī'a* difficult and impractical. Third, there was a process of questioning and self-reflection within Islam in the wake of the Mongol invasions of the Islamic East in the early thirteenth century. The annihilation of Islamic power by a pagan ruler destroyed the unquestioning confidence in existing Islamic orthodoxy.

This self-questioning can be seen among the Sufis as well. It is in the post-Mongol era that the Sufi intervention in politics becomes more manifest. In discussing *taṣawwuf* my focus, as we will see in the third chapter, will not simply be on Sufism as a mechanism for incorporating Indic influence into Islam, but on how, in the course of these incorporative attempts, a deliberate Sufi intervention arises in politics as Sufis attempt to define the direction of political processes in India. Sufism has been defined in various ways: for our purposes here, Sufism is an assertion of the right of the individual to experiment with Islamic religious truth, even if such experimentation is independent of the *sharī'a*. Initially, Sufis were individual wanderers and marginal people who claimed no allegiance to a well-defined set of regulations. But in the course of time, as has been spelt out by a number of historians of Sufism, there was a coalescence—first of groups (*ṭā'ifa*) and then of orders (*ṭarīqa*).[7] In the post-Mongol period we see another level of transformation: Sufis

[6] For a comprehensive discussion on the *Yāsā* of Chengiz Khan, see David Ayalon's articles in *Studia Islamica*, 33 and 34 (1971); 36 (1972); and 38 (1973), pp. 97–8, 99–140, 151–80, 113–58, and 107–56, reproduced in *idem, Outsiders in the Lands of Islam: Mamluks, Mongols, and Eunuchs*, London, 1988, chaps IVa, IVb, IVc, and IVd.

[7] Compare J.S. Trimingham, *The Sufi Orders in Islam*, Oxford, 1971, chaps 1–3; for definitions of Sufism and its historical developments, see Annemarie

now see the need to intervene in politics, and, more than that, there is an attempt in the Sufi world to appropriate and portray the political course as being shaped and determined by Sufi masters. These two levels of change within Sufism can be seen in India by the time of the compilation of Nizam-al-Din Auliya's conversations in the *Fawā'id al-Fu'ād*.

Underlying all this is a series of tensions in the trajectory of political Islam which also had a close bearing on the course of its history in the subcontinent. One of these tensions is to be found in the historical contradiction—starting from early Islamic history—between the claims of 'Ajam (the Persian world, broadly speaking) and that of the Arabs. 'Ajam, from the very beginning, refused to accept the Arabs as their masters—the military and political superiority of the latter notwithstanding. Proud of their Perso-Islamic past, the vanquished people of 'Ajam struggled to offset their military defeat at the hands of the Arabs by clinging stubbornly to their own culture, and by vigorously reviving their language, literary traditions and social practices. The result was a long-drawn-out movement—*shu-'ūbiya* and *mawālī*—which culminated in the overthrow of Arabic in favour of Persian as the language of power.

A second tension is to be seen from the time of the rise of the Mongols, who both literally shatter Muslim power as well as pose vast conceptual problems with which later centuries must grapple. The 'detours' of Islam, which include Sufism and the language of politics in India in the medieval period, should be seen in this context.

I address these issues primarily out of materials in Persian, the most significant language of political—and even perhaps cultural—discourse in the Indo-Islamic context of the period. This central role played by Persian cannot, however, be simply seen as 'natural', and I shall also be concerned to demonstrate how and why it came to play the role it did in the discussions of our epoch.

The *sharī'a* occupied a significant position in medieval Islamic

---

Schimmel, *Mystical Dimensions of Islam*, Chapel Hill, NC, 1975, chaps 1–2, pp. 3–97.

political formations, and therefore it must be given due consideration in any serious discussion on Indo-Islamic politics too. However, it seems to me that several historians use the term only in its juristic sense, and thus overlook the import and implications of the varieties of its use in non-juridical literature. The result is that an important context is left out when the rigidity and bigotry associated with *sharī'a* are highlighted. We encounter this problem in both the so-called 'secular' as well as in communal writings on medieval and early modern India. We know that even in juristic *sharī'a* there was, and is, a measure of flexibility. The consensus of Muslim jurists and divines over the significance of diversity (*ikhtilāf*) in the readings of the Prophetic traditions led to the emergence of more than one school in jurisprudence (*fiqh*) and scholasticism (*kalām*). Above all there is clear evidence of the juristic recognition and legitimation of diversity within Islamic schools. This is illustrated by the institution of *fatwā*, which was intended to create a space for interpretation and the enforcement of a juristic position in diverse contexts.

As a matter of fact, much of the rigidity in the *sharī'a* in South Asia begins with the colonial period, following the codifications effected under the aegis of early British rulers. East India Company officials often felt uncomfortable with the interventions of traditional *qāẓī*s and *muftī*s in civil and criminal matters. They attributed the variety and flexibility in indigenous styles of pronouncing judgment to what they called the 'culpable bias' of these *muftī*s and *qāẓī*s. To them, the latter's discretion emanated from a lack of 'integrity' in the natives. They thought that considerations in the *sharī'a* for the prevailing local customs and social practices created an uncalled-for space of 'arbitrariness'. They thus felt that there should be a fixed code, authoritative and authentic, based on original legal texts, with which they intended to counter the interference of native *maulavi*s. Thus emerged a condition which nurtured the assumption that authority rested only within texts selected at their behest.[8]

[8] Muhammad Qasim Zaman, *The Ulama in Contemporary Islam: Custodians*

Another factor which reinforced this impression of rigidity and resistance to change with reference to *sharī'a* has been the understanding that there was no possibility or space left for innovations in *sharī'a* after the first centuries of Islam. This is something which pertains to what has come to be known as 'the closure of the gate of *ijtihād*', a view which began with Joseph Schacht's studies of the history of Islamic law.[9] This view has already been convincingly called into question,[10] and for such questioning there is some evidence, as we will see later, from Mughal India as well.

However, I am not concerned here with the resilience and tolerance that jurists themselves demonstrate in the enforcement of *sharī'a*. Such resilience, we know, remained confined within the accepted ambit of the four juridical principles, namely, the Qur'an; the traditions of the Prophet (*ḥadīṣ*); the consensus among the *'ulama'* and the jurists (*ijmā'*); and analogy (*qiyās*) often extending

---

*of Change*, Princeton, 2002, pp. 21–7; Ayesha Jalal, *Self and Sovereignty: Individual and Community in South Asian Islam since 1850*, London, 2000, pp. 139–53, and also pp. 153–86 for a discussion on how colonial manoeuvres in the legal domain promoted conditions for a new Muslim identity. See also J.D.M. Derrett, *Religion, Law, and State in India*, London, 1968, pp. 229ff for a discussion on similar problems with reference to Hindu law and *dharmashastra*; Radhika Singha, *A Despotism of Law: Crime and Justice in Early Colonial India*, Delhi, 1998, pp. 1–35, for a discussion on the problem of 'Rule of Law' and judicial discretion with reference to criminal law; David Gilmartin, 'Customary Law and *Shari'at* in British Punjab', in Katherine P. Ewing, ed., *Shari'at and Ambiguity in South Asian Islam*, Berkeley, 1988, pp. 43–62.

[9] Joseph Schacht, *An Introduction to Islamic Law*, Oxford, 1964, in particular pp. 69–75.

[10] Wael B. Hallaq, 'Was the Gate of *Ijtihād* Closed?' *International Journal of Middle Eastern Studies*, 16 (1984), pp. 3–41, and 'On the Origins of the Controversy about the Existence of *Mujtahids* and the Gate of *Ijtihād*', *Studia Islamica*, 63 (1986), pp. 129–41, reproduced in *idem, Law and Legal Theory in Classical and Medieval Islam*, London, 1995, chaps V and VI. See also his *Authority, Continuity, and Change in Islamic Law*, Cambridge, 2001, pp. 166–235; and Baber Johansen, *Contingency in a Sacred Law: Legal and Ethical Norms in the Muslim Fiqh*, Leiden, 1999.

within the boundaries of the known schools of jurisprudence.[11] Changes were to be with reference to the authority of their earlier masters. Further, while jurists tolerated a non-*sharī'a* act, they simultaneously regarded it as an offence and suggested its expiation (*kaffāra*).

I have in mind, rather, the sense in which Muslim philosophers and intellectuals used the term *sharī'a* in their politico-cultural writings. Some of these, even when they initially formed part of a literature of dissent, were gradually integrated into the larger body of Islamic literature. Thus, like the *sharī'a* of the jurists, the *sharī'a* of these philosophers and intellectuals deserves equal notice for a truer appreciation of premodern Muslim politics. For when we use the term in its juridical sense alone, we emphasize the validity of an uncompromising and fixed meaning and concede the ground entirely to that meaning of the term. As a consequence, the legitimacy or illegitimacy of a political act tends to be explained in the light of religion, i.e. as either religious or irreligious. The *sharī'a*, it is true, did occupy a significant position in medieval Indian Muslim politics, but we need to clearly recognize that the term did not carry the same meaning in every context.

In some political writings, e.g. the *Fatāwa-i Jahāndārī* of Ziya al-Din Barani (the noted fourteenth-century historian and political theorist), state legislation or *ẓawābiṭ* was seen as totally opposed to the *sharī'a*. Yet state legislation was here countenanced on the basis of pragmatism: for Barani the vicissitudes of the time required this secular intervention of legislation for the preservation of the Muslim community. On the other hand, in the literature produced in the Persian world, e.g. in the *Akhlāq-i Nāṣirī* of Nasir al-Din Tusi (in the post-Mongol period), there was no such compromise. State

[11] These were the four sources of law that Muslim jurists recognized as the foundation of the *sharī'a*. By the tenth century they had reached such rigour in interpretation that, according to one author, the text was sovereign. See Schacht, *An Introduction to Islamic Law*, pp. 60 and 114–15; Wael B. Hallaq, *A History of Islamic Legal Theories*, Cambridge, 1997, pp. 1–124 for a reformulated discussion of the early phases of the formation and articulation of Islamic legal theory.

legislation was not necessarily a contravention of the *sharī'a*. In fact, here the distinction between 'secular' and *sharī'a* regulations merged into a grey area. These two traditions of writing thus use *sharī'a* in different senses. While one is largely within the ambit of the theological meaning of the term, the other is a distinct deviation from the theological or orthodox position. I will discuss these two sets of political writings in the second chapter with a view to understand the principles—and also something of the practice—of governance under the sultans of Delhi and the rulers of Mughal India.

These two sets of texts belong to the Perso-Islamic world into which India had been integrated by the thirteenth century. But it may be noted at the outset that they represent two distinct and diverse traditions of political writing. The writings of Barani, broadly speaking, represent a literary style that one would classify as *ādāb*,[12] while the writings of Tusi and the texts that follow his tradition need to be differentiated as *a<u>kh</u>lāq*—which I will discuss later. These two traditions have often been classified indiscriminately under the term 'mirrors of princes' literature, without regard for the distinction between the two.[13]

The *a<u>kh</u>lāq* texts—in particular the writings which took Tusi's work as a model—represented in fact the best example of the appropriation into the medieval Muslim intellectual world of non-Islamic—and in strictly juristic terms even anti-Islamic—ideas. The effort in

[12] Compare Louise Marlow, *Hierarchy and Egalitarianism in Islamic Thought*, Cambridge, 1997, pp. 117–42; Tarif Khalidi, *Arabic Historical Thought in the Classical Period*, Cambridge, 1994, pp. 171–6 and 193–200; Sunil Kumar, 'The Value of *Ādāb al-Mulūk* as a Historical Source: An Insight into the Ideals and Expectations of Islamic Society in the Middle Period (AD 945–1500)', *The Indian Economic and Social History Review*, vol. 22, no. 3, July–September 1985, pp. 307–27.

[13] See, for example, E.I.J. Rosenthal, *Political Thought in Medieval Islam: An Introductory Outline*, Cambridge, 1985; A.K.S. Lambton, *Theory and Practice in Medieval Persian Government*, London, 1980; for Muhammad Baqir Khan Najm-i Sani's *Mau'iẓah-i Jahāngīrī*, see Sajida Sultana Alvi, ed. & tr., *Advice on the Art of Governance: Mau'iẓah-i Jahāngīrī of Muḥammad Bāqir Najm-i <u>S</u>ānī: An Indo-Islamic Mirror for Princes*, Albany, 1989, especially the editor's Introduction.

these writings was, as we will see, to provide a philosophical, non-sectarian and humane solution to emergent problems that India's Muslim society encountered. *Sharī'a* here is redefined, in part to signify a kind of protest against an overly legalistic approach. This protest is couched in a language that paves the way for much of the dissidence which gradually became part of generally acceptable 'orthodox' Islam.

On the other hand, in the other set of texts on norms of governance, the term *sharī'a* is used in its narrow and legalistic sense. Among Barani's precursors one can list, in this category, the political treatises of Nizam al-Mulk Tusi and Ghazali; and then, in India, of Fakhr-i Mudabbir. In this tradition of writings, too, there are certain unmistakeable borrowings from the non-Islamic world. In many cases their authors support their viewpoints with wise sayings from the ancient world, illustrating them with stories and anecdotes from Sassanid Persia. Yet, crucially, they fail to question the basis of juridical *sharī'a* or provide a new definition of it. For this reason it seems to me unjustified to club the two sets of writings together within the same category.

The literature which came to be known as *ādāb*, and which originated in the first Arabic translations and adaptations of Greek and Iranian texts, continued to be produced until the end of our period. It had a considerable impact on the political and intellectual history of Islam, in the Perso-Turkic ecumene in particular. The *akhlāq* literature of the post-Mongol period marked a significant advance in the evolution of such literature. Its concerns, as we will see later, were statecraft, political culture, and philosophy, not merely practical and pragmatic, but also theoretical. More than being mere digests of norms of individual good behaviour, ethics, and urbanity, these texts were intended to articulate and transmit what ought to constitute correct conduct and action in varying political contexts. The writers of the ideals propagated in these texts were a comparatively small group, but on occasion effective and significant. In actual practice, jurists and theologians rarely had supreme legal authority, despite their numerical advantage over the writers of this *akhlāq* literature. Throughout our period, theologians' positions were greeted by the political élites with what has been characterized as either 'indifference',[14] silent resistance, or even direct contestation by a parallel theoretical construct. The power accorded to theologians in some modern writings on Islamic political theory[15] actually has no precedent in the history of premodern political Islam.

This *a<u>kh</u>lāqī* tradition received nourishment from the Greek legacy, the rationalism of which had earlier been incorporated into Islam through the writings of, say, Ibn Sina and Farabi. To what extent this implied the subjection of revelation to reason is a moot question that I prefer not to address here. This much, though, is clear—that in our texts there is a consistent attempt to show harmony between the sacred and the secular. The fact that the Mughals' claim to rulership did not emanate from their religious position also reinforced this variety of non-juristic articulation of power and its enforcement. In Mughal India, both in the military and civil departments, 'non-believers' such as Rajputs, Kayasthas, and Khattris (whom the jurists regarded as infidels) occupied a most crucial position, without regard to the reaction of jurists. There is in fact little juristic discussion around the validity or invalidity of, for instance, the matrimonial alliances of Mughals with local Hindu Rajputs, or of Akbar's decisions to abolish the *jizya* and pilgrimage taxes on non-Muslims. True, Aurangzeb extended patronage to the compilation of the *Fatāwā-i 'Ālamgīrī*; but again there is no evidence of this ever being put into practice. Indeed, Aurangzeb's decision to reimpose *jizya* was not in reference to the demands of holy law.[16]

[14] This expression comes from Stephen Humphreys, 'Islam in the Political Arena: Three Paradigms for the Future', cited in Barbara D. Metcalf, 'Presidential Address: Too Little and Too Much: Reflections on Muslims in the History of India', *Journal of Asian Studies*, 54, 4, 1995, pp. 951–67.

[15] Cf. Ayatullah Ruhullah Khomeini, *Wilayat-i Faqih*, English trans. by Hamid Algar, *Islam and Revolution*, Berkeley, 1981, pp. 27–166. Lewis suggests that *ādāb* died out very early and that it had a limited impact on later generations.

[16] For Mughal–Rajput matrimonial alliances and Akbar's decisions to abolish *jizya* and pilgrimage tax, and Aurangzeb's reversal of these decisions, see S.R. Sharma, *Religious Policy of the Mughal Emperors*, New York, 1972, pp. 30–74 and 191–8; Satish Chandra, *Historiography, Religion, and State in Medieval India*, New Delhi, 1996, pp. 153–73.

It is only much later, in the second half of the eighteenth century, that we have an overt statement regarding the position of Hindus in juristic terms, and, as we will see in the fifth chapter, this statement was not from a jurist but from a Sufi. What is more curious is that Aurangzeb inflicted *jizya* upon a community within which a large number were still ready to spill blood on the battlefield in defence of his power, and who also figured prominently in his secretariat and administration.

All this was in a realm where the seats of power, Delhi and Agra, were designated respectively as *dār al-khilāfa* and *mustaqarr al-khilāfa*, and the Mughal emperor was also not infrequently called *khalīfa*.[17] Yet it would be unfair to assume that Mughal historians ever regarded Mughal rulers as the caliphs of the Muslim community, in the line of succession of the Umayyads (661–750) and Abbasids (750–1517); or that they considered Delhi and Agra centres of the entire Muslim world in the way that Damascus and Baghdad had been. The reality of the *khilāfa* had died, and, though its romance and symbolic significance lived on, none of these words used in earlier Islam denoted the meaning they once did. Muslims in India cohabited with non-Muslims, Muslim rulers with non-Muslim subjects, and later, in the eighteenth century, even Muslim subjects with non-Muslim rulers, all without reference to what earlier jurists had advocated regarding such social situations.

Since the language of the *akhlāq* texts—wherein I have located the redefinition of *sharī'a*—is invariably Persian, and since these texts represent an important genre of Persian literature, I ask in the fourth chapter if there was something in the world of Persian literary culture—in the images and metaphors that Persian authors (in particular poets) chose or invented—which further buttressed such a re-definition of the concept of *sharī'a*. By posing this question and answering it, I seek to add some detail on the trajectories of Islam's language of governance in India, in particular Mughal India. I have tried to explain the reasons for the widespread use of this developing

[17] Muhammad Hadi Kamwar Khan, *Tazkirat al-Salāṭīn-i Chaghtā*, ed. Muzaffar Alam, Bombay, 1980, for instance, pp. 10, 11, 12, 13, 21, 28, 38.

language, and sought to assess the strengths and weaknesses implied by this vocabulary for the medieval Muslim state in India. Did language have any bearing on questions of identity formation, and thereby have a bearing upon the nature of the Muslim state? In what manner did religion enter this picture?

The other texts that I have used in my discussion, within which the term *sharī'a* continues to be used in a juridical sense, are also in Persian. We will see that it was in Persian that a number of treatises similar to the *akhlāq* texts were compiled—as late as in the seventeenth century—in order to contest the positions and content of the latter. The terms and contents of these debates, in which redefinitions of key Islamic terms were first met by opposition, and then by a movement towards reaffirmation, will form the subject matter of the fifth chapter.

This book is focused on materials from the premodern history of India's Islamic past. Yet, though my discussions and illustrations are from such relatively distant times, they are relevant to an understanding of the trajectory of Islam in our own time.

For the past two hundred years and more, political Islam has been passing through a critical phase, in the sense that the social and political tensions that Muslims in different parts of the world have encountered during this period have been much more serious than in any earlier phase—including those that were witnessed during the immediate post-Mongol phase. At the hands of the West, Islam has over this modern colonial and postcolonial era experienced an unprecedented onslaught at every level: in relation to politics, military matters, culture, aesthetics, and morality, and even in the most basic ways in which people live their routine lives and conduct themselves. The original ideas and hegemonies of Islam—its worldview—once so dominant via its own conquests, have in all these realms been overwhelmed by Europe. The value that its once magnificent political symbols held have perished as America and Europe have pushed their cultures abroad, clothing much of the world that we experience today in Western garb. In India, by the mid-nineteenth century, the Mughal empire ended conclusively. In the Near East, Iran, and West and Central Asia, these entire regions were subjugated to one or the other Western power. In the twentieth century was shattered whatever remained of the Ottoman Empire.[18]

One enduring consequence of this encounter was the production of a stereotype of Islam, which defined not only the West's perception of Islam but also began to shape the way in which Muslims themselves perceived their religion. Islam appeared as a closed, dogmatic, intolerant faith whose doctrines were fixed and unchanging, their authority deriving from texts not subject to interpretation. This is the image that continues to haunt us even today.

Muslim clerics have explained this humiliating state of affairs theocratically, in terms of Muslim deviance from the true path of their blessed faith. The ignominy of Muslims, they claim, is the consequence of a divine scourge, God's punishment for their having lost the true faith. The result of this school of explanation has been the emergence of a powerful puritanism and movement for religious reform and revivalism.[19] Alongside this argument, there have also appeared some religious intellectuals who have pleaded for a taste of modernity, for genuine reform and the reformulation of Islamic tradition, but their influence has remained limited.[20] It is possible—one can speculate—that these modernists could have mobilized

[18] For a brief and useful survey, see Arthur Gold Schmidt Jr., 'The Colonial Period', and John O. Voll, 'Muslim Responses to Colonialism', in Marjorie Kelly, ed., *Islam: The Religious and Political Life of a World Community*, New York, 1984, pp. 137–72; John L. Esposito, *Islam and Politics*, Syracuse NY, 1991, pp. 32–59. See also Bernard Lewis, *What Went Wrong: The Clash between Islam and Modernity in the Middle East*, New York, 2002.

[19] Barbara D. Metcalf, *Islamic Revival in British India: Deoband, 1860–1900*, Princeton, 1982; Usha Sanyal, *Devotional Islam and Politics in British India: Ahmad Riza Khan Barelwi and His Movement, 1870–1920*, Delhi, 1996; Francis Robinson, *The Ulama of Farangi Mahall and Islamic Culture in South Asia*, Delhi, 2001, pp. 177–210.

[20] In South Asia's context, among the several important studies of modernist Islamic thought are: Aziz Ahmad, *Islamic Modernism in India and Pakistan, 1857–1967*, London, 1967; Christian W. Troll, *Sayyid Ahmad Khan: A Reinterpretation of Muslim Theology*, Delhi, 1978; David Lelyveld, *Aligarh's First*

some strength within the world Islamic community had there been a strong Muslim political regime to lend support to their ideas, as had happened in the past. There might perhaps have been more of an eclectic culture of borrowing and exchanging from the Western world if the Muslim world had felt more secure—as historically it did, for instance, when the early Arabs encountered Greco-Hellenic and Iranian traditions. In those older examples of cultural exchange, Muslims had been the conquerors.[21] In recent times, in the wake of their utter defeat, even the Islamic modernists have been too overwhelmed by a sense of insecurity to gain much acceptability for their ideas. By and large, their efforts have ironically resulted only in squeezing all ideologies of rational reform out of the public debate, while their insecurity has forced them into a kind of crisis of identity.

Of graver consequence has been the growing image of these modernists as allies of Islam's subjugators. Of interest in this connection are the charges that the '*ulamā*' levelled, for instance, against Sir Sayyid Ahmad Khan (d.1898), who was projected as a mere puppet of the British. This image gained wide currency, much beyond the circle of his opponents.[22] As a matter of fact, some of

*Generation: Muslim Solidarity in British India*, Princeton, 1978. See also Fazlur Rahman, *Islam and Modernity: Transformation of an Intellectual Tradition*, Chicago, 1982; and Daniel Brown, *Rethinking in Modern Islamic Thought*, Cambridge, 1996.

[21] I appreciate the fact that many scholars would look askance at such empathetic and apologetic views as mine. For one explanation of the failure of modernity in the Muslim world, see Bernard Lewis, *What Went Wrong*.

[22] For the types of charges levelled against Sayyid Ahmad, see Altaf Husain Hali, *Ḥayāt-i Jāved*, Lahore, 1965, pp. 508–46. It may also be noted here that many believed that the story of the native hero who cooperated with the British in *Ibn ul-Waqt* (lit. 'time server')—a novel by Nazir Ahmad (d.1912), author of *Taubat un-Nasūḥ* and *Mir'āt ul-'Urūs*—was built around Sayyid Ahmad. This impression was evidently wrong. Not only was Nazir Ahmad himself a modernist and a close associate of Sayyid Ahmad, he also publicly denied the allegation. There have been several editions of *Ibn ul-Waqt*, which is now also available in an excellent English translation by Muhammad Zakir, titled *The Man of the Moment*, Delhi, 2001.

these modernists have sought the support of Western powers to enforce reform. We have also seen, most notably in the case of Turkey in the twentieth century, that some modernist Islamic states have sought change by claiming to throw away the past entirely. The claims of revivalists have, as a consequence, been further emboldened at various politically opportune conjunctures within such states: modernists have, at such times, been projected as mere puppets and blind imitators of the West. The situation has been aggravated by the fact that revivalists—many of whom were also rank reactionary sectarians—as well as Muslim nationalists who fought the West for their political freedom, have all ironically come to find themselves sharing virtually the same platform. This has meant that, at one level, there has been little to distinguish the fight against Western colonialism on the one hand, and on the other the movement to mobilize Muslims as a separate community by rejuvenating their lost traditions and glory.

The conditions, therefore, have been rife for nourishment of the belief that it is only *within* the Islamic tradition that the solution to the new challenges of the West can be found: any other strategy to combat cultural and religious defeat would be not merely un-Islamic but also anti-Islam. Thus in South Asia, Sayyid Abu'l A'la Mawdudi (d.1979)—a protégé and spokesman of the '*ulamā*' of Deoband, and an editor of their organ, *Al-Jamī'at*, broke with them in 1928 and established himself as an independent editor and writer for *Tarjuman al-Quran*, finally creating in 1941 an organization of his own named *Jamā'at-i Islāmī*. He also engaged in polemic with a major Deobandi '*ālim*, Husain Ahmad Madani (d.1957), who advocated a united Hindu and Muslim approach to nationalism.[23] This particular thread of religious revivalism has created the space for what has come to be known as 'Islamism'. In this view—which is completely at odds with the entire history of Muslim civilizational

[23] For Mawdudi, see S.V.R. Nasr, *Mawdudi and the Making of Islamic Revivalism*, New York, 1996, pp. 14–21 and 32–41. For a collection of Mawdudi's writings from the period of his editorship of *Al-Jamī'at*, see Khalid Ahmad Hamidi, ed., *Āftāb-i Tāza*, Lahore, 1993.

borrowing and appropriation from the various cultures it has encountered—the way forward for the subjugated Muslim world has been narrowly and stultifyingly understood as lying only within an all-encompassing Islam, which has itself been narrowly defined and theologically constrained by this school of Islamic thought. The struggle of Islam, from this narrow perspective, requires the acquisition of political power in order to implement an ideology for re-creating the rule of Allah on earth.[24] This worldview has only resulted in a violent and radical form of political Islam, which has been nourished by memories and the observation of injustice at the hands of Western colonialism and neo-colonialism. The West was not merely targeted as the principal enemy, it was also identified as the new *Jāhiliya* (barbarity, unbelief, ignorance), politically more dangerous and culturally more contaminated than the one that prevailed in pre-Islamic Arabia. The elimination of this *Jāhiliya* was regarded as a part of the prophetic mission, and the West was deemed degenerate and devilish. Not only was this new *Jāhiliya* incompatible with Islam, it was also the duty of Muslims to stamp it out.[25]

Religious revivalism in the Islamic world had earlier sought to purify Islam itself from social practices that had gradually been incorporated into Islam through cultural borrowing. Now, it seemed time to cast its gaze outside the faith, to purify its world by eliminating not merely the internal enemy but the enemy outside. This radical notion of purification now turned to violence, using the call to *jihād* as a call to arms. We may see an illustration of this in the internal history of Indian Islam.

[24] Nasr, *Mawdudi*, pp. 81–106; *idem, The Vanguard of Islamic Revolution: The Jamī'at-i Islami of Pakistan*, Berkeley, 1994. Abu'l A'la Mawdudi, *Islāmī Riyāsat*, ed. Khurshid Ahmad, Lahore, 1962, pp. 17–115. See also Roxanne Euben, *Enemy in the Mirror: Islamic Fundamentalism and the Limits of Modern Rationalism*, Princeton, 1999; Richard P. Mitchell, *The Society of the Muslim Brothers*, New York, 1993; Emmanuel Sivan, *Radical Islam: Medieval Theology and Modern Politics*, New Haven, 1990; R. Scott Applebee, ed., *Spokesmen for the Despised: Fundamentalist Leaders of the Middle East*, Chicago, 1997.

[25] Compare Sivan, *Radical Islam*, pp. 21–8, for a discussion of the views of Mawdudi and Sayyid Qutb.

Islamic revivalism in India was in the nineteenth century largely a movement for piety, not for political power. Islamic revivalists sought to strengthen themselves and their belief systems by establishing religious seminaries, such as the Deoband *madrasa* in Uttar Pradesh, for further study and purification. These seminaries were supported entirely through donations from within the community and remained independent of the state. It was this same movement that, earlier in Indian history, sided with non-Muslims against the British for the object of self-rule. And it was this same movement that rejected the movement for a separate Muslim state because it rejected the notion of an authority—the nation-state—other than the will of God. All this was despite the fact that pan-Islamism had fired the imagination of many Deobandis.[26] There was no single voice among the Deobandis. While Husain Ahmad Madani supported the Congress for a united India, Shabbir Ahmad Usmani (d.1949) and Mufti Muhammad Shafi (d.1976) were in the forefront of the struggle for a separate homeland for Muslims. The Deoband *madrasa* was, however, controlled by the Madani faction. Besides this, it is also interesting that the '*ulamā*' associated with this *madrasa* repudiated Mawdudi's version of Islam as far down the road as the late 1970s.[27] It is only much later, in the 1990s, that the disciples of some of those '*ulamā*' who had opposed Madani's position allowed their seminaries in Pakistan to groom and support young students who became part of the Taliban in Afghanistan. It was they who now controlled and led a new movement for Islamic purification that saw political power as its means of fulfilment.[28]

[26] Husain Ahmad Madani, *Muttaḥida Qaumiyat aur Islam*, second edition, Delhi, n.d.; *idem, Pakistan Kya Hai?*, I & II, Delhi, 1946; Ziyaul Hasan, *The Deoband School and Demand for Pakistan*, Bombay, 1963.

[27] See for instance Madani, *Mawdudi Dastūr aur 'Aqā'id ki Haqīqat*, Deoband, n.d.; Muhammad Akhtar, *Mawdudi Ṣāḥib Akābir-e Ummat kī Naẓr mein*, Karachi, 1976; Karimuddin, *Mawlānā Mawdūdī ke Ghalaṭ Naẓriyāt*, Multan, 1976.

[28] See Zaman, *The Ulama in Contemporary Islam*, pp. 87–110; and Jamal Malik, *Colonialization of Islam: The Dissolution of Traditional Institutions in Pakistan*, Delhi, 1996, pp. 120–226 for some relevant details. Neither of these

It is true that, much earlier, in the Arabian peninsula, Islamic puritans and political strategists had come together. This combine, however, represented only one version of Islam, limited to a region and a group of Muslims. Politically and spiritually it stayed on the periphery for nearly the whole of the nineteenth century. Only recently, after it allied its interests with the West, has Arabian Islam acquired its formidable position as the putative sole spokesman of Islam, with Saudia Arabia occupying centre stage.[29] The interventions of Great Power politics within the world of Islam have contributed substantially to legitimizing certain groups over others. Many of the changes, including an understanding of what constitutes Islam, have taken place not in a vacuum but within this political context. Added to this has been the West's invariable support to authoritarian regimes, including contemporary Islamic kingdoms. In short, it is not simply that the 'Islamist position' (as Bruce Lawrence

---

two books makes this distinction, but see also Barbara D. Metcalf, preface to the paperback edition of *Islamic Revival*, Delhi, 2002, for a more sensitive, though brief, treatment of these details.

[29] For instance, aside from a couple of individual opinions, the '*ulamā*' of Deoband—even as they were often accused, or rather abused, of being 'Wahhabis' by their Barelwi opponents—for long maintained a distance from and also disapproved of Muhammad bin Abd al-Wahhab's teachings. It was only in the mid-1970s that they made a kind of official statement in appreciation of his religious ideas as enforced by the Saudis. Cf. Manzur Ahmad Numani, *Shaikh Muḥammad bin 'Abd al-Wahhāb ke Khilāf Propaganda, aur Hindustān ke 'Ulamā'-i Ḥaqq par Us ke Aṣarāt*, Lucknow, 1978. For some idea of the reception of 'Wahhabi' Islam in South Asia, see also the polemical, though not academically serious, Sunni and Shi'a treatises by Hakim Muhammad Ramzan Ali Qadiri, *Tārīkh-i Wahhābiya*, Lyallpur, 1976; Farogh Kazimi, *Fitna-i Wahhābiyat*, Lucknow, 1998.

For the rise of Wahhabi power in Arabia and the Saudi rulers' relations with Britain and the United States of America, see L.A.O. de Corancez, *The History of the Wahhabis, from their Origin until the End of 1809*, Reading, 1995; Madavi al-Rasheed, *A History of Saudi Arabia*, Cambridge, 2002; Cary Fraser, 'In Defense of Allah's Realm: Religion and Statecraft in Saudi Foreign Policy Strategy', in Susanne H. Rudolph and James Piscatori, eds, *Transnational Religion and Fading States*, Boulder, CO, 1997, pp. 212–40. See also Anthony Cave

notes) was a product of modern Westernized institutions.[30] Rather, the West has played no insignificant role in lending legitimacy to radical Islam and providing additional fodder for the violent claims of *jihād* to take root.

Technology has been another contributing factor shaping the way the Muslim world saw itself and its place in the new world. The rise of global media has, in a historically unprecedented fashion, permitted the creation of a radical Muslim *imaginaire*. All of a sudden it has become possible for Muslims in different corners of the world to possess a near-simultaneous understanding of the struggles faced by Islam in different parts of the globe. Muslim consciousness, having gained knowledge of Muslim persecution globally, has been further fuelled by the idea that the enemy is external. In earlier times, this was never so: the struggle between various Muslim regimes was a reality, while the idea of the *ummah*—the body of the faithful as a whole—was limited. With the exception of the age of the Prophet and the early years of the Pious Caliphate, no Muslim ruler could ever be accepted as the unchallenged political head (*amīr*) of the entire community. The Kharijites challenged even the later Pious Caliphs, the Shi'ites defied the Umayyads, and the Great Abbasids feared and faced resistance from the Umayyads of Spain and later from regional Perso-Turkic rulers. The subsequent sultanates and empires, including the Ottomans, the Safavids, the Uzbeks and Mughals, all rivalled one another. It is only in the wake of Islam's confrontation with the West, and the emergence of pan-Islamism, that the Ottoman claim to be the head of the world Muslim community has come to acquire some appeal.[31] And only in the past

Brown, *Oil, God, and Gold: The Story of Aramco and the Saudi Kings*, Boston, 1999.

30 Bruce B. Lawrence, *Defenders of God: The Fundamentalist Revolt against the Modern Age*, Columbia, 1995.

31 Cf. Lewis, *Political Language of Islam*, pp. 48–50. For the Mughal attitude towards the Ottomans, see Naimur Rahman Farooqi, *Mughal–Ottoman Relations: A Study of Political & Diplomatic Relations between Mughal India and the Ottoman Empire, 1556–1748*, Delhi, 1989. There was a marked change in the attitude

few decades—parallel to the alternative articulations of the reformers, the revivalists, and finally of the Islamist notion of a new political Islam—have we so starkly seen the growth of a mental map in which the Muslim world is united in its victimhood while being radically differentiated from Western perpetrators of violence.

In this context, the idea that the world is *and has always been* divided into two has become rather easily legitimized by world events. The Muslim world has begun to speak of a world divided into two—Islam and the rest. From the West have emerged theories such as Samuel Huntington's 'clash of civilizations',[32] which, though perhaps proffered as a phrase of explanatory convenience, has become a prophecy for the Muslim world to move further from the West. In the eyes of the West, on the other hand, terrorism carried out in Islam's name has served to reaffirm the stereotypes that emerged and gained legitimacy during the early phases of European colonial expansion. The result has been a collapse of the entire practice of the faith into one terrible and frightening image of Islam as synonymous with the*mujāhidīn*. Both camps have then projected these new understandings of the relationship between the Muslim world and the West backwards into time, arriving thereby at an interpretation of unending and ongoing conflict throughout history. There has thus been a kind of mutual slandering, and it seems as though it is only now, ironically in the wake of the current global

---

of Indian Muslims towards the Ottomans with the waning and final collapse of Mughal power. See Khwaja Abd al-Qadir,*Waqā'-i' Manāzil-i Rūm*, ed. Mohibbul Hasan, Bombay, 1968; Saiyid Sulaiman Nadvi, *Khilāfat aur Hindustān* in *idem, Maqālāt-i Sulaimān*, Azamgarh, 1966, pp. 112–84.

[32] Samuel P. Huntington, *The Clash of Civilizations and the Remaking of World Order*, reprint, New Delhi, 1997. See in particular pp. 209–18. It is unfortunate to find echoes of this view in the writings of some of the best scholars of the history of Islam: cf. Bernard Lewis, 'The Roots of Muslim Rage',*Atlantic Monthly*, September 1990; *idem, The Crisis of Islam: Holy War and Unholy Terror*, New York, 2003. In 'The Roots of Muslim Rage', Lewis writes: 'The struggle between Islam and the West has now lasted fourteen centuries. It has consisted of a long series of attacks and counterattacks, jihads and crusades, conquests and reconquests . . .' While there is no doubt a measure of truth here,

order, that the medieval juridical theory of the world as divided into two—*dār al-Islam* and *dār al-ḥarb*—is finally gaining practical acceptance.[33]

This is, in some ways, the point of departure for the present book. Implicitly, and at points explicitly, it contests this erroneous interpretation of the history and nature of Islam. It shows a different history via a careful documentation of key examples and texts from the political history of Indian Islam. I seek to demonstrate in this book that it was not simply in its earlier phases that Islam borrowed from and interacted with non-Islamic worlds. In its entire history, I suggest, Islam appropriated and welcomed ideas from the world outside. Islamic ideals and doctrines were open to interpretation. They were refigured and rethought over the centuries, even when texts were cited and doctrines referred to, to authenticate action. Islam's politics endeavoured to narrow the bridge between communities; its religious leaders tried to appreciate the traditions of the 'Other' as well. Focusing on complex practices of cultural and political exchange and appropriation that existed substantially in India's Muslim world, I try to show here that Islam's history was far more a kind of dialogue with the worlds it reached—and reached out to. And in the process Muslims, like most religious communities, have picked up various strategies to devise a politics informed, though not always driven by, the sacral.

---

the dangerous potential inherent in such a generalization—which implies that confrontation was always initiated by the Muslims, and that violence is somehow inherent in Islam—is self-evident. I must add that Lewis's own details and evidence, available in his serious historical works, contradict the sweeping statements and conclusions that he makes in his journalistic writings.

[33] I should mention here that many Western scholars of Islam are also ill at ease with this view. They have shown variety in Islamic traditions in their researches on both history and modern politics. For some studies along these lines, see John O. Voll, *Islam, Continuity and Change in the Modern World*, Boulder CO, 1982; John L. Esposito, *Islam: The Straight Path*, New York, 1991; *idem, The Islamic Threat: Myth or Reality?*, New York, 1999; *idem, Unholy War: Terror in the Name of Islam*, New York, 2002; Bruce B. Lawrence, *Shattering the Myth: Islam Beyond Violence*, Princeton, 1998; Yohanan Friedmann, *Tolerance and Coercion in Islam*, Cambridge, 2003.

In this sense, in trying to dispel the stereotype of Islam's eternal clash with Christianity, Hinduism and the other faiths—with which, I argue, it has long coexisted, taught, and learned from—I believe this book of history speaks as much to historians as to serious readers who, like myself, are worried by both the 'threat of Islam' and the 'threat to Islam'.[34]

[34] I have taken this expression from Fred Halliday's *Islam and the Myth of Confrontation: Religion and Politics in the Middle East*, new edn, London, 2003.

CHAPTER 2

# *Sharīʻa*, *Akhlāq* and Governance

## *Sharīʻa* in Early *Ādāb* Writings

The expansion of Islam brought not just new lands and peoples within the ambit of its power, but also a variety of new social and political ideas. With these came significant changes in the theocratic foundation of early political Islam. Societies conquered by Islam retained memories of their own past; they valued their old modes of life, social practices, mores and traditions.[1] Islam's contact with these societies was bound to affect Islam itself: domination affects both conqueror and vanquished. Parallel to the compilation and codification of the *sharīʻa*, thus, there also set in a process of the evolution of political ideals outside the *sharīʻa*'s strict confines.[2] These ideals were often in opposition to the ones upheld by jurists, even though the authors who introduced and compiled these ideals tried to integrate them into the body politic of Islam. They did not question the authority of the jurists in matters pertaining to religion. In some cases, as a matter of fact, they themselves were the jurists. The treatises on principles and practices of government compiled in this early phase thus virtually conformed to the ideals of the *sharīʻa*.

[1] H.A.R. Gibb, *Studies on the Civilization of Islam*, eds Stanford Shaw and William Polk, London, 1962, esp. chap. 4; R.P. Mottahedeh, 'The *Shuʻūbiyah* Controversy and the Social History of Early Islamic Iran', *International Journal of Middle Eastern Studies*, vol. 7, no. 2, 1976, pp. 161–82; *Encyclopaedia of Islam*, vol. II, Leiden, 1983, pp. 918–31; vol. III, Leiden, 1986, pp. 883–5.

[2] Schacht, *An Introduction to Islamic Law*, pp. 28–75; N.G. Coulson, *History of Islamic Law*, Edinburgh, 1964, pp. 86–102.

The first oft-cited and notable of such treatises, which cleverly integrated the demands of the *sharī'a* and the heritage of the classical Islamic past while subtly manipulating prevailing opinions was the *al-Aḥkām al-Sulṭāniya* of Abu'l Hasan al-Mawardi (d.1058), written in Arabic. Mawardi was a *qāẓī*, a defender of the tradition. For him the authority of the caliph was supreme, and among his important duties was the defence of the *sharī'a*, the dispensation of justice according to the *sharī'a*, and the organization of *jihād*.[3] Nizam al-Mulk Tusi, another notable political theorist of the eleventh century, wrote his *Siyāsat Nāma* or *Siyar al-Mulūk* in the time of Malik Shah Saljuq (1027–92). His views were, at one level, completely different from Mawardi's position. The ideals and models Nizam al-Mulk cited in his book were most often ancient Persian ones. The caliph, for him and for his Saljuq master, was little more than a pension-holder, while the ruler was the absolute *Pādshāh*.[4] Even in the case of those institutions for which he could have cited precedents from the classical Islamic period, Nizam al-Mulk looked instead to ancient Persia. While Mawardi legitimized heredity from the case of the nomination of Caliph 'Umar by Abu Bakr,[5] Nizam al-Mulk did so by drawing upon examples from ancient Persia.[6] But for Nizam al-Mulk, too, defence of the *sharī'a* and the keeping alive of religion and the true faith were among the most important duties of an Islamic king. He thus characterized the Batinis, the Qarmatis, and other such groups as 'heretics' and as 'enemies of state and Islam', and made a strong plea for their ruthless suppression.[7]

Between Mawardi's apologia for the caliphate and Nizam al-Mulk's appropriation of Persian kingship was Ghazali's (d.1111)

[3] Abu'l Hasan ibn Muhammad al-Mawardi, *Al-Aḥkām al-Sulṭāniya*, ed. Muhammad Badr al-Din al-Na'sani, Cairo, 1909, pp. 3–18; H.A.R. Gibb, 'Al-Mawardi's Theory of the Caliphate', in *Studies on the Civilization of Islam*, ed. Stanford Shaw and William Polk, London, 1962, pp. 151–65.

[4] Nizam al-Mulk, *Siyāsat Nāma*, ed. Hubert Darke, Tehran, 1962, pp. 13–16 and 41.

[5] *Al-Aḥkām al-Sulṭāniya*, pp. 7–8.

[6] *Siyāsat Nāma*, p. 151.

[7] Ibid., pp. 74–5.

position of compromise in his celebrated *Naṣīḥat al-Mulūk*, written around the same time, and also addressed to a Saljuq sultan, Sanjar bin Malik Shah (r.1105–18).[8] 'Constituent authority', in Ghazali's view, belonged to the sultan, but the validity of the sultan's government was dependent upon his oath of allegiance to the caliph and the latter's appointment of him. Ghazali's principal concern was the proper execution of *sharī'a*,[9] but his ideas are also influenced by Sufi notions of ethics. What is of greater significance for our purpose is the fact that, along with his emphasis on the maintenance of *sharī'a*, Ghazali lays equal emphasis on the need for a ruler to perform practical duties according to the principles of 'justice'.[10]

In some measure, then, Ghazali laid the theoretical grounds for the acceptability of later writers who argued for the primacy of the ordinary duties of the king on grounds of political expediency.[11] All the same the debate on political norms was at this time governed by the demands of *sharī'a* in its narrow juridical sense. While many aspects of politics juristically in opposition to the *sharī'a* were tolerated, they were largely connived at as necessary evils. There was

[8] Ghazali wrote the text in Persian; it was later translated into Arabic. Most manuscripts of the Arabic version bear the title *Al-Tibr al-Masbūk fi Naṣīḥat al-Mulūk*. The Persian text has been edited by Jalal Humai (Tehran, 1972/1351 *sh.*) and an Arabic text has been published by H.D. Isaacs. Compare F.R.C. Bagley's Introduction to his English translation, which appears as *Counsel for Kings*, London, 1964.

[9] *Counsel for Kings*, pp. 51–6.

[10] Ibid., pp. 45–7; A.K.S. Lambton, 'The Theory of Kingship in *Naṣīḥat ul-Mulūk* of Ghazali', in A.K.S. Lambton, *Theory and Practice in Medieval Persian Government*, chap. v.

[11] Ghazali is also notable for the impact of Greek writings on his political theory. Even in the *Naṣīḥat* he cites Aristotle in support of the qualities he recommends as essential for kings: 'Aristotle was asked, "What great man is worthy to be called king, or is God alone (worthy)?" He answered, "The man in whom you will find certain things, however lacking he be in other qualities." Then he continued, "First of all knowledge, and[then] forbearance, compassion, clemency, generosity and the like; because great men owe their greatness to the divine effulgence and to their radiance of soul, pureness of body, and breadth of intellect and knowledge, as well as the domain which has long been in their family." '

no systematic attempt at giving the *sharī'a* a meaning different from the one developed in law books.

Early Indo-Islamic political theory, such as that enunciated for example in the thirteenth century in Fakhr-i Mudabbir's *Ādāb al-Ḥarb wa'l-Shujā'a*, and more definitely and clearly in the fourteenth century in Ziya al-Din Barani's *Fatāwā-i Jahāndārī*, is in many respects an extension of this tradition. What becomes clear also is that, in the Indian environment, in the midst of 'hostile' and 'infidel' surroundings—with early Muslim rulers uncertain of their position—the limitations of these traditions become increasingly manifest.

## Fakhr-i Mudabbir's *Ādāb al-Ḥarb*

Fakhr-i Mudabbir's work[12] was not compiled in India, but as it was dedicated to Sultan Shams al-Din Iltutmish (r.1211–36), the first sovereign Muslim ruler of Delhi, it has a strong bearing on the history of early Muslim states in northern India. The book comprises over thirty-five chapters. Twenty-seven of these pertain principally to warfare, army organisation, the drawing of battle-lines, and weaponry. Seven others, which have also been edited and published separately as *Ā'īn-i Kishwardārī*,[13] relate to what we may term 'norms of governance'. At the start of his book the author emphasizes the finality of the word of Islam. The mission of the prophets—124,000 in all, according to this author—was to rescue humanity from 'the darkness of infidelity to the light of Islam'. With the advent of Muhammad, the last and most revered of prophets, the world was finally embellished by *Sharī'a-i Islāmia*: and thus all other faiths were deemed annulled. In subsequent sections of the text, the *sharī'a* of Islam provides the structure within which Fakhr-i Mudabbir locates various categories of battles. The most 'sacred' and holiest

[12] Fakhr al-Din Muhammad bin Mubarak Shah (Fakhr-i Mudabbir), *Ādāb al-Ḥarb wa'l Shujā'a*, ed. Ahmad Suhaili Khwansari, Tehran, 1967/1346 *sh*. For a discussion see Sunil Kumar, 'The Value of *Ādāb al-Mulūk* as a Historical Source'.

[13] *Ā'īn-i Kishwardārī*, ed. Muhammad Sarwar Maulai, Tehran, 1975/1354 *sh*.

of battles are those that were fought against infidels for the glory of Islam; those killed in these 'holy' battles are martyrs (*shahīds*), those who survived are *ghāzīs*. All other battles—namely those fought by Muslims against Muslims to gain power, or those fought to ensure the smooth flow of revenue, or those launched against criminals—are deemed inferior and avoidable.[14]

The huge importance given to upholding the *sharī'a* of Islam in Fakhr-i Mudabbir's text is once again evident from the fact that it devotes an entire chapter to enumerating the merits of *jihād*. Then, chapter twenty-six of the work details the manner in which *jizya* is to be collected from non-Muslims (*zimmīs*): 'The people of the *zimma* should not ride on horses, should not wear clothes like Muslims or live like Muslims.'[15] Mudabbir adds that Muslims who turn away from Islam become renegades or apostates; if they maintain their heresy for three days they may be persuaded to return to the fold; if they refuse there should be no option other than their execution.[16]

Mudabbir recommends state offices only for religious, pious, and godfearing Muslims whose prime concern is to protect and promote the rights of Muslims (*ḥaqq-i Musalmānī*) and to avoid cirumstances in which Muslims are liable to be offended (*āzār-i dil-i Musalmān*). In the final analysis it is the personal religiosity and piety of the official which determines his ability to discharge his responsibility of promoting the Faith.[17] This is illustrated by Mudabbir's chapter on justice. Here, the qualities that he lists for such officials (*amīr-i dād*) are revealing. The office of the *amīr-i dād* is seen as next in importance only to the exalted position of the king, and thus it is only fitting that the person adorning such an office should come from the royal family, or at least from the families of high-ranking officials—such as Sayyids and other members of noble lineages. Further, it is important that he be kindhearted, considerate and sensitive, and familiar with details of the *sharī'a*. Again,

[14] Fakhr-i Mudabbir, *Ādāb al-Ḥarb*, p. 336.

[15] Ibid., chap. 25, pp. 388–97; for *jihād*, pp. 404–5.

[16] Ibid., p. 405.

[17] *Ā'īn-i Kishwardārī*, pp. 25, 30 and 33.

Mudabbir stresses that during court petitions and hearings the *amīr-i dād* should take special care of the rights of Muslims; he should see to it that these are not violated.[18]

In order to stress the point that all 'virtues' rest ultimately with the followers of Islam alone, Mudabbir recommends that the judiciary be entrusted with the charge of pious and godfearing Muslims. Those responsible for presenting the cases of petitioners and respondents to the court of the *amīr-i dād* are again required to be good Muslims. This he believes to be necessary to ensure that the judicial apparatus of a Muslim state functions primarily to benefit Muslims.[19] Fakhr-i Mudabbir's king—even if emulating the examples of ancient Sassanid kings—has thus to manage the state for the sole purpose of protecting and promoting the interests of Muslims and their *sharī'a*.

## Barani's *Fatāwā-i Jahāndārī*: The Construction of a Past

Ziya al-Din Barani is undoubtedly one of the most extensively read and cited authors of pre-Mughal India. He not merely continues the Nizam al-Mulk-Ghazali tradition, he builds his own theory in the new Indian context with a view to protect and promote the interests of the *sharī'a*. In one modern evaluation, he is 'the first theoretician to justify secular laws among the Mussalmans.'[20] There is no doubt

[18] Ibid., p. 38.

[19] Ibid., pp. 39–40.

[20] Muhammad Habib, 'Life and Thought of Ziauddin Barani', *Medieval India Quarterly*, IV, January-April 1958, reprinted in Muhammad Habib and Afsar Umar Salim Khan, *Political Theory of the Delhi Sultanate* (*Including a Translation of Ziyauddin Barani's 'Fatāwā-i Jahāndārī*, circa AD 1398), Allahabad, n.d., pp. 117–72. For some other relevant and useful studies of Barani, see Peter Hardy, *Historians of Medieval India: Studies in Indo-Muslim Historical Writing*, London, 1960; *idem*, 'Didactic Historical Writing in Indian Islam', in *Islam in Asia*, I; *idem*, 'Force and Violence in Indo-Persian Writing on History and Government in Medieval South Asia', in Milton Israel and N.K. Wagle, eds, *Islamic Society and Culture: Essays in Honour of Professor Aziz Ahmad*, Delhi, 1983, pp. 165–208.

that Barani said something radically different from his predecessors as well as from his contemporaries. Yet there is a need to carefully scrutinize his political views, together with the circumstances in which such laws as he advocated were allowed; and, more significantly, we need to look carefully at Barani's view of the despicably sinful repercussions for the Muslim ruler who enacted, or lived with, such laws. I have tried here to study his thought in the light of his *Fatāwā-i Jahāndārī*, even though I concede that without a comprehensive examination of his history and other works an assessment of his ideas can only be tentative.

The *Fatāwā* is principally a text on abstract principles, but almost throughout it the discussion on principles is followed by detailed historical anecdotes to illustrate and seek legitimacy for these principles. The discussion on almost every theme is thus divided into two parts, intimately interwoven. Each shapes the other, and together they bring into relief Barani's political thought. We cannot come to a proper understanding of Barani's doctrine if we separate the section on historical anecdotes—whether deemed 'authentic' or otherwise—from the one on abstract principles. By choosing and selecting his historical characters, Barani attempts to resolve—in theory at least—the conflict between the demands of *sharī'a* and the problems of governance in his own time. He therefore creates the past with a purpose.

In this context, I must add that, in the available study and English translation of the text of the *Fatāwā*, much of Barani's construction of the past has been dismissed summarily. The translator, (Mrs) Afsar Salim Khan, justifies her dismissal on the grounds of the dubious authenticity and chronological discrepancies within the events that Barani describes. She rejects a large portion of the historical part of his text as 'fallacious', 'fictitious', a 'figment of Barani's imagination', 'historically impossible', and as stemming from his 'stupendous' and 'frightful ignorance' of history and geography.[21]

It is difficult to accept this view. Barani was no ordinary writer.

[21] Habib and Salim Khan, *Political Theory of the Delhi Sultanate*, pp. 7 and 67.

He was in fact one of the most literate historians and theorists of his time. As a courtier and companion (*nadīm*) of Muhammad bin Tughlaq (r.1324–51)—a most literate ruler of pre-Mughal times—Barani could not have been ignorant of what had and had not been documented, nor of what Mrs Khan considers the authentic historical past. Further, Barani compiled a biography of the Prophet Muhammad (*Na't-i Muḥammadī*), and translated into Persian an Arabic history of the Barmaki *wazīrs* of the Abbasids (*Tārīkh-i Barāmika*). It may be mentioned here that his original plan was to write a world history, which he abandoned because such a task, in his understanding, had been performed successfully in the thirteenth century by his predecessor Minhaj al-Siraj, in his *Ṭabaqāt-i Nāṣirī*. Barani therefore decided to pick up the threads where Minhaj had left them. Amir Khwurd and Shams-i Siraj 'Afif, Barani's two eminent younger contemporaries, admired his knowledge of history and literary brilliance.[22] It seems that Barani exercized careful choice not only in relation to what he intended to include in his *Fatāwā*, but also in relation to the ways in which past events were to be presented and projected in the text.

Barani thus constructs his own history, which then governs his choice of heroes and villains. Barani's al-Mamun (r.813–33), the illustrious Abbasid caliph, for instance, emerges in the *Fatāwā* as a protector of Sunni Islam, and as an admirer of orthodox religious scholars like Imam Ahmad bin Hanbal (d.855). Evidently, Barani's portrayal of al-Mamun is contrary to what we know from 'authentic' histories of the time about the caliph and his Mu'tazilite leanings, and of the treatment meted out to the two imams who disagreed with him in public and expressed their indignation over his religious views. In Barani's reading, however, Sunni orthodox Islam achieved brilliance in al-Mumun's time. The caliph therefore is his hero, and is shown in the company of the imams Barani adored. For Barani there is not even the remote possibility of al-Mamun being anywhere

[22] Shams-i Siraj 'Afif, *Tārīkh-i Fīrūz Shāhī*, ed. Maulavi Wilayat Husain, Calcutta, 1890, pp. 29–30, and 177; Amir Khwurd Kirmani, *Siyar al-Auliyā'*, Delhi, 1884–85/1302 H, pp. 312–13.

close to the Mu'tazilites, whom he despised and regarded as heretics.[23]

Barani's portrayal of the celebrated ruler of Ghazna, Mahmud (r.998–1030), best illustrates how his theoretical conceptions are linked to the history he creates. Barani's Mahmud is, from childhood, inspired with the desire to extirpate infidels and idolatry, and thus launches campaigns into India to annihilate the Brahmans, the leaders of a false religion. This Mahmud is not remotely influenced by the love of wealth; instead, a desire for martyrdom always illuminates his noble soul. He never accepts presents or bribes from any non-Muslim—bribes he is offered to spare a man's life or let him go unharmed. If only Mahmud had been able to launch one more campaign into India, he would have exterminated all Hindus with his holy sword.

Barani's Mahmud, like Barani himself, detests the Mu'tazilites and the philosophers, and considers them the carriers of a false creed and the worst enemies of the 'true faith'. If only Bu Ali Sina (Avicenna)—the progenitor of Hellenistic philosophy in the lands of Islam—had fallen into Mahmud's hands, Mahmud would have cut him into pieces, minced his flesh and fed it to the kites, says Barani. In this portrayal, Mahmud never misses congregational prayers, lives the life of a missionary, and mobilizes all to propagate the truth of Islam. One of the most powerful rulers of his time, Qadr Khan of Khita, embraced Islam at his behest.[24]

Now, there is little purpose in looking for evidence of this Mahmud in 'authentic' accounts of Mahmud's contemporaries. Barani's Mahmud is possibly close to the traditions and legends which had come to surround the memory of the sultan. In the *Fatāwā* Mahmud is picked up as a model of the ruler of an ideal Muslim state—the kind that Barani wished to see built in India. Justice was to be the hallmark of this state. In Barani's view, it must be noted, justice was to be ensured only at the hands of a strong, pious, and *sharī'a*-protecting Muslim king. Thus, in his *Tārīkh*, the prime concerns of even

[23] Zia al-Din Barani, *Fatāwā-i Jahāndārī*, ed. Afsar Salim Khan, Lahore, 1972, pp. 125–30.

[24] Ibid., pp. 15–20, for instance.

a relatively weak sultan like Jalal al-Din Khalji (r.1290–96) are shown as the suppression of infidels (Hindus) and the promotion of *dīn* and *sharī'a*.[25]

## Barani on *Dīndārī* and *Jahāndārī*

Barani's definition of a Muslim ruler deserves special attention. An anecdote mentioned in the *Fatāwā* is particularly helpful for this purpose. It relates to the conflict between two political figures of the Islamic world—Ya'qub al-Lais al-Saffar (r.861–79) and Isma'il Samani (r.892–907). For Barani, Ya'qub was not a Muslim in the true sense of the term because he had created difficulties for the caliph in Baghdad. Isma'il Samani, on the other hand, was a good Muslim because he had delivered the caliph and Baghdad—the capital city of the Islamic world at the time—from the terrors Ya'qub had unleashed. Isma'il Samani's memory further endeared itself to Barani because he, in Barani's evaluation, took pride in the fact that he never violated the injunctions of the *sharī'a*.[26] A political, non-religious precedent was thus being used to define an ideal Muslim ruler. This, however, was not an easy exercise for Barani, even though he embarked upon it frequently in his writings.

Barani was naturally uncomfortable at the intrusion into the Muslim world of the hierarchically conceived, aristocratic, non-Islamic Sassanid state model. Throughout his *Fatāwā*, an unmistakeable unease prevails in this regard. It might even be asserted that the whole text, including the portions where he discusses 'secular principles', seems an attempt to suggest devices to undo or at least check this intrusive malaise. Unlike Fakhr-i Mudabbir, Barani is very clearly intervening to resolve the dilemma in accordance with the challenges that concrete social reality posed to the inherited tradition of the *sharī'a*. Theorists had in the past attempted to resolve this dilemma either by silently accepting and accommodating that which was non-Islamic—as was the case in the political commentary

[25] Compare *Tārīkh-i Fīrūz Shāhi*, ed. Sayyid Ahmad Khan, Calcutta, 1860, pp. 214–19, the dialogue between the Sultan and Ahmad Chap on the occasion of their expedition to Ranthambor.

[26] *Fatāwā*, pp. 5–9.

of Nizam al-Mulk Tusi—or else by attempting to reinterpret the *sharī'a* and thus adjusting it to non-Islamic accretions. An illustration of the latter can be found in the political writings of Ghazali.

Barani reacts to this problem by an outright repudiation of all that is non-Islamic. The Iranian pattern of governance or *pādshāhī*, legitimated to a degree by earlier writers, is to him a sin; the ruler who practices this system of governance is a sinner. True religion, according to him, consists only in following in the footsteps of the Prophet Muhammad, son of 'Abdullah Quraishi. Barani does concede that the ruler who desires to govern effectively has to follow the policies of the ancient Iranian kings: but since 'between the traditions of the Prophet and his mode of life and living, and the customs of the Iranian emperors, and their mode of life and living, there is a complete contradiction and total opposition',[27] the appropriation of the latter by a Muslim ruler is an offence against the law. The good sultan must therefore keep performing religious duties in an exaggerated manner in order to atone for this offence and to ensure his own salvation.

There are other points that Barani illustrates and develops in his *Tārīkh*. First, he cites the sermon and the advice of Shaikh Nur al-Din Mubarak Ghaznavi at the court of Sultan Shams al-Din Iltutmish. The shaikh wanted the sultan to be more vigilant in matters of the enforcement (*tarwīj*) of the *sharī'a* than in those pertaining to personal piety and prayers. Second, Barani dislikes 'Ala al-Din Khalji (r.1296–1316) but is full of praise for his reign because it was blessed by the grace of the presence of Shaikh Nizam al-Din Auliya (d.1325), and also because the sultan's efficient administration and powerful army broke the back of the infidels, checked the menace of the Mongols, and thus turned Delhi into an enviable abode of the faith and the faithful.[28] Third, one of the principal objectives of writing history, as far as Barani was concerned, was to highlight the achievements of Islam, contrasting these with the defects and failures of infidels. In the preface to *Tārīkh*, he summarily evaluates the

[27] Ibid., pp. 139–40; English transl., p. 39.

[28] *Tārīkh-i Fīrūz Shāhī*, pp. 41–4, 265–9, and 322.

period of the Pious Caliphs (r.632–61) solely in terms of their success in uprooting the enemies of the faith and of their evil practices of 'infidelity' and idolatry.[29]

Barani thus defines, with great rigidity, the schism between the political and the religious, and by reducing the scope for ambiguity he also reduces the margin for political manoeuvre. He sketches a rather impractical framework for governance and declares that the ruler who does not follow this does not deserve to be called a Muslim.[30] He does so because the theologian in him surfaces each time he theorizes on a political doctrine. Despite his realization of the benefits of drawing on political precedent, he is sceptical of their durability in the long term for true upholders of Islam. He is aware of the implications of this approach for his own time as he suggests specific measures for governance in Hindustan: the good Muslim king should not be content with merely levying the *jizya* and *kharāj* on Hindus, he should instead establish the supreme position of Islam by overthrowing infidelity and slaughtering its leaders (*imams*), the Brahmans.[31] Barani sometimes invokes the name of his hero, Mahmud of Ghazna, to reinforce his view, providing details of his invasions, his demolition of temples, the humiliation of Hindus, and so forth.[32]

In Barani's world there could only be two life patterns diametrically opposed to each other, one in conformity with the *sharī'a*—as theologians understood the term—and the other against it. Even the normal, universal, human qualities are slotted by him as binary oppositions: Islamic and anti-Islamic, or *shar'ī* and *ghair-shar'ī*. This is indicated in the chapters in the *Fatāwā* on royal determination (*'azm*), tyranny and despotism (*satīhash-o-istibdād*), and justice (*'adl*). For Barani, royal determination or royal will has no independent character; it is determined by the nature of the objectives it aims at achieving. A political act intended to promote the interests

[29] Ibid., pp. 1 and 3–4.

[30] *Fatāwā*, pp. 142–3; English transl., p. 40.

[31] Ibid., pp. 165–6; English transl., p. 46.

[32] Ibid., pp. 57–8.

of Muslims is thus praiseworthy, however injurious it may be for others. No royal action taken in the cause of Islam can be despotic. On the other hand, the royal resolve that offends, ignores, or overlooks the demands of Sunni Islam is nothing but tyranny.[33]

Again, according to Barani, only a pious Muslim ruler can deliver justice to the people. Justice is to be sought because its enforcement creates conditions in which 'the molesters of the faith (*dīn*) and *sharī'a* are disgraced and overthrown . . . the glory of Islam is raised.' Justice is established only when the king truthfully follows the commands of religion.[34]

Barani is familiar with Plato and Aristotle, the two Greek philosophers oft cited in medieval Islamic writings, but he contents himself with mere hints at the importance of reason and rationality. He draws on the prevailing memory of the legendary justice of the Sassanid ruler Anushirwan, a pre-Islamic Zoroastrian, but he quickly balances this by describing anecdotes of the justice associated with 'Umar bin al-Khattab, the Second Pious Caliph of Islam (r.634–44). What is more significant still is that he is uneasy with the fact that it was Anushirwan, a pagan, who commanded the ultimate image of an impeccably just ruler. Barani postulates a formula to resolve this difficulty. He divides justice into two categories: justice which guarantees universal equality (*'adl-i musāwāt-i ṯalabī-yi 'ām*) and justice which ensures only special or limited equality (*'adl-i musāwāt-i ṯalabī-yi khāṣṣ*). The former is represented by the Pious Caliph 'Umar. This implies a situation in which the ruler obliterates the distinction between the ruler and the ruled, imparting justice by mingling with them as one. The latter—which, according to Barani, is represented by Anushirwan—entailed a system in which the king, retaining his privileged regal status, delivers justice to people from the exalted portals of his royal court. The ruler here merely ensures equality among litigants.[35] Justice that guarantees universal

[33] Ibid., pp. 50–1; English transl., pp. 13–14 and 15.

[34] Ibid., p. 68; English transl., p. 17.

[35] Ibid., English transl., pp. 37–8.

equality can only be Islamic; and even though such equality ended with the Pious Caliphs, for a Muslim king this should be the ideal—not the sort demonstrated by Anushirwan. This superior model of justice is not easy to emulate, but it is to be constantly sought after and used to convince unbelievers of the finality and truth of the faith.[36]

In this chapter, Barani also discusses the close connection between *dīndārī* (looking to the faith) and *jahāndārī* (concern with the world). The two are to him inseparable; their combination creates and sustains ideal conditions for the promotion of Islam. His discussion of the principles of governance thus revolves around key concepts such as *sharī'a*, *kufr*, *jihād*, and *jizya*, where all that is good originates in Islam, while a non-Muslim is nothing but evil embodied. The practice of *iḥtikār*—that is, hoarding goods purchased at low prices to sell at critical times when prices have soared—was usually considered an evil as such, independent of the wrongdoer's religious affiliation. Barani, however, attributes such evil to the religion of the Hindus and tends to explain the practice in religious terms,[37] basically because he has noticed this among Hindus. He refuses to link hoarding to the simple secular fact that Hindus dominate and control trade in his time. Thus, hoarding must be suppressed not because it is bad for people across faiths but because Muslim rulers may thus deprive Hindus of their ill-gotten gains. The sultan will then serve an important cause within the true faith.

On grounds of necessity, however, Barani also advises that non-Muslims be taken into Muslim state service—within limits. The evidence of Hindu soldiers in the army of his hero, Mahmud, to fight the enemies of Islam is enough reason for him not to abhor their presence in the armies of the sultans of his own time. Barani does emphasize the compelling need under which Mahmud found himself, and hastens to enumerate the disadvantages of Hindu soldiers as well: 'The disadvantages of collecting slaves and keeping them

[36] Ibid., pp. 75–81.

[37] Ibid., pp. 136–7; English transl., pp. 37–8.

together are these: Most of these slaves are reckless and shameless. Fear of God and the characteristics of hereditary Islam . . . cannot be implanted in the minds of Hindu slaves even during the many years they grow from childhood to maturity among the Mussalmans.'[38]

The logic of necessity also extends to his plea for the *ẓawābiṭ* or secular state regulations to be framed by the ruler. He makes it very clear that *ẓawābiṭ* were to be justified on grounds of political expediency, in situations when Muslim rulers are unable to implement the regulations of the *sharī'a* in full. The aim of framing the *ẓawābiṭ* was hence to reinforce the *sharī'a*, to complement it; the *ẓawābiṭ* were not meant to work separately from, let alone contrary to, the *sharī'a*.[39] An anecdote on the meeting between Sultan Mahmud and Qadr Khan (the ruler of Khita), in which the two rulers inform each other of the laws and regulations in vogue in their respective domains—and thereby account for the success and stability of their regimes—is revealing. Mrs Khan dismisses this anecdote as historically impossible, for, as she says, the kingdom of Khita (or Qara Khita) was founded only in 1123, much after Mahmud's death in 1030.[40] Mrs Khan is right, and the incident of the meeting of the two sultans is obviously Barani's imaginative construction, but it is precisely for this reason significant for our purposes. Barani writes that, having heard from Qadr Khan of the features of his laws, Mahmud outlined the secrets of the success of his own *ẓawābiṭ* (among other things) as follows:

> We belong to Mohammad's Faith; he was the last of the prophets. In every law I frame concerning the affairs of my state, my real object is the enforcement of the Prophet's *sharī'at* to which my laws are not opposed. The first law of my government is this. Thirty-eight years have passed since I became king, and it has been my strong resolve and firm determination ever since my accession to put the

[38] Ibid., pp. 104–5; English transl., p. 25.
[39] Ibid., p. 217; English transl., p. 64.
[40] English transl., p. 67, notes.

> opponents of the Prophet's religion to the sword, to take the orders of the Muslim *sharīʻat* to the ends of the earth and to illuminate all territories with the light of Islam. I assign the duty of enforcing the orders of the *sharīʻat* to pious, religious and God-fearing men.[41]

Barani's emphasis on high birth, heredity and class is generally seen as among the secular or non-religious features of his political theory. For Barani, it has been suggested, virtues such as political acumen, administrative skill and statesmanship are not acquired traits but genetic ones. He attributes the longevity of the rule of the Sassanids to the fact that they upheld the principle of heredity when allocating positions to their officials.[42] However, it is also important to keep in mind that Barani's discussions on heredity are all geared towards ensuring the stability of Islamic regimes. The principal aim is not, as has been suggested, to build legitimacy for a 'class state'.[43] Rather, the interests of the Muslim community define the contours of his ideas on the heredity question.

In fact, Barani's narrow horizons, within which the discussion of heredity is structured, can be located in the historical developments of the period with which he is concerned. Barani covers about a century and a half in his book. For him, this is a particularly unnerving period. Ideally, during this long stretch of time, Islam and the rule of *sharīʻa* should have been firmly established in India. Yet, to the contrary, he sees that this period is rocked with political revolution and ethnic strife. Muslim ruling families are continuously under threat and becoming weak. This obviously troubles Barani; the only solution that he sees lies in the principle of heredity. This article of faith is further illustrated by a long passage which reads like a pathetic sermon, wherein he highlights the view that frequent changes within ruling classes lead to the ruination of illustrious Muslim families. He makes a plea for 'think[ing] of a policy (*tadbīr*) owing

[41] Ibid., pp. 228–31; English transl., pp. 69–70.

[42] Ibid., p. 305; English transl., p. 93.

[43] See Irfan Habib, 'Barani's Theory of the History of the Delhi Sultanate', *India Historical Review*, vol. 7, nos 1–2, 1980–1, pp. 99–115.

to which Musalmans . . . and their families and followers may not be deprived of their lives and properties.'[44] Barani's invocation of the heredity principle, or the appropriation of a non-Islamic, Iranian and Indian principle, can thus hardly be taken as an index of the socialization of the Delhi Sultanate. It was a conscious choice exercized by Barani to serve the narrowly sectarian interests of the early Islamic regime in India.

How much the practice of the Delhi sultans conformed to or deviated from this theory is an altogether different question. Our aim here has been principally to assess the ideal positions that a noted Indo-Muslim political theorist advocated with reference to both the *sharī'a* and notions of expediency. We know perfectly well that these ideas could hardly have influenced the policies of even the most powerful of the early Turkish rulers of northern India. Shams al-Din Iltutmish thus took shelter behind the plea that the Muslims, in terms of strength, were still like salt in a dish and thus unable to wage an all-out war either to force infidels to accept Islam or to exterminate them because of their refusal. Ghiyas al-Din Balban (r.1266–87), who dominated Delhi politics first as a powerful faction leader and then as sultan, kept theologians and theorists like Barani at a distance by dismissing them as mere seekers after narrow worldly gain (*'ulamā'-i dunyā*). 'Ala al-Din Khalji did have celebrated discussions on such questions with his *qāẓī*, but in practice followed the rule which, in his calculation, best served the interest of his power and people. Muhammad bin Tughlaq (r.1324–51), far from degrading them, accorded high positions to Hindus; while his successor, Firuz Tughlaq (r.1351–88), showed interest in Hindu traditions and monuments despite his orthodox religious leanings. Sikandar Lodi (r.1489–1517), even if sometimes remembered as a bigot, encouraged Hindus to learn Persian for their fuller participation in state management.[45] Such being the practice, Barani's *Fatāwā* represents merely one point of view, and it is surely

[44] *Fatāwā*, p. 309; English transl., p. 104.

[45] Cf. K.A. Nizami, *Some Aspects of Religion and Politics in India during the Thirteenth Century*, reprint, Delhi, 1974, pp. 152, 315–16; A.B.M. Habibullah, *The Foundation of Muslim Rule in India*, reprint, Allahabad, 1976, pp. 264–76.

misleading to give it the title that appears on its English translation by Mrs Khan, namely, *The Political Theory of the Delhi Sultanate*.

## The *Zakhīrat al-Mulūk* of Mir Sayyid 'Ali Hamadani (d.1384)

Before turning to later materials from the Mughal period, it may be in order to briefly consider Sayyid 'Ali bin Shihab Hamadani's *Zakhīrat al-Mulūk*.[46] This is not strictly an Indo-Islamic text, despite the fact that Hamadani's name is often associated with the history of Islam in Kashmir.[47] Hamadani wrote the *Zakhīrat* with the aim of discussing and elaborating the principles of the form and substance of power and governance (*lawāzim-i qawā'id-i salṭanat-i ṣuwarī-o-ma'nawī*) for those Muslim rulers and state officials who wished to set right the affairs of religion (*istiṣlāḥ-i umūr-i dīn*). The book, divided into ten chapters, opens with a discussion on the institutes and requirements of faith in God, the Prophet and the Qur'an, and on the requirement for their perfection. The second chapter—which deals with the principal pillars of Islam, prayers and duties that man owes God—begins with a tradition of the Prophet on prayer (*namāz*). Chapter three deals with moral standards and etiquettes for rulers; chapter four with rights and duties of members of a family; the fifth with statecraft. Of the remaining five chapters, only one, the ninth, deals with regulations of governance (*salṭanat* and *wilāyat*); the rest are all concerned with matters spiritual.[48]

The thrust and content of the passages on the principles of *salṭanat*, the qualities and duties recommended for the king, and the

[46] 'Zakhīrat al-Mulūk', MS. Bibliothèque Nationale (BN), Paris, no. 760, ff. 2a, 6a, and 19b.

[47] See, for instance, A.Q. Rafiqi, *History of Sufism in Kashmir*, Delhi, n.d., pp. 80ff; Aziz Ahmad, 'Conversion to Islam in the Valley of Kashmir', *Central Asiatique Journal*, vol. XXIII, nos 1–2, 1979. M. Ishaq Khan, however, does not agree with this position. See his *Kashmir's Transition to Islam: The Role of the Muslim Rishis (Fifteenth to Eighteenth Centuries)*, Delhi, 1994, pp. 4–21, 22–35 and 221–40.

[48] See S.M. Azizuddin, 'Political Ideas of Mir Sayyid Ali Hamadani', *Hamdard Islamicus*, vol. XIII, no. 4, pp. 31–41.

categories of people (or *ri'āyā*) are all discussed with reference to *sharī'a*. The ruler who does not have a benign attitude towards his people and transgresses the limits of the *sharī'a* is the enemy of God and the Prophet.[49] Hamadani calls such a ruler 'the Caliph of the Devil'. Further, he delineates ten necessary conditions to ensure the stability of the state, among which the first two are that 'while dealing with matters involving his people he should place himself as one of them; treat the Muslims in the way he would like himself to be treated; and that the best prayer for him is the fulfilment of the needs of the Muslim (*qaẕā-i ḥajāt-i Musalmānān*).'[50]

Muslims have twenty special rights which rulers are obliged to guard.[51] The principal concern of the state, for Hamadani, is enforcement of the institutes of the *sharī'a* with a view to providing justice to Muslims, to reward and honour them in a manner commensurate with the excellences they have achieved in faith (*īmān*). He divides the subjects (*ra'iyat*) of the ruler into two categories, *Kāfir* and Muslim, but then dwells only on the latter (*ahl-i īmañ*).[52] The rights of the *ri'āyā*, according to Hamadani, should follow from their respective religions. Muslims and *Kāfirs* both enjoy divine compassion (*raḥmat-i Ḥaqq*); nonetheless, they have to be treated differently by Muslim rulers. *Kāfirs* living in a Muslim territory are *ahl-i ẕimma*; Muslim rulers should protect their lives and properties provided they (*ahl-i ẕimma*) maintain the following somewhat elaborate conditions laid down in the agreement (*'ahd-nāma*) that the Second Pious Caliph 'Umar had made with the People of the Book and the fire-worshippers (*majūs wa ahl-i kitāb*):

> (1) They should not build places of worship, (2) nor should they renew or rebuild the old and desolate ones. (3) Muslim travellers should be allowed to enter and stay in their religious buildings, and (4) if any Muslim wants, he can also stay as a guest for three or four days in their houses. (5) The *ẕimmīs* should not act as spies. (6) If a

49 Ibid., p. 33.
50 *Ẕakhīrat al-Mulūk*, ff. 87.
51 Ibid., f. 88a.
52 Ibid., ff. 19b and 92.

relative of theirs is inclined to accept Islam, he should not be discouraged and dissuaded from doing so. (7) They should give due respect to Muslims, and (8) if a Muslim happens to visit a place where a non-Muslim occupies a seat, the latter must vacate it for the Muslim. (9) They should not dress like the Muslims. (10) They should not use Muslim names. (11) They should ride on horses without reins and saddles. (12) They should not carry weapons. (13) They should not use rings with engraved stones (*muhr-o-nagin*). (14) They should not sell wine, nor should they drink in public. (15) In order to look different from the Muslims, they should wear clothes in their own old style. (16) There should be no public demonstrations of their rituals and customs before the Muslims. (17) They should not live in the neighbourhood of Muslims. (18) They should not carry their dead bodies through Muslim graveyards. (19) They should not mourn their dead in public; and (20) they cannot buy Muslim slaves.[53]

From Mawardi and Nizam al-Mulk to Barani and Hamadani, a long distance is traversed with regard to the evolution of the theory and practice of governance. Nizam al-Mulk was a *wazīr*, a man at the helm; his heroes included the pre-Islamic Anushirwan, Buzurchmehr and Ardeshir. Ghazali, a theologian-Sufi, was in a way a middle-of-the-road thinker. These writers advocated maintenance of the *sharī'a* and its defence against enemies. For Mawardi, the caliph defended *sharī'a* the best; for Nizam al-Mulk, the king was to guarantee its maintenance; and Ghazali struck a compromise between the two. For Barani, kingship with all its attendant attributes was a sin for which the king had to make compensation (*kaffāra*). In the process, bigotry and narrow religious sectarianism became integral to his political theory. Hamadani's prime concern, wherever he discussed statecraft, was also to advise Muslim rulers to ensure the welfare of the people of the faith.

There is scarcely any sign of the impact of Hellenic writings on the discussions of statecraft in these writers. Further, they all saw the king as a Muslim ruler whose role it was, in the first place, to

[53] Ibid., ff. 90 and 91a.

manage the interests of Muslims. The aim of their discussion around terms like *sharī'a* and *siyāsa*—as also their desire to resolve the conflict between the two—was above all to maintain the integrity of the community of Muslims.

This was, however, only one tradition that influenced the formation of Indo-Islamic principles of governance.

## *Sharī'a* in Nasirean *Akhlāq*

### Nasir al-Din Tusi and His *Akhlāq*

It may be argued that Nizam al-Mulk and Barani also, in a measure, represent 'dissent'—but only to the extent that they, in varying degrees, tolerate the existence of kingship in Muslim society. In religious matters, they adhere to Sunni orthodox traditions, using the term *sharī'a* in its conventional juristic sense. But there were simultaneous movements of dissent in the domain of religion as well, and since the proponents of these movements considered the existing dominant power structures a form of tyranny, they developed alternative norms and principles.[54] The theories of these writers were more prominently based on thinkers from the Byzantine tradition. Initially, these trends found favour with extremist groups of so-called 'deviationists', but they were soon integrated into a general theory of state. For an evaluation of this process, Khwaja Nasir al-Din Tusi's *Akhlāq-i Nāṣirī*[55] deserves special notice. Through this work, and especially its section on state and politics, a good part of the ideas of erstwhile dissenters gradually entered the general fabric of Sunni political Islam. The *sharī'a*, all the same, continued as the reference point.

Tusi was a philosopher and scientist with well over a dozen books to his credit. He was the builder of the celebrated observatory

[54] Bernard Lewis, *The Assassins: A Radical Sect in Islam*, London, 1967; P.J. Vatikiotis, *The Fatimid Theory of State*, 2nd edn, Lahore, 1981; Wilfred Madelung, *Religious Trends in Early Islamic Iran*, Albany, New York, 1988.

[55] Several editions of this book are available. I have used the edition prepared by Mujtaba Minavi and 'Ali Riza Haidari, Tehran, 1976; G.M. Wickens has translated the text into English as *The Nasirean Ethics*, London, 1964.

and library at Maraghah in Azarbaijan in 1259. He organized a large number of savants around it and thus compiled a work entitled the *Zij-i Īlkhānī*.[56] He published the *Akhlāq-i Nāṣirī* in Persian,[57] first in 1235 at the instance of the Isma'ili prince Nasir al-Din 'Abd al-Rahim bin Abi Mansur, who was the *wālī* (ruler) of Quhistan during the reign of 'Ala al-Din Muhammad (1221–55) of Alamut. We are aware that Tusi was commissioned to translate Ibn Miskawaih's *Tahẕīb al-Akhlāq* or *Kitāb al-Ṭahāra* from the Arabic, but his work eventually turned into much more than a translation. Besides the first discourse, which was a summary arranged anew of Ibn Miskawaih's *Tahẕīb*, Tusi added two new discourses—one on the household and family management (*tadbīr-i manzil*), the other on politics (*siyāsat-i mudun*)—as parts of practical wisdom (*ḥikmat-i 'amalī*). He drew on Hellenic philosophical writings and blended them with his own 'Islamic' view of man and society. His synthesis represented 'a subtle transcending of both'.[58]

The king was for Tusi the sustainer of existing things, the one who completes that which is incomplete. Since men (*insān*) by their nature (*uns-i ṭaba'ī*) were social beings and needed other men, it was necessary that an arrangement be made for the right working of their relationships. The individual who had attained perfection through equipoise (*i'tidāl*) and through a perception of union with the Supreme Being was thus selected for kingship. The ideal king

[56] Edward G. Browne, *Literary History of Persia*, II, Cambridge, 1969, p. 485. Abdus Salam Nadvi, *Ḥukamā'-i Islām* (Urdu), Azamgarh, II, p. 256. For an account of the Maraghah Observatory, see Aydin Sayilli, *The Observatory in Islam*, Ankara, 1960, pp. 189–223.

[57] The book was reissued with a second preface wherein Tusi is severely critical of the religious milieu in which it is originally written. Tusi alludes to his enforced service with the Isma'ilis and his rescue from them by the Mongols. (Cf. the edition published by The Punjab University Lahore Press, Lahore, 1955.) This was, however, as G.M. Wickens points out, only to cover a revised preface and dedication.

[58] G.M. Wickens, 'Akhlaq-i Naseri', *Encyclopaedia Iranica*, vol. I, ed. Ehsan Yarshater, London, Boston and Henley, 1985, p. 725. Qustantin Zurayq has prepared a new edition of the Arabic *Tahẕīb al-Akhlāq*, Beyrut, American University, 1966.

was the philosopher-king: his noble aim was to help his subjects 'reach potential wisdom by the use of their mental powers'. In his discussion on the categories of social order, Tusi followed the classification of the noted Islamic philosopher Farabi. Civil society (*tamaddun*), according to him, is first to be divided into two categories: first, the ideal and excellent city or state (*al-madīnat al-fāẓila*); second, the bad and unrighteous city. The second sort of state was again sub-divided into three categories; the misguided city which had gone astray (*al-madīnat al-ẓālla*), the evil-doing city (*al-madīnat al-fāsiqa*), and the ignorant city (*al-madīnat al-jāhila*).[59] Like Farabi, Tusi also suggested that it was possible for the ideal city to be composed of peoples with diverse social and religious practices.[60] The leader of the ideal city was ideally to be the philosopher-king, under whose care and protection each member of society, secure in the place best suited for him, was to aspire and struggle to achieve perfection.[61]

The *Akhlāq-i Nāṣirī* is a work of theory, idealistic and normative in character, and it is naturally difficult to take the text as evidence of the circumstances that actually obtained when it was prepared. Still, one is tempted to point to the fact that the book was composed at a time when the religious views of rulers did not correspond with those of large numbers of their subjects. In 1235, Tusi dedicated the book to an Isma'ili prince of a region which, in Nizam al-Mulk's *Siyāsat Nāma*, had been portrayed as especially disturbed and misguided.[62] Later, when the 'pagan' Mongols, having shattered the caliphate and the power of Muslim rulers, rose to become kings of the erstwhile world of Islam, Tusi wrote a new preface to his work

[59] M.M. Sharif, ed., *A History of Muslim Philosophy*, 2 vols, Wiesbaden, 1963–6, I, pp. 704–14.

[60] *Akhlāq-i Nāṣirī*, pp. 286–7. 'The People of the Virtuous City, however, albeit diversified throughout the world, are in reality agreed, for their hearts are upright one towards another and they are adorned with love for each other. In their close-knit affection they are like one individual.' *The Nasirean Ethics*, p. 215.

[61] Ibid., pp. 286 and 288.

[62] *Siyāsat Nāma*, pp. 262–7, for the Qaramitas and the Batinis in Quhistan.

and dedicated it to the non-Muslim Mongol ruler of Maraghah, without changing its contents.

It was in this sort of situation that Tusi envisaged an ideal ruler who would harmonize the conflicting interests of diverse social and religious groups in the state. The crisis which the Muslim world encountered in the face of the Mongol disaster created conditions for the acceptability of Tusi's idea.[63] This is not to suggest that in the state which Tusi—or for that matter similarly inclined writers—envisaged, religion and the *sharīʻa* occupied no important place. Tusi indicates that the nomos or the Divine Institute (*Nāmūs-i Ilāhī*), which occupied a premier position among the three prerequisites for the maintenance of an ideal civil society, manifests itself in *sharīʻa*.[64] The Divine Institute in Nasirean ethics appears to be the same as the universal metaphysical ideal. And if a divergence was noticed between the two anywhere, the proponents of Nasirean ethics, like certain early Muslim philosophers, took support from the principle of *tāwīl* (interpretation) to get at the real inner meanings (*bāṭin*) behind mere words and appearance (*ẓāhir*).[65]

They invoked the *sharīʻa* and illustrated their discourses by citing such anecdotes from the classical Islamic period as they found supporting their ideals. This was intended to serve as an effective device to promote and enhance the prospects of their 'radical' views. However, the connotations of the *sharīʻa*, in these cases, were not the same as those that a jurist intended when he used the term. The ideal ruler in the Nasirean tradition was the one who ensured the well being of the people of diverse religious groups, and not Muslims alone.

Before proceeding further we should be clear that there was no

[63] M. Khalid Masud, 'The Doctrine of *Siyasa* in Islamic Law', *Recht van de Islam*, vol. 18, 2001, pp. 1–29.

[64] *Akhlāq-i Nāṣirī*, p. 134.

[65] M.M. Sharif, ed., *A History of Muslim Philosophy*, I, pp. 544–64 and 592–616, for an illustration, for instance, from Ibn Rushd's *Tahāfat al-tahāfah* (Repudiation of the Repudiation), which he wrote in reply to Ghazali's *Tahāfat al-Falāsifah*.

uniformity of political concepts and ideas which emerged after the Mongol invasion of the Islamic world. In the writings of Ibn Taimiyya (d.1328) and Ibn Qayyim (d.1350), for instance, there was a totally different response to the crisis, even as they allowed greater power to rulers *vis-à-vis* jurists.[66] In the ruling mileux of the Perso-Islamic world, Ibn Taimiyya had little impact. In the Indian context the early references to Ibn Taimiyya's ideas remain unacknowledged, surfacing only much later in the writings of Shaikh Ahmad Sirhindi and Shah Wali-Allah, in the seventeenth and eighteenth centuries. Tusi's norms of governance, in contrast, were read, articulated, and rearticulated off and on in the Perso-Islamic world from his time to the heyday of the Mughals.

## The *Akhlāq-i Nāṣirī* in Mughal India

There is not much in the available writings on medieval Indian intellectual and literary history to indicate the exact time and place of the first entry of Tusi's *Akhlāq* into the subcontinent. The book was certainly widely read in Mughal India.[67] One may surmise that it reached India through Gujarat or the Deccan, where several Persian scholars, including some pupils of Jalal al-Din al-Dawwani (who had prepared a recension of the book under the title *Akhlāq-i Jalālī* in the late fifteenth century), had migrated in the late fifteenth and sixteenth centuries. Sikandar Lodi (r.1489–1517) is reported to have invited one Mir Sayyid Rafi al-Din, a disciple of Dawwani from Gujarat, to his court.[68] But it should be noted that both Dawwani and Rafi al-Din were primarily theologians, and that the latter lent active support to the orthodox Sunni sectarian '*ulamā*' in India.[69]

[66] Compare M. Khalid Masud, 'The Doctrine of *Siyasa* in Islamic Law'; see also Fazlur Rahman, *Revival and Reform in Islam: A Study of Islamic Fundamentalism*, Oxford, 2000, pp. 133–65.

[67] S.A.A. Rizvi, *Religious and Intellectual History of the Muslims in Akbar's Reign (1556–1605) with Special Reference to Abul Fazl*, Delhi, 1975, pp. 355–6 and 366–9.

[68] Ibid., pp. 42 and 80.

[69] Ibid., p. 42.

It is likely that the Mughals appropriated Nasirean ethics as a legacy of Babur, the founder of their rule in India, who in turn inherited it from the Timurids of Herat after their extirpation by the Shaibanis. Sultan Husain Bayqara (r.1470–1506), the last great Timurid in Herat, even though a Sunni, seems to have disapproved of his government being run exclusively on narrow Sunni Islamic lines.[70] In consonance with his policies, at least two versions of Tusi's work—*Akhlāq-i Muḥsinī* by Husain Wa'iz al-Kashifi and *Dastūr al-Wizārat* or *Akhlāq-i Humāyūnī* by Qazi Ikhtiyar al-Din Hasan al-Husaini—were prepared at his behest.[71] Of these two, a detour through Ikhtiyar al-Husaini's treatise helps us, in particular, to comprehend some of the reasons for Tusi's special status within the body of Mughal Persian authors.

*Akhlāq-i Humāyūnī* was initially titled *Dastūr al-Wizārat*, a book of modest size on ethics and politics. The author claims he has described and summed up (*ba-ikhtiṣār*) in 'elegant' and 'eloquent' Persian, and also tabulated 'the subtle, abstruse, complex and

[70] According to Rizvi, Sultan Husain Bayqara had decided to have the *khuṭba* read in the names of the twelve *imams*, but his prime minister Mir 'Ali Sher Nawa'i (d.1501) and certain other authorities stopped him from doing so. Cf. his *A Socio-Intellectual History of the Isna 'Ashari Shi'is in India*, Canberra, 1986, vol. I, pp. 165–6. Rizvi cites Nurullah Shustari's *Majālis al-Mūminīn*. Using several contemporary chronicles, Jean Calmard has recently shown that Bayqara discouraged strictly legalistic Sunni Islam, had Shi'ite leanings, and also proposed to proclaim Shi'ism as the state religion. See his 'Les rituels shi'ite et le pouvoir: L'imposition du shi'ism safavide, eulogies et malédictions canoniques', in J. Calmard, ed., *Etudes Safavides*, Paris-Tehran, 1993, p. 113.

[71] Kashifi's *Akhlāq-i Muḥsinī* is available in print; among its several editions is the one published from Bombay in 1890/1308 H. An English translation of another version by Jalal al-Din has also been published as *Practical Philosophy of the Muhammadan People: Exhibited in its Professed Connexion with the European, so as to Render either an Introduction to the Other: Being a Translation of the Akhlak-i Jalaly from the Persian of Fakir Jany Muhammad Asaad, with References and Notes by W.F. Thompson*, Karachi, 1977 (reprint of 1880 edition); Husaini's *Dastūr al-Wizārat* has not been published. Manuscript copies (nos 767 and 768) are preserved in the Bibliothèque Nationale (BN), Paris. For a description, see Edgar Blochet, *Catalogues de Manuscripts Persans*, vol. 2, Paris, Imprimerie nationale (etc.), 1905–34, pp. 37–8.

convoluted' discourses on themes (*rashḥāt-i masā'il rā dar mashāri'-i jadāwīl jaryān dād*) which he had read in numerous books, including, and in particular, those by Ibn Miskawaih and Nasir al-Din Tusi on human nature, the family, household and government. The purpose of writing his book, he tells us, is to provide state officials with a manual for day-to-day activities (*dastūr al-'amal-i rūznāma-i ayyām; aṣḥāb-i riyāsat wa arbāb-i siyāsat*), as a means towards the consolidation of their religious and worldly fortunes as well as for the stability of the state (*sabab-i ṣalāḥ-o-falāḥ-i ṣuwarī-o-ma'nawī wa bā'iṡ-i dawām-o-khulūd-i mulk-o-daulat*).

The book is divided into three parts, called *qānūns* (laws), and each is divided further into two sections, called *qā'idas* (rules). These again are divided into two chapters termed *baḥs̱* (debates, enquiries). Part One is on ethics or the correction of disposition (*tahẕīb-i akhlāq wa farhang*), with discussions on virtues and vices, and on methods of their acquisition and removal, respectively. In the introduction to Part Two, the author proposes to discuss the family, and the regulation of households and properties. But in the main text the discussion is devoted only to the regulation of properties (*tadbīr-i amwāl*)—the ways they should be acquired, the heads under which one should spend one's wealth, the categories of properties one should never seek to build, etc. Part Three discusses the principles of rulership (*taqwīm-i ri'āyā wa mamlikat-dārī*), with a section on the king's servants and with discourses on nobles and the army in two separate chapters. Section Two of this part considers the subject population, with a discussion on those who are accomplished (*khawāṣṣ*) in Chapter One, and those that comprise the ordinary *ri'āyā* in Chapter Two.[72]

The author, Ikhtiyar al-Din al-Husaini, the chief *qāẓī* of Herat and a *wazīr* in the time of the Timurid Sultan Husain Bayqara,[73] came from an eminent family of '*ulamā*' of Turbat-i Jam, and had held

72 *Akhlāq-i Humāyūnī*, BN, Paris, MS. No. 767 and 768, fols. 6a-8b.

73 Khwandmir, *Ḥabīb al-Siyar*, Tehran, 1973/1352 *sh.*, vol. IV, pp. 355–6; and pp. 311, 376, 377, 382, 398, 514 and 685, for his biographical notices; see also Blochet, *Catalogue*, vol. 2, p. 37.

high positions in Timurid Central Asia. He prepared the earlier version of his book in the time of Sultan Abu Sa‘id Mirza (1459–69), for the young prince Husain Mirza (later Sultan Husain Bayqara) who was, at the time, the chief prop and support of the *salṭanat* and acted virtually like the *wazīr*.[74] Subsequently, after the collapse of Timurid power in Herat, our author, lucky to escape the fate (‘imprisonment and execution’) of many of his contemporaries, chose a life of retirement in his home town of Turbat, ‘accompanied and favoured there by the souls of the great saints and of his ancestors’.[75] Then a day came when he heard that ‘the lamp of the illustrious Timurid house’ had again been lit in Kabul with the valiant efforts of Zahir al-Din Muhammad Babur. Subsequently, he arrived at the court of Babur, accompanied by several ‘princes and great men of Herat’.

The young Babur impressed our author with his unusual accomplishments, support for learning, and active participation in learned debates. Ikhtiyar had long discussions with Babur on the diverse branches of science and on the laws and forms (*qawānīn-o-ādāb*) of government. The result, he claims in the second preface to his book, was a treatise, the title of which he thought should appropriately be *A<u>kh</u>lāq-i Humāyūnī*, since it represented the high ethical ideals of the king, Babur (*chūn īn risāla partawīst az natā’ij-i a<u>kh</u>lāq-i humāyūn-i ḥaẓrat-i ‘ālī, ān rā Risāla-i A<u>kh</u>lāq-i Humāyūnī nām nihād*). We know that this treatise was the very same that the author had earlier compiled for Prince Husain Mirza. At any rate, our author is very conscious of the value of his work, and, just as he had earlier advised Husain Mirza to keep it constantly with him, he now hopes it will prove a source of strength for Babur, and later for his ‘illustrious descendants’, in running their government.[76]

Ikhtiyar al-Husaini wrote a couple of other books as well. Babur,

[74] *A<u>kh</u>lāq-i Humāyūnī*, MS. 768, fols. 4a–6b.

[75] Khwandmir says that Abu’l Fath Muhammad Shaibani retained him in the office of *qāẓī*. But after his death he was dismissed. Ikhtiyar then retired to Turbat to lead a life of an agriculturist there. See *Ḥabīb al-Siyar*, p. 355.

[76] *A<u>kh</u>lāq-i Humāyūnī*, fols. 2a–6a.

in his memoirs, cites his *Asās al-Iqtibās*, a collection of Qur'anic verses and traditions of the Prophet with comments;[77] this is the same work that Khwandmir calls *Iqtibāsāt*. Another work written by our author is titled *Mukhtār al-Ikhtiyār*, this being on jurisprudence,[78] suggesting that he conceived a division between the law meant for prayers and other private matters on the one hand, and the one discussed in the *Akhlāq-i Humāyūnī* on the other, within which a significant part deals with public issues.

## Political Norms in *Akhlāq* Literature

The main body of an *akhlāq* text generally begins with a discussion on human dispositions and the need for their disciplining and sublimation. The discussion is interspersed with Qur'anic verses and the traditions of the Prophet, with a bearing on universal human values. Thus the reference points are unequivocally 'man' (*bashar, insān, banī ādam*), his living (*amr-i ma'āsh*) and the world (*'ālam, āfāq*). The perfection of man, according to the authors of these texts, is to be achieved by the admiration and adulation of divinity, but is impossible to attain without a peaceful social organization wherein everyone earns his living cooperatively and by helping others. Thus:

> If one is engaged in managing the means of his living, and seeks no help from anyone else, he will spend all his life arranging merely a part of his food and clothing. The affairs of living must thus be administered through cooperation (*shirkat-o-mu'āwanat*) which [in turn] depends on justice (*'adl*). If *'adl* disappears, each man will pursue his own desires. Therefore there has to be an institute (*dastūr*) and a balancing agency (*mīzān*) to ensure cooperation. The *sharī'a*—the protectors of which have been the prophets (*anbiyā' wa*

[77] Blochet, *Catalogues*, vol. 2, p. 37.

[78] See *Ḥabīb al-Siyar*, p. 356; see also W. Ivanow, *Descriptive Catalogue of the Persian Manuscripts in the Collection of the Asiatic Society of Bengal*, vol. I, Calcutta, 1924, pp. 449 and 662, for a description of a manuscript copy of this work titled *Mukhtār al-Ikhtiyār 'alā al-Mazāhib al-Mukhtār* of Qazi Ikhtiyar al-Din bin Ghiyas al-Din al-Husaini. The work is dedicated to Babur.

*rusul*)—serves this purpose. But the *sharī'a* cannot work without being administered by a just king, whose principal duty it is to keep people in control through affection and favours.[79]

The goal in the discourse on political organization in *a<u>kh</u>lāq* literature is thus 'cooperation', to be achieved through justice (*'adl*) administered in accordance with a law which is protected and promoted by a king whose principal instrument of control should be affection and favours (*rāfat-o-imtinān*), not command and obedience (*amr-o-imtiṣāl*). The *sharī'a* here connotes, as one could speculate from its elaboration, something other than the jurist's notion of strict Islamic law. The reader here is reminded of the Qur'anic verse that there is a single God who has sent prophets to different communities, with *sharī'a* to suit their time and climes.

Justice (*'adl*) emerges as the cornerstone of social organization. But how 'cooperation' was sought to be achieved could be gauged from the fact that Tusi initially suggests mutual love (*maḥabbat*)—a much higher and nobler means—as the ultimate and most powerful guarantor of such cooperation. Justice occupies second place in his order of preference; it is not the natural way to achieve social balance, it is artificial because it is attained only through the king's exercise of power and through a coercive government machinery.

> Justice leads to artificial union, whereas love generates natural unity, and the artificial in relation to the natural is compulsive, like an imposition. The artificial comes after the natural, and thus it is obvious that the need for justice, which is the most accomplished human virtue, is because of the absence of love. If love among the people were available, *inṣāf* [justice] would not have been needed. [The word] *inṣāf* comes from *naṣf* [which means taking the half, reaching towards the middle]. The *munṣif* [the dispenser of justice] is called so because [he] divides the disputed object into two equal parts (*munaṣafa*); division into halves (*tanṣīf*) implies multiplicity (*taka<u>ss</u>ur*) whereas love is the cause of oneness.[80]

[79] *A<u>kh</u>lāq-i Humāyūnī*, BN, MS. No. 767, ff. 2.

[80] *A<u>kh</u>lāq-i Nāṣirī*, pp. 258–9; also pp. 251–74 for further elaboration and a discussion on different categories of love. See also *The Nasirean Ethics*, pp. 195–211.

*Akhlāq* literature hence recommends the evaluation of behaviour among men of strength, and their level of natural goodness or ill disposition (*khair-o-sharr-i ṭab'ī*).[81]

The rights of the *ri'āyā* do not follow from their religion. Muslim and *kāfir* both enjoy divine compassion (*raḥmat-i Ḥaqq*) in equal measure. Notions of *kāfir*, *kufr*, *zimma* and discrimination on such grounds find no place in *akhlāq* treatises. The true representative and the shadow of God on earth is the king who guarantees the undisturbed management of the affairs of His 'slaves', so that each achieves perfection (*kamāl*) in consonance with his competence and ability. This pattern of governance is called *siyāsat-i fāẓila* (ideal politics), which establishes, on firm foundations, the leadership (*imāmat*) of the true king. There is also a flawed and blemished politics (*siyāsat-i nāqiṣa*) against which the ruler is warned to guard himself, for the practice of faulty and perfunctory politics leads eventually to the ruination of the country and its people.[82]

> The man of ideal politics is always on the right path, considers the *ri'āyā* as his sons and friends and has control over his greed and lust (*ḥirṣ-o-shahwat*) through his intellect. The man of faulty politics resorts to coercion, takes the *ri'āyā* as his slaves, nay, even as women, while he himself is a slave of greed, lust and desire for wealth.[83]

Justice occupies a central place in discussions on medieval Islamic political theory, but its implications are not always the same. Mawardi defines '*adālat*, the quality of '*adl*, 'as a state of moral and religious perfection', while Ibn Yusuf equates religious piety with justice. The latter even advised the Abbasid Caliph Harun al-Rashid to reject the ancient Sassanian tradition of justice. For Nizam al-Mulk, on the other hand, the Sassanian Anushirwan was the best model of a just ruler. Kingship, he stated, cannot survive without justice; for the ruler it meant observation, in all matters, of

[81] *Akhlāq-i Humāyūnī*, BN, MS. No. 767, ff. 37b-38b.
[82] Ibid., f. 28b.
[83] Ibid., f. 29a.

the 'mean'. However, the most important objective that the ruler must achieve by administering justice is to set right the affairs of religion, 'so that God most high may accomplish for him the affairs of religion and of the world and fulfill his desires in both worlds.'[84] Nizam al-Mulk counts the ruthless execution of Mazdak and his 1200 followers (who had threatened the end of kingship in the Sassanian line) as the most notable achievement of Anushirwan towards establishing a just regime.[85] Silencing the opposition and the suppression of dissent by a king would therefore also, in Nizam al-Mulk's theory, count among the principal features of justice. In Ghazali, too, the importance of a religious ethic is obviously the principal reason for the maintenance of justice. But interestingly, Ghazali also gives some weight to expediency, which to Kaikā'us ibn Iskandar—the author of the noted eleventh-century text *Qābūs-nāma*—was the sole reason for justice.[86] Religion does not figure in Kaikā'us's definition of the aims of justice. Justice, to him, was meant to ensure the effective authority of the king, the well being of the *ri'āyā*, and the prosperity of the country.[87]

In *akhlāq* texts, on the other hand, justice in the ideal state is defined as social harmony, and the coordination and balance of the conflicting claims of diverse interest groups that may comprise people of various religions. The ruler, like the good physician, must know the diseases that afflict society, their symptoms and their correct treatment. Since society is composed of groups of diverse interests and of individuals of conflicting dispositions, the king must take all possible care for *'adl* to work smoothly, to maintain the

[84] A.K.S. Lambton, 'Justice in the Medieval Persian Theory of Kingship', *Theory and Practice in Medieval Persian Government*, chap. IV, pp. 91–119.

[85] *Siyāsat Nāma*, pp. 239–59.

[86] Lambton, 'Justice in the Medieval Persian Theory of Kingship'. As a matter of fact, Kaika'us's discussion on *ā'īn-o-sharṯ-i Bādshāhī* (rules and regulations of kingship) is one of the first examples in Persian of the later 'practical wisdom'. Compare, *Qābūs-nāma*, ed. Ghulam Husain Yusufi, Tehran, 1966/1345 *sh.*, pp. 227–39.

[87] Ibid.

health of society and the equipoise (*i'tidāl*) within it. This is how the state can be brought together into a single unit. Divergence from *'adl* causes clashes and thus destruction. No one should get either less or more than he deserves as a member of his class. Excess and shortfall (*ifrāṭ-o-tafrīṭ*) both dislocate the nature of the union and social relations of companionship.[88]

This emphasis on the desirability of justice is throughout argued from the point of view of a secular ethic. The state, its apparatus, its army, its wealth and the law are all taken as a means to achieve this ideal social balance. The king should have this goal in mind in all his actions, including the appointment of officials. In consideration of *'adl*, the king should in person investigate the conditions of the *ri'āyā* and make sure they have direct access to him. If perchance he cannot be available every day, he must fix a day for the populace to approach him direct for the redressal of grievances.[89] The author of the *Akhlāq-i Humāyūnī* thus reminds the ruler that the kings of ancient Persia allowed direct access to commoners, and that 'Umar, the Second Pious Caliph, made regular night tours through the city of Medina and around it, to find out for himself the conditions of his subjects.[90] Anecdotes from classical Islam are then mentioned to motivate the king to keep alive the means of 'justice' for all, and not—as we notice in other treatises on politics—to legitimate and invoke discrimination against one or the other section of the *ri'āyā*.

The intentions of the king, who emerges in these texts as the all-powerful centre of societal organization, turn out to be the most important factor for just rule. According to Husain Wa'iz al-Kashifi, in matters of the management of people and their welfare the intentions of the king play a crucial part. 'If his [the king's] intention is justice, the result will be blessing and the country will become populous, prosperous and well managed; but if, God forbid,

[88] *Akhlāq-i Humāyūnī*, ff. 30a–30b.

[89] Ibid., f. 30b.

[90] Ibid., ff. 39b–40a. The author mentions the famous anecdote of the caliph's encounter with the cursing widow who had nothing for her hungry children, and as they cried of hunger she pretended to cook something for them until they slept.

the contrary is the case, blessing will depart, the revenues will cease to grow, and the people will be in a quandary.'[91] A just king is the shadow of God, the source of all that is good for society. The emphasis is on the maintenance of balance in society, not on the eradication of infidelity and idolatry. A primary advice to the king is to consider his subjects as 'sons and friends', irrespective of their faith.

Deserving our special attention is the fact that justice had an independent existence, with the objective of serving a real public interest. Muslim or non-Muslim, a ruler must be just. A non-Muslim but just ruler will serve society better than an unjust Muslim sultan. The inherent excellence of justice and its intrinsic strength kept the ancient Sassanid kings entrenched in power for well over 5,000 years, even though they were all fire-worshippers and infidels.[92]

So, it was in the light of human reason (*ʻaql*) and not any religious legal code that the performance of the ruler, in relation to his concern for justice, was to be weighed. This view of justice echoes the early Muʻtazilite theory of values. In the early Abbasid period, there were two principal theories or values that opposed each other. One, of the Muʻtazilites and the philosophers, held that values such as justice and goodness have a real existence, independent of anyone's will. The other, of the Ashʻarites, said all values are determined by the will of God, who decides what shall be just or good or otherwise.[93] Following an intense competition between these two doctrines, that of the Ashʻarites finally prevailed in most Sunnite theological writings. The Muʻtazilite position survived principally as one of dissent, but it also found its way, with some modification, into the circles of some learned elites, including the authors of the *akhlāq* treatises, which are of great interest in part for this reason. Against this

[91] Husain Waʻiz al-Kashifi, *Akhlāq-i Muḥsinī*, Bombay, 1890/1308 H, pp. 56–7.

[92] Nur al-Din Qazi al-Khaqani, *Akhlāq-i Jahāngīrī*, British Library, London, Oriental and India Office Collections (OIOC), MS. 2207, f. 274b.

[93] G.F. Hourani, *Reason and Tradition in Islamic Ethics*, Cambridge, 1985, pp. 57–8.

background, it is a matter of considerable significance that these treatises, in course of time, began to be taught at the Sunni *madrasas* of Mughal India.

In these texts, terms such as *nāmūs*, *sharī'a* and the *sharī'a* of the prophets are often used interchangeably. The reference to the *sharī'a* of the prophets is fascinating because it allows Muslims to accept the laws and codes of all prophets on par with Islam. In Dawwani's recension of Tusi's *akhlāq*, the *sharī'a* is termed the greatest *nāmūs*, with the sultan being the second, and money the third.[94] The attempt at identifying *nāmūs*, a non-Islamic concept, with *sharī'a*, emerges more clearly in a treatise compiled in the Deccan in the seventeenth century. The objective of the state (*salṭanat*), according to its author, is to fulfill worldly human needs, but since human beings follow diverse religions because of their varied temperaments and social milieux, conflict (*niẓā'*) in this endeavour is inevitable. The role of the *nāmūs* or *sharī'a* then is to avoid conditions of conflict.

> To avoid this conflict there is thus the need of a perfect person, God-sent and God-supported. The philosophers call him *nāmūs* and the method he adopts is called *nāmūs-i Ilāhī*. To the *'ulamā'* of Islam, he is known as *rasūl*, *nabī* and *shāri'* and the method as *sharī'a*.[95]

The term *sharī'a*, in such treatises, does not then imply the same as in works of jurisprudence. The term even for jurists, it must be admitted, was not always so narrow as to refuse admission to every alien social practice. In the early Islamic period there are some cases of legislation in matters of police, taxation and criminal justice for the sake of *siyāsat*, even though, in general, such legislations were often rejected as *siyāsiya*, as distinct from *sharī'iya*, and hence did not have the same sanctity or authority.[96] Some consideration was also given to usage and custom (*'urf* and *'ādat*). But

[94] Jalal al-Din Dawwani, *Akhlāq-i Jalālī*, Lucknow, 1916, p. 114.

[95] 'Ali bin Taifur al-Bistami, *Tuḥfa-i Quṭb-Shāhī*, Bodleian Library, Oxford, MS. 1471, ff. 6b–71a.

[96] Fauzi M. Najjar, '*Siyasa* in Islamic Political Philosophy', in Michael E. Marmura, ed., *Islamic Theology and Philosophy*, Albany, 1984, pp. 92–110.

here again the *sharī'a* of the jurists allowed such custom on the pretext of *qiyās* and *maṣlaḥa*—which meant reasoning by analogy, and expediency, exigency; or, in other words, justification through texts or their implications from the Qur'an and its traditions. *Qiyās* and *maṣlaḥa* did not involve an independent moral opinion. For all this, categories like *qiyās, maṣlaḥa, 'urf*, and *'ādat* did introduce and reinforce resilience and a degree of ambiguity in *sharī'a*, which in turn proved a factor in facilitating the acceptability of these *akhlāq* texts.

### Ethical Norms in Mughal Politics

Babur's 'illustrious descendants', however, do not seem to have greatly relished Ikhtiyar al-Husaini's simplified recension of the works of Ibn Miskawaih and Tusi. Introduced to that world through the *A<u>kh</u>lāq-i Humāyūnī*, they preferred to read and understand for themselves the fuller (even if convoluted) original texts. Tusi's book was not simply among the five most important books that Abu'l Fazl wanted Emperor Akbar to have read out to him regularly, it was among the most favoured readings of the Mughal political élites: the emperor issued instructions to his officials to read Tusi and Rumi, in particular.[97] The imprint of *a<u>kh</u>lāq* literature is unmistakeable also in discourses on justice, *i'tidāl*, harmony, *siyāsat*, reason and religion—and more generally on norms of governance—in texts such as the *Ā'īn-i Akbarī*, the *Mau'i<u>z</u>ah-i Jahāngīrī* and a large number of Mughal edicts.

One hardly needs to reiterate here the similarity of this account within discourses on justice, politics, reason and religion in Abu'l Fazl's writings on the one hand, and in treatises on Nasirean ethics on the other.[98] I would still wish to quote here, at some length, a passage from a letter that has generally gone unnoticed in Abu'l Fazl's *Inshā'*. Abu'l Fazl mentions this letter as a proclamation of the royal code of conduct and a working manual (*manshūr al-ādāb-i Ilāhī wa*

---

[97] Muhammad Amin Bani Isra'il, *Majma' al-Inshā'*, BN, MS. No. 708, f. 38a; see also *Inshā'-i Abu'l Fa<u>z</u>l*, Lucknow, 1863/1280 H, pp. 57–8.

[98] See Rizvi, *Religious and Intellectual History of Muslims in Akbar's Reign*, pp. 197, 355–6 and 366–9.

*dastūr al-'amal-i āgāhī*) issued by Akbar to the managers (*muntaẓimān*) and officials (*kārpardāzān*), including princes, high nobles, *manṣabdārs*, *'āmils*, and *kotwāls* in charge of towns and villages throughout the empire.

> In all works, from routine mundane duties to prayers, they should endeavour to please God . . . They should not seek solitude(*khalwat-dost*) like recluses, nor should they mix freely with the commoners as the people of the bazaar do; they should always adhere to the balanced middle, and should never abandon the path of equipoise (*miyāna-rawī, sarishta-i i'tidāl*) . . .
>
> When they are free from their public work, they should read books written by the pious and saintly, such as the ones on *akhlāq* that cure moral and spiritual ailments . . . They should appreciate the truth of religion (*dīndārī*) so that they do not fall into the trap of impostors (*arbāb-i tazwīr-o-khud'a*).
>
> The best prayer is service to humanity. They should welcome all with generosity, whether friends, foes, relatives or strangers; in particular they should be kind to the recluse and seek the company and advice of the pious.
>
> They should investigate the nature of crimes and offences among people judiciously (*ba-mīzān-i 'adālat*), assess which of these is worth punishing(*sazā dādanī*), which is forgivable and to be ignored (*poshīdanī-o-guzashtanī*). Most crimes which seem of lower magnitude may require to be dealt with drastically, while others which appear serious may need to be ignored. They should first try to admonish and reprove the culpable, and should resort to tying, beating, severing limbs and execution only after they fail to correct by admonition and reproof. They should never resort hastily to killing; and should refer cases of execution to the royal court, even if they fear mischief [due to delay in execution] by their dispatch and imprisonment. They should refrain from skinning, and from the trampling of offenders under the feet of elephants, and from other practices of barbarous rulers. The punishment should be commensurate with the nature of the offender, for an angry look (*nigāh-i tund*) works like killing among the good, while among the ignoble even a heavy blow is ineffective.

. . . They should not encourage flattery; most works are left undone because of [the evil influence of] flatterers. They should personally look into the grievances of people, should note the names of the aggrieved, and should not allow delay in providing them with redressal.

. . . In moments of anger they should not give up the threat of reason (*sarishta-i 'aql*). They should instruct the wise among their servants to check them when they are full of rage or overwhelmed with grief (*dar zamān-i hujūm-i gham-o-ghuṣṣa*). They should not swear habitually, as this inspires lack of trust (*saugand khurdan khwud rā muttahim dāshtan ast*); they should not resort to abusive words which behove only the ignoble. Their troopers should not occupy the houses of the people without their consent . . . They should be ever watchful of the conditions of people, the big and the small [for] chiefship or rulership means to guard and protect (*sardārī 'ibārat az pāsbānī ast*).

. . . And they should not interfere (*muta'arriẓ*) in any person's religion (*dīn-o-mazhab*). For, wise people in this worldly matter—which is transient—do not prefer that which harms. How can they then choose the disadvantageous way in matters of faith—which pertains to the world of eternity? If he [the subject] is right, they [state officials], would oppose the truth [if they interfere]; and if they have the truth with them and he is unwittingly on the wrong side, he is a victim of ignorance (*bīmār-i nādānī*) and deserves compassion and help, not interference and resistance (*maḥall-i taraḥḥum-o-i'ānat ast na jā-'i ta'arruẓ-o-inkār*). They should be pleasant, well-wishing and friendly to all (*nekū-kār, khair-andīsh wa dostdār-i har guroh*).

. . . They should not eat like animals, beyond the necessary limit. They should not indulge in jocularity and frivolousness. They should regularly receive information through more than a single source of intelligence; they should never rely on the information given by any one person, since people are generally not absolutely honest and free from greed. Intelligence agents should follow and check each other without their knowing that each is under surveillance (*bar har amr chand jāsūs ta'ayyun kunad ki az yak dīgar khabardār nabāshand*). They should not let wicked and ill-natured men come close to them, even if such men are useful and may be utilized in chastizing evildoers. They should be careful that those close to them be not oppressive, and they should refrain from the company of the unsound and glib-tongued (*charb-zubān-i nādurust*) who are dangerous, and enemies in the guise of friends. There should be adequate arrangements to disseminate and promote learning, to generously encourage the learned and the accomplished, and to tutor and train [the scions of] reputed [lit. ancient] families.

Their expenditure should always be less than their income. Those who spend in excess of their income are fools, while those whose expenses equal their income are neither fools nor wise. And they should not lie and should always honour their word. They should go for hunting only occasionally as a pastime and for drilling and the exercise of soldiers.

In each town (*qaṣba*), city (*shahr*) and village (*dih*), officials should work in tandem to find out the number and the kind of inhabitants there, depute an *amīr* (chief) of the *maḥalla* (quarter, locality) to supervise the local business, and appoint intelligence agents to supply news of daily developments. They should see to it that in case of mishaps or fire, neighbours should help each other; in case of thefts the goods stolen should be recovered; and that if they fail in this they should lose their jobs. They should see that the properties of the deceased and missing persons go to their rightful heirs or else are deposited in the treasury. Sale, distilling and drinking of wine should be allowed only as a medicine. They should try to ensure a reasonable price (*arzānī-yi nirkh*) for goods, and should not allow the practice of hoarding.[99]

Clearly, this *dastūr* is inspired by *akhlāq* texts. A close examination might show that even the words employed, the language and style, all show such an impact. The following passage from *Akhlāq-i Humāyūnī*, which relates to the king's comportment, shows the nature and extent of such influences:

In each matter which the king takes up, he should regard himself as a subject and the other as the king. He should not tolerate for others what he considers improper for himself. He should not wait for the

[99] Abu'l Fazl, *Inshā'-i Abu'l Faẓl*, vol. I, Lucknow, 1280 AH, pp. 57–67 (my translation).

time when the needy approach his court. He should not be given totally to bodily joy and pleasures. Benevolence and favour, and not force and violence, should be the cornerstone of his activities.

He should endeavour to please his people for God's sake. He should not disobey God for the people's sake. He should be just and fair when people ask him for his decision, and be forgiving when they expect mercy from him.

He should seek the company of the pious and thus obtain peace of heart. Each person should be kept within the limits of his ability. It is not enough that he [the king] not be a tyrant. He should manage the country in such manner that none in his territory can afford to be cruel.[100]

The Mughal concern for *akhlāq* norms is also reflected in their extraordinary interest in understanding as well as facilitating conditions for their subjects (*jamhūr anām*) to appreciate each other's religion and traditions. It is interesting to note here the precise terms in which Abu'l Fazl accounts for Akbar's encouragement of the translation of Hindu scriptures. In his introduction to the Persian translation of the *Mahābhārat* he writes:

> The generous heart [of His Excellency] is temperamentally inclined towards the well being of all classes of people (*iṣlāḥ-i aḥwāl-i jamī' ṭabaqāt-i barāyā*), friend and foe, relations and strangers are all equal in his farsighted view. This [consideration for all] is the best method for the physicians of bodies, and should be highly appropriate for the physician of the soul [as well]. Why should this beneficence then not be the [distinctive] feature of [His Excellence], the chief physician of the chronic ailments of the human soul (*pas shīma-i karīma-i sar-i daftar-i mu'ālijān-i amrāẓ-i muzmana-i nufūs chira nabāshad*)? He has noticed the increasing conflict (*nizā'*) between the different sects of Muslims (*farā'iq-i millat-i Muḥammadī*), on the one hand, and the Jews and the Hindus (*Juhūd-o-Hunūd*), on the other, and also the endless show of repudiation of each other's [faith] among them. The sagacious mind [of His Excellence] then decided to arrange the translations of the sacred books of both the communities (*farīqain*), so that with the blessing of the most revered and perfect

[100] *Akhlāq-i Humāyūnī*, ff. 37b–38b (my translation).

soul [the Emperor] of the age, they both refrain from indulging in hostility and disputes, seek the truth, find out each other's virtues and vices and endeavour to correct themselves. Also in each community (*ṭā'ifa*), a group of illiterates, fanatics and triflers have gained prominence. Pretending to be leaders of religion, they have misguided people with their frauds and fallacies (*tazwīrāt-o talbīsāt*) to take as significant those matters which are far from the path of wisdom and prudence. These inauspicious impostors (*muzawwirān-i bī-sa'ādat*), because of their ignorance or dishonesty, their hankering after carnal desire, misinterpret the ancient scriptures, the wise sayings and doing of sages of the past. When books of both these communities are rendered in a simple, clear, and pleasant style, simple-hearted folks will appreciate the truth and be free from the [traps of] trivialities (*fuẓūliyāt*) of the fools who go around posing as learned and wise (*nādānān-i dānā-numā*). It was therefore ordered that a translation in a plain style of the *Mahābhārat*, which consists of most of the basic principles and rites of the Brahmans of India and is their most honoured, most sacred and most detailed book, be prepared in collaboration with the experts of [both the Persian and the Sanskrit] languages and under the judicious scrutiny of the learned and the wise of both communities.[101]

It is naturally difficult to measure the impact of the translations of such books on the manner in which the two communities viewed each other. We may only note here that, in seventeenth-century

[101] *Mahābhārat*, Persian transl. by Mir Ghiyas al-Din 'Ali Qazvini, ed. S.M. Reza and N.S. Shukla, vol. I, Tehran, 1358 H, Abu'l Fazl's Introduction, pp. 18–19.

The word *Juhūd* (Jews) may have been used here as it rhymes with the word *Hunūd*. The Jews in Mughal India, however, occupied a significant position, even as there is not much work on the theme. For some useful information, see Walter G. Fischel, 'Jews and Judaism at the Court of the Mughal Emperors in Medieval India', *Proceedings of American Academy for Jewish Research*, vol. XVIII, 1948–9, pp. 137–77. Similarly the use of the word, '*ṭā'ifa*' for the community may have been intended to undermine the sanctity of '*millat*' and '*kesh*', words generally used for the purpose. All these communities, Abu'l Fazl may have meant to convey, are mere 'groups' (like the different spiritual orders) of the one community of humanity—something in tune with his general religious outlook.

Mughal India, a number of Muslim scholars included the pre-Muslim Indian past in histories they wrote, and thus gave a message to their readers to appreciate and appropriate Indian tradition as part of human history. Indeed, Abu'l Fazl stated that this too was one of the objectives of the translation of the *Mahābhārat*. He wanted Muslims in general, who believed that the world is only 7,000 years old, to know how old was the history of the world and its people (*kuhnagī-yi 'ālam wa 'ālamiyān*). He wanted kings, who loved to listen to histories, to learn from the experiences of the past.[102]

Among such histories was the *Rauẓat al-Ṭāhirīn*, compiled in 1603 by Tahir Muhammad 'Imad al-Din Hasan Sabzawari. This book is divided into five chapters. Chapter One deals with the histories of pre-Islamic prophets, Greek philosophers, and Persian and Arab kings. The second describes histories of the Pious Muslim Caliphs and subsequent developments in the lands of Islam. The third gives the history of the Turks and the Mongols. The fourth gives the histories of pre-Islamic Indian rulers, the *Mahābhārat*, the Surajbansi and Chandrabansi (Solar and Lunar) kings and their successors, an account of Nandghosh, Gautam and their sons, an account of Kamdev, and histories of Bengal, Pegu, Ceylon, Martaban and other lands and islands. The final chapter is a history of Muslim rulers in India down to the age of Akbar, with an account of contemporary nobles, scholars and poets.[103] It is noteworthy that all those whom Sabzawari included in his history were, as the title suggests, intended to be among the *ṭāhirīn*—the pure, clean and holy. Sabzawari's book was a history of mankind, and the author saw himself as an inheritor of the heritage of universal humankind.

My purpose is not to suggest that these norms were the sole feature of community relations that developed in the seventeenth century. For example, as I discuss later, translation and commentary of an ancient Hindu text by a noted divine and seventeenth-century Chishti Sufi, Shaikh 'Abd al-Rahman, contains even the Prophet

[102] Ibid.

[103] Tahir Muhammad Imad al-Din Hasan Sabzawari, *Rauẓat al-Ṭāhirīn*, Bodleian Library, Oxford, MS., Arch. Swinton, Elliot 314, preface of the author.

and Imam Husain as key figures, this being the assertion that Islamic truth had been anticipated in Indic-Brahmanic scriptures. In another text, *Ḥujjat al-Hind*, the erotic stories of the *Mahābhārat* were interpreted as obscene, thereby suggesting the immoral nature of the cultures which sustained them.[104]

It is clear, all the same, that Nasirean ethics contested the norms of governance which we summarized above in Barani's *Fatāwā*, and thereby proved to be an important support to stable and enduring Mughal rule within the multifaceted religio-cultural conditions of India. By integrating Nasirean norms into their politics, the Mughals also emphatically distanced themselves from the ambience of another Central Asian political code which developed around the court of the Shaibanid dynasty of the Uzbeks in the early sixteenth century—by Fazl-Allah ibn Ruzbihani Isfahani in his *Sulūk al-Mulūk*.[105] This latter book is virtually on Islamic jurisprudence, and its ambit in political terms is narrow, in fact narrower than that found in the works of Nizam al-Mulk, Ghazali, and Barani. The author, Ruzbihani, obsessed with his own brand of Sunni Islam, regarded the Shi'ites of Iran as apostate and believed that an all-out war (*jihād*) against them was obligatory.[106] What was particularly abhorrent for the Mughals, within Ruzbihani's digest, was the way in which Babur, the founder of their power in India, was portrayed in this work. Ruzbihani contended that in spreading heresy in Transoxiana, Babur, like the Iranian Shi'i leaders, had played a 'detestable' role. According to him the region was afire with *fitna* (sedition), for Babur had invited the red-capped Safavid Qizilbash to come to his help in his fight against the Uzbeks to recover Samarqand and Bukhara. And, but for the Uzbek king 'Ubaid-Allah Khan's gallant

[104] I will discuss these questions in my work on Persian translations of some Hindu scriptures, at a later date.

[105] Fazl-Allah ibn Ruzbihani Isfahani, *Sulūk al-Mulūk*, British Library, London MS. Or. 253, preface. See also the printed edition edited by Muhammad Ali Muvahhid, Tehran, 1984/1362 *sh.* For an English translation, see M. Aslam, *Muslim Conduct of State*, Islamabad, 1974, pp. 31–2.

[106] Ibid., fol. 3a; English transl., pp. 33–4.

struggle (*jihād*), the rites and symbols of the true faith would have been completely rooted out of the region.[107]

## Religion and Mughal Political Culture

The Mughals did not simply repudiate Ruzbihani's code, they went even further and took pride in the fact that the followers of different religions lived in peace in their empire. Jahangir (r.1605–27) proudly contrasts this situation with the conditions of intolerance and bigotry that then obtained in territories under the Uzbeks and the Safavids, in Central Asia and Iran, respectively.[108] In the assessment of Shaikh 'Abd al-Rahman, the Mughals ensured the supremacy of *dīn* by their exaggerated concern for social harmony (*mashrab-i i'tidāl*). In Mughal India, he noted—unlike in Uzbek Central Asia and Safavid Iran—the followers of all religions (*adyān-o-maẕāhib*) lived in peace and performed their rites and social practices freely. And yet the Mughals acted in complete accord with the injunctions of their faith (*nuṣūṣ*).[109] Further, Jahangir, in keeping with the tradition set by his father Akbar, also commissioned a translation, perhaps the first, into Persian, of Ibn Miskawaih's celebrated work *al-Ḥikmat al-Khālida*. The book, originally written in Arabic, consisted of the maxims of the Greeks, the Persians, the Indians and the Arabs. One Taqi al-Din Muhammad bin Shaikh Muhammad al-Arjani al-Tushtari rendered it into Persian under the title *Jāwidān Khirad* ('The Eternal Wisdom').[110] It was a measure of its popularity that, later in 1655, Hajji Shams al-Din Muhammad Husain Hakim

[107] Ibid., fols. 3b–4a; English transl., 33–4, 37–46.

[108] Nur al-Din Muhammad Jahangir, *Tūzak-i Jahāngīrī*, ed. Sayyid Ahmad Khan, Aligarh, 1964, p. 16. Significantly, Jahangir mentions here the Jews (Yahūdi) also.

[109] 'Abd al-Rahman Chishti, *Mir'āt al-Asrār*, British Library, Or. 216, fol. 507a.

[110] Taqi al-Din Muhammad al-Arjani al-Tushtari, *Jāwidān Khirad*, British Library, London, MS., Or. 457. I have used the BL, MS. See also the printed edition, ed. Bihruz Sarvatiyan, Tehran, 1976, and the Arabic edition, ed. Abd al-Rahman Badawi, Beyrut, 1983.

prepared a compact recension of the book on the instructions of the noted Mughal noble Shayista Khan. This version is known as *Intikhāb-i Shāyista Khānī.*[111] Highlighting the value of his translation, Taqi al-Din noted that the book comprised the truths and experiences of the past and that he translated the work so that,

> those among the heaven-like powerful kings, the prudent *wazīrs* and the high ranking *amīrs*, who have a majestic nature, penetrating sight, and keen intellect to appreciate the mysteries of the East and West and the sciences of both the worlds, may make the counsels contained in these truthful maxims and the splendours of [their] sublime realities, their manual for their works and activities which would beget and strengthen power, and thus may earn eternal fortune.[112]

A life in conformity with these ancient Islamic and non-Islamic counsels, significantly, ensured both mundane (*dunyawī*) and sacred (*dīnī*) excellence. Again, *dīn* and *sharī'a* in the sense of Islam alone figure nowhere in the four essential features (*ādāb-o-sharā'iṭ*) which, according to Hajji Shams al-Din, were integral (*arkān-o-sutūn*) to state management. The Hajji delineates these features as: (1) hard work and independent and intelligent application of mind (*koshish-o-ijtihād*) to evaluate the ability of incumbents for different state works, with due consideration of their skill, trustworthiness, prudence, honesty, integrity, kindheartedness and concern for justice; (2) insistence on prioritizing issues and policies, and quick follow-up for their execution; (3) constant vigilance so that no official dare neglect his duties or be oppressive and unkind to the *ri'āyā*; (4) adequate reward for efficiency and excellence, and punishment for the wicked and evil-doers.[113]

The unmistakeable imprint of Nasirean ethics that one discerns is thus not simply on the norms or principles of governance but on

[111] Haji Shams al-Din Muhammad Husain Hakim, *Intikhāb-i Shāyista Khānī*, British Library, London, Oriental and India Office Collections, MS. 2210.

[112] *Jāwidān Khirad*, fol. 4a (my translation).

[113] *Intikhāb-i Shāyista Khānī*, fols. 50.

a very wide area of Mughal politico-cultural life. Nasirean ethical norms in fact occupy a distinct position even in some *akhlāq* texts compiled in the opposed tradition. This may be demonstrated through an examination of certain Mughal texts of this genre.

Nur al-Din Qazi al-Khaqani's *Akhlāq-i Jahāngīrī*[114] is a major book on *akhlāq* compiled under the Mughals. The author, a *qāẓī* of Lahore, was a grandson of Hasan 'Ali ibn Ashraf al-Munshi al-Khaqani, who was the chief secretary of Akbar's half brother, Mirza Hakim, the ruler of Kabul; he had himself written a book on *akhlāq* and dedicated it to the prince under the title *Akhlāq-i Ḥakīmī*.[115] Nur al-Din Qazi's work, *Akhlāq-i Jahāngīrī*, is an expanded and enlarged edition of *Akhlāq-i Ḥakīmī*. In his text, Munshi discusses the merits of good behaviour, courage, reliance on God, justice, bravery, politics, compassion, patience, determination, keeping one's word, and the need for mutual consultation, in thirteen separate chapters (*maqālas*); the fourteenth and last chapter is on diverse sub-themes (*fawā'id-i mutafarriqa*). Qazi copies all the Munshi chapters verbatim while integrating them into his enlarged chapters. He also adds eight new chapters on the merits of the Sufic concept of love, learning and the learned, fear and hope, humility and affection, repentance, honesty, truthfulness, and contentedness. He also throws in some lighthearted anecdotes (*muṯā'bāt*). Both Munshi and Qazi intended their works to be on religious ethics. An agreeable and ideal disposition for both is identical with Islamic belief (*īmān*), and the ruler in both texts is exhorted to maintain justice—which has been used in the routine sense of mercy and munificence—for all Muslims. In the chapter on justice, the acceptance of Islam by the Mongol king Ghazan Khan (r.1295–1304) and his people has even been represented as an instance of justice.[116]

Clearly then, these books were not modelled on the works of Tusi or Ikhtiyar al-Husaini. In treatises in the Nasirean tradition, the term

[114] Nur al-Din Qazi al-Khaqani, *Akhlāq-i Jahāngīrī*, OIOC, MS. 2207.

[115] Hasan 'Ali ibn Ashraf al-Munshi al-Khaqani, *Akhlāq-i Ḥakīmī*, OIOC, MS. 2203.

[116] *Akhlāq-i Ḥakīmī*, ff. 3b–4a and 46b; *Akhlāq-i Jahāngīrī*, ff. 7a and 273a.

*siyāsat* is used to denote discipline, control and management. The ruler is often advised to discipline, in the first place, his own self, and thereby acquire the moral authority to control and discipline others by conferring on them either rewards or punishments. The ruler must be strong enough to overawe the bad and the ill natured, as well as fulfill the expectations of the good.[117] For Munshi, however, there are two principal categories of *siyāsat*: first and foremost is the effort to propagate the faith and manage the community of believers by eliminating enemies of the faith. The second category of *siyāsat* involves restricting the ambitions of high officials and keeping ordinary state servants overawed.[118] Qazi has no comments to add on these observations.

As a matter of fact, there is on a couple of points a difference between these two books. Munshi begins with the statement that the life and teachings of the Prophet of Islam offer the best in human culture; that only by following his path can man excel in ethics; and that the best human act be deemed the effort to please the heart of a Muslim.[119] In the *Akhlāq-i Jahāngīrī*, this part of Munshi's preface is dropped. What further deserves notice in Qazi's work is a passage that he adds in the chapter on justice. Here Qazi, like Tusi, reiterates the independent goodness of justice, saying that justice, and not Islam or infidelity, occupies principal place in matters of governance, and that a non-Muslim but just ruler serves society better than an unjust Muslim. Justice, he adds, on account of its inherent strength and goodness, sustained power in ancient Persia for 5,000 years in the same dynasty, even though all the rulers of this dynasty were infidels and worshipped fire:

> The reason why state power remained in their house [for 5,000 years] was because they . . . tolerated no injustice to their *ri'āyā*. The Prophet of Islam reports (*khabar*) that God revealed to the Prophet David that he should instruct his people not to abuse and

[117] *Akhlāq-i Humāyūnī*, ff. 31b–32a.

[118] *Akhlāq-i Ḥakīmī*, f. 96a.

[119] Ibid., f. 4.

speak evil of the kings of 'Ajam. 'For they filled the world with justice so that my slaves may live in safety.'[120]

> *'Adl-o-inṣāf dān na kufr-o-na dīn*
> *ānchi dar ḥifẓ-i mulk darkār ast*
> *'Adl-i bī-dīn niẓām-i 'ālam rā*
> *bihtar az ẓulm-i shāh-i dīndār ast*
>
> (Know that it is Justice, not Infidelity or Faith
> that ensures the safety of the country;
> for the world is better served by justice without Faith,
> than by the tyranny of a Faithful king.)

Also of relevance here is the tradition (*ḥadīṣ*), noted in several *akhlāq* digests, emphasizing the primacy of justice:

> Even though Anushirwan is outside the circle of Islam, his justice was of such a high order that the Prophet [boastfully] said: 'I was born in the age of Naushirwan, the just'! . . . Hajjaj bin Yusuf [the Umayyid governor of Iraq] was a born Muslim, companion of the companions of the Prophet. Still, people mention his name spitefully because of his cruelties, while Anushirwan, a fire-worshipper infidel, is always remembered with adulation.[121]

Qazi also recorded anecdotes to illustrate the meaning of justice and the crucial place he thought it should be given within state management. One such anecdote pertains to the time of Sultan 'Ala al-Din Khalji and relates the encounter of the noted Sufi of Panipat, Shaikh Sharaf al-Din, with the principal official (*ḥākim*) of the town. Dular, the eunuch, the *ḥākim* of Panipat, had imprisoned a Hindu on the pretext of a crime and then released him on payment of a huge sum. But the *ḥākim*'s greed was not yet quenched; he pressed for more money. The Hindu then fled and took shelter in the hospice of the shaikh. When Dular heard about this, he insisted that the shaikh hand over the fugitive and threatened him with dire consequences in case he failed to comply with his order. The shaikh did

[120] *Akhlāq-i Jahāngīrī*, f. 274b.

[121] 'Ali ibn Taifur al-Bistami, *Tuḥfa-i Quṭb Shāhī Akhlāq-i Bādshāhī*, f. 11a.

not budge. Subsequently, the *ḥākim* decided to ride to the hospice. Terrified, and in a panic, the hospice attendants implored the shaikh to yield and told him of the irate *ḥākim*'s imminent approach. But no sooner did he enter the threshold of the hospice than the *ḥākim* was thrown from his horse's back, dashed to the ground, and instantly killed. This was mysterious, for the shaikh did not touch him; he had simply hit the wall with his prayer carpet when he noticed Dular entering the hospice. And then he wrote to the sultan:

> Brother 'Ala al-Din Khalji, keeper (*shaḥna*) of Delhi territory, accept greetings from Sharaf of Panipat, and then note that I have slapped Dular and sent him up to the sky. He had turned insane and had begun giving trouble to the people of God. Send another person here as soon as you get this letter or else the *shaḥna* of Delhi will also be dismissed.

The sultan immediately appointed his son as *ḥākim* of the town and sent him to the shaikh with the request that if he did not approve the appointment, another officer would follow.[122]

The story is probably apocryphal, yet the message of the Qazi is clear. Constant vigil and close watch over developments throughout the domain, far beyond the immediate vicinity of his capital, is necessary for the good king; and all, irrespective of creed, should be equal in the eye of the ruler.

The difference between the *Akhlāq-i Ḥakīmī* and the *Akhlāq-i Jahāngīrī* could be explained in terms of the evolving political and intellectual milieu of Mughal India. Manuals on Nasirean ethics, together with the liberal Sufic tradition and Persian poetry, contributed significantly to the making of this milieu and provided guidance for an acceptable pattern of living in a heavily religious but multicultural medieval set-up. Non-sectarianism, as well as a serious concern for justice and harmony, were desired among the élite; were especially remarked upon and highlighted. Shayista Khan, according to the compiler of *Intikhāb-i Shāyista Khānī*, was head and shoulders above his contemporaries because he was totally free of bigotry. He was a man of *sulḥ-i kull* (the Akbari ideological position of 'absolute

[122] *Akhlāq-i Jahāngīrī*, ff. 387b–388a.

peace'), he saw all as his friends and possible allies, whatever their personal faith or religion.[123] Shayista Khan's *dīn* was thus not in conflict with his liberal and open-minded approach.

In Mughal India there were thus significant numbers of texts laying down norms of governance—in addition to books of Islamic law. These texts had become integral to the literary and cultural Indo-Persian tradition. Apart from the texts already mentioned, it seems worth noting that Husain Wa'iz al-Kashifi's *Anwār-i Suhailī*, a Persian translation of the legendary Indian text *Panchatantra*, was among the few illustrated manuscripts that Akbar and Jahangir commissioned. Akbar also commissioned a translation of the Jain version of the same text, which is now available as *Panchākiyāna*. Akbar's chief ideologue Abu'l Fazl prepared his own recension of the text as *'Iyār-i Dānish*. Even the noted political text of Jahangir's time, *Mau'iẓah-i Jahāngīrī*, is comprised in different places of a verbatim copying from either Munshi Nasrullah Abu'l Ma'ali's *Kalīla Damna* or Kashifi's *Anwār-i Suhailī*; both, we know, are oft-cited Persian translations of the *Panchatantra*.[124] The *Panchatantra* thus occupied a major place in Mughal political culture and in the Mughal political imagination.

It would, however, be a travesty of the facts if one were to assert that high Mughal officials generally believed in, and practised, religious tolerance. Noteworthy here are two contemporaneous observations on the existing religious atmosphere: these help us get some

[123] *Intikhāb-i Shāyista Khānī*, f. 3a.

[124] For a description of the *Anwār-i Suhailī* manuscript with illustrations, preserved in the British Museum in London, see J.V.S. Wilkinson, *The Light of Canopus: Anwar i Suhaili*, New York, London, *c.* 1929; for an English translation of the *Anwar-i Suhaili*, see *Anwár-i Suhaili*, or *Lights of Canopus: Commonly Known as Kalilah and Damnah*, translated by Arthur N. Wollaston, London, 1904; for *Panchākiyāna*, see *Panchakiyanah*, edited by Tara Chand and Sayyid Amir Hasan 'Abidi, Aligarh, 1973; for *Kalila Damna*, see Mujtaba Minavi, ed. Tehran, 1964/1343 *sh.* For passages from *Kalīla Damna* and *Anwār-i Suhailī* in *Mau'iẓah-i Jahāngīrī*, see Heshmat Moyyad's review of Sajida Sultana Alvi's *Advice on the Art of Governance: Mau'iẓah-i Jahāngīrī of Muhammad Bāqir Najm-i Sānī. An Indo-Islamic Mirror for Princes* in *Īrānshenāsī*, vol. III, no. 3 (Autumn 1991), pp. 621–8.

idea of the extent to which the Mughal state either followed or disregarded the demands of narrow religious considerations. One of these is a remark by 'Abd al-Qadir Badauni, the unofficial historian of Akbar's time, about the reception accorded in India to Mir Muhammad Sharif Amuli, the Iranian scholar and Nuqtawi leader who had to flee Iran for fear of persecution. Badauni, as we know, disliked non-Sunni ideas and considered them heretic. He detested the non-orthodox ideas of Amuli and disapproved of the prevailing situation wherein deviants such as Amuli were welcomed. He writes: 'Hindustan is a wide place, where there is an open field for all manner of licentiousness, and no one interferes in another's business, so that every one can do just as he pleases.'[125]

The other observations relevant for us are those of the French traveller François Bernier, who visited India decades later, in Aurangzeb's time. After commenting disapprovingly on 'strange' Hindu beliefs and rituals regarding eclipses, Bernier remarks: 'The Great Mogol, though a Mahometan, permits these ancient and superstitious practices; not wishing or not daring to disturb the Gentiles in the free exercise of their religion.'[126] It was noted by Bernier, among others, that even in matters like *satī* the Mughals intervened only indirectly: 'They [the Mughals] do not, indeed, forbid it (*satī*) by a positive law, because it is a part of their policy to leave the idolatrous population, which is so much more numerous than their own, in the free exercise of its religion; but the practice is checked by indirect means.'[127]

All this does not mean that the Mughals were not concerned with

[125] Abd al-Qadir Badauni, *Muntakhab al-Tawārīkh*, vol. II, ed. W.N. Lees and Ahmad Ali, Calcutta, 1865, p. 246; English transl. W.H. Lowe, reprint, Delhi, 1973, p. 253; Riazul Islam, 'Akbar's Intellectual Contacts with Iran', in Milton Israel and N.K. Wagle, eds, *Islamic Society and Culture: Essays in Honour of Aziz Ahmad*, New Delhi, 1983, pp. 351–73; for Nuqtawis, see K.A. Nizami, *Akbar and Religion*, Delhi, 1989, pp. 54–61.

[126] François Bernier, *Travels in the Mogul Empire, 1656–1668*, English transl. by A. Constable, reprint, New Delhi, 1972, p. 303.

[127] Ibid., p. 306.

Islam. Consolidation of the bases of their glorious community (*tāsīs-i mabāni-yi millat-i baiẓā'*), and enforcement of the injunction of the illustrious *sharī'a* (*tarwīj-i aḥkām-i sharī'at-i gharrā'*) have been listed equally among the significant achievements of Jahangir's reign.[128]

Yet it is clear that the *sharī'a* which guided the Mughal pattern of governance bore the impact of the tradition of Nasirean *akhlāq*, this being reinforced by the world that the poets and Sufis had in their own domains delineated in Persian, a world in which it became possible to use the term *sharī'a* not necessarily or merely in its narrow legalistic sense. The Muslims of these domains thus found a way out after the supposed 'closure of the door of *ijtihād*'. It was not simply that infidels, like all sects of Muslims, had freedom of belief in the regime of this *sharī'a*; it went further, in that they were not treated as the people of ordinary *ẕimma*. In the regime of this *sharī'a*, infidels, like Muslims, could build their own places of worship and could even sometimes demolish mosques—even when this implied to purists a significant threat to the faith and a grave sign of weakness in Islamic rule. An observation of Shaikh Ahmad Sirhindi, the famous Naqshbandi saint-theologian of the early seventeenth century, is worth noting:

> The spread of the illustrious *sharī'a* comes from the efficient care and good administration of the great sultans, which has lately slackened, causing an inevitable weakness in Islam. The infidels of India [thus] fearlessly destroy mosques and build their own places of worship in their stead. In Thanesar in the Krukhet [Kurukshetra] tank there was a mosque and a shrine of a saint. Both have been pulled down by the infidels and in their place they have now built a big temple. Again, the infidels freely observed the rituals of infidelity, while Muslims are unable to execute most Islamic ordinances. On the day of *Ekādashī* when the Hindus abstain from eating and drinking, they see to it that no Muslim bakes or sells bread or any other

[128] Muhammad Baqir Najm-i Sani, *Mau'iẓah-i Jahāngīrī*, ed. and transl. S.S. Alvi, text, 145, translation, p. 43.

> food in the bazaar. On the contrary, in the blessed month of Ramazan, they cook and sell food openly. Due to the weakness of Islam, nobody can stop them from doing this. Alas, a thousand times alas![129]

Nonetheless the Mughal rulers—in whose times Sirhindi thought the *sharī'a* (as he understood it) had ebbed so low—still prided in calling themselves the Majesty and Light of the Faith (Jalal al-Din Akbar, Nur al-Din Jahangir). The *qāẓī* and the *ṣadr* of Mughal times, as in all other Islamic states, occupied high positions; and Muslim divines, among others, had land or cash grants to pay for the stability of the empire and to maintain and keep aloft the symbols of Islam (*sha'ā'ir-i Islāmī*) through the length and breadth of their territory. The periodic dispatch of rich donations to the holy cities of Mecca and Medina, with the official delegates of the *hajjīs*, continued. What is significant is also that Sirhindi's addressee, Mir Muhammad Nu'man, also an important divine of the time, saw the reigning ruler, Jahangir, not only as a man of piety and justice but also as someone who ensured compliance with the ordinances of the *sharī'a*.[130] For Sirhindi, like Barani, the rule of the *sharī'a* meant not only total dominance by Muslims but also the humiliation of infidelity and infidels—if not their elimination and annihilation. But to the Mughals, the *sharī'a* came to be synonymous with the *nāmūs-i Ilāhī* (divine law), the most important task of which was to ensure a balance of conflicting interests, of harmony between groups and communities, of non-interference in their personal beliefs.

Before we end this chapter, it may not be out of place to take note of the recent debate about the issue of what has often been described as 'the closure of the gate of *ijtihād*', in particular because the term figures in Taqi al-Din Shustari's *Jāwidān Khirad*. The support for this comes from some other Mughal Indian writings as well. Badauni, for instance, who is known in particular for his conservative

[129] *Maktūbāt-i Imām Rabbānī*, letter no. 92 to Mir Muhammad Nu'man, p. 118, vol. II, reprint, Istanbul, 1977, pp. 233–44 (my translation); see also Yohanan Friedmann, *Shaykh Ahmad Sirhindi, An Outline of His Thought and a Study of His Image in the Eyes of Posterity*, Montreal, 1971, p. 82.

[130] *Maktūbāt-i Imām Rabbānī*, op. cit., p. 233.

and reactionary approach and bigotry, extols *ijtihād.* According to him,

> it is not permissible (*najaiz*) for a *mujtahid* to follow others (*taqlid*). It is incumbent upon him to strive and exert himself to draw his own conclusions in the light of Koran and hadith both in matters relating to fundamentals (*usūl*) and details (*fara*) . . . [A] *mujtahid* following others would amount to eating alms (*sadquah*). As it is not permitted for a rich man to take alms from others, similarly it is prohibited for a *mujtahid* to follow the conclusions and findings of others. If a *mujtahid* arrives at correct conclusions, he will receive ten fold recompense, but even if he fails he will be entitled to recompense.[131]

The debate revolves not simply around questions of the principles and rules of jurisprudence; it equally covers the nature of the relationship between religious law (*sharī'a*) and politics (*siyāsa*). Now *ijtihād* has been defined as 'the exertion of mental energy for a legal opinion to the extent that the faculties of the jurists become incapable of further effort.' This activity of Muslim jurists has been considered by many modern scholars as having ceased at the end of the ninth century. By the beginning of the fourth century of the *hijra*, says the Muslim legal specialist Joseph Schacht,

> the point had been reached when the scholars of all schools felt that all essential questions had been thoroughly discussed and finally settled, and a consensus gradually established itself to the effect that from that time onwards no one might be deemed to have the necessary qualifications for independent reasoning in law, and that all future activity would have to be confined to the explanation, application, and, at the most, interpretation of the doctrine as it had been laid down once and for all.[132]

Wael B. Hallaq, as we noted above, has however expressed serious doubts about the validity of this view. Through a systematic and

[131] Abd al-Qadir Badauni, *Najat al-Rashid*, ed., S. Moinul Haq, Lahore, 1972, cited in Ishtiyaq Ahmad Zilli, 'Badauni Revisited: An Analytical Study of *Najat ur Rashid*', in Iqtidar Husain Siddiqui, ed., *Medieval India: Essays in Intellectual Thought and Culture*, vol. 1, Delhi, 2003, p. 156.

[132] Schacht, *An Introduction to Islamic Law*, pp. 70–1.

chronological study of the original legal texts, he has shown that '*ijtihād* was deemed a perennial duty, and the actual practice of Muslim jurists, and that *ijtihād* was not only exercised in reality, but that all groups and individuals who opposed it were finally excluded from Sunnism.'[133]

Indeed, the four schools of Islamic jurisprudence continued to develop even after the deaths of their original founders. There were many who differed from the masters, and many others claimed to be *mujtahid*s even though they remained within the ambit of the regulations of existing schools. Some modern scholars have illustrated this revisionist view from discussions in legal and political writings on court judgements and state legislation.[134] Badayuni's remark on *ijtihād* and Shustari's use of the term may also be cited to show that many, if not all, Mughal India scholars regarded the door of *ijtihād* as still open. However, while Badauni recommends *ijtihād* only for theologians and *'ulamā* of high calibre, Shustari makes a plea not only for the accomplished *'ulamā'*, but also for the king, nobles and state officials to be given permission to engage in *ijtihād* in political and administrative matters. We may note that Shustari here does not speak as a narrow sectarian Shī'i. We can also speculate that this was one of the reasons why *akhlāq* norms—which had their beginnings in a dissident tradition—were gradually integrated in the broadly Sunni Islamic edifice of India. These norms represented the pre-colonial South Asian Muslim search for a 'practical philosophy', as also a considered political theory which was not necessarily within the limits of the conventional principles of jurisprudence.

[133] Wael B. Hallaq, 'Was the Gate of *Ijtihād* Closed?', pp. 3–41. See also note 10 of the Introduction.

[134] M. Khalid Masud, 'The Doctrine of *Siyasa* in Islamic Law', pp. 1–29.

CHAPTER 3

# The Sufi Intervention

The *sharī'a*, whether juristic or as defined within Nasirean ethics, was not alone in shaping medieval and Mughal political culture. From the beginning, the Timurids gave due regard in their political system to the received code of their 'pagan' ancestors, the Mongols. Babur's testimony bears out the fact that he considered the *Tūra-i Chengīzī* (or 'Law of Chengiz Khan') an important component of his heritage:

> My forefathers had always sacredly observed the rules of Chingez. In their parties, their courts, their festivals and their entertainments, in their sitting down and in their rising up, they never acted contrary to the *Tūra-i Chengīzī*. The *Tūra-i Chengīzī* certainly possessed no divine authority, so that any one should be obliged to conform to them; every man who has a good rule of conduct ought to observe it. If the father has done what is wrong, the son ought to change it for what is right.[1]

Over and above this, there was also the powerful influence of Sufi ideas and beliefs on the Mughals. While the *bā shar'* Sufi orders generally emphasized that true mystical experience did not legitimize a violation of religious law, the *sharī'a* itself was supposed not to occupy a very crucial place in the path of spiritual progress. We will see here how Sufism is relevant for an appreciation of one or the other feature of the idioms of power in the medieval and Mughal worlds.

[1] Cf. *Bābur-Nāma*, translated by John Layden and William Erskine, vol. II, Oxford, 1921, p. 7, cited in Iqtidar Alam Khan, 'The Turko-Mongol Theory of Kingship', *Medieval India: A Miscellany*, vol. II, Bombay, 1972, p. 14.

## Another Vision of Power: The Sufis of North India

The first Sufic centres in north India were built in the wake of Ghaznavid rule over Punjab during the eleventh-twelfth centuries. Then, with the establishment of the Delhi Sultanate at the beginning of the thirteenth century, Sufi orders (*silsilas*) began to expand, encouraging and promoting many beliefs held in common by Hindus and Muslims. Even among those Sufis who were puritanical in their attitude and uncompromising on questions of adherence to the *sharī'a* in purely juridical terms, there were examples of general charity and tolerance. They shunned ritual and ceremony, they spoke the language of the common people, they gave an impetus to linguistic and cultural assimilation. All types of people are reported to have visited the *jamā'at-khānas* (hospices) of the early Chishtī mystics, who believed and preached that the highest form of prayer was the removal of misery among those in distress.[2]

There is also evidence of an attitude of understanding and admiration by Sufis towards Hindu cults and creeds. In the words of an early Sufi, infidelity and faith, orthodoxy and heresy were all mere expressions: there was no such thing as absolute opposition or antagonism; everything was conceived in relative terms because in the final analysis all were God's creatures.[3] The earlier Hindu and Buddhist influence on Islamic mysticism apart, many practices—such as bowing before the shaikh (head of a Sufi order), offering water to visitors, circulating *zanbīl*, shaving the heads of new initiates, audition parties (*samā'*), and inverted penances (*chilla-i ma'kūs*)—were borrowed from the practices of local Hindus; they encouraged conditions for accommodation to local non-Muslim religious attitudes and aspirations.[4] Several Sufis interacted and had ideological

[2] Amir Hasan Sijzi, *Fawā'id al-Fu'ād*, Lucknow, pp. 13–14, 68 and 147; Amir Khwurd, *Siyar al-Auliyā'*, Delhi, 1884/1302 H, pp. 38–9 and 46.

[3] The statement is attributed to Shaikh Sharaf al-Din Yahya Maneri, an eminent fourteenth-century Sufi of Bihar. Cf. Maulana Ni'matullah, *Ganj-i Lāyakhfā*, Khuda Bakhsh Library, Patna, MS., ff. 34–5.

[4] *Fawā'id al-Fu'ād*, pp. 137, 158–9; K.A. Nizami, ed., *Khair al-Majālis*, Aligarh, 1959, pp. 65, 66 and 150; also K.A. Nizami, *Some Aspects of Religion and*

discourses with Indian ascetics and saints (*yogīs* and *bhaktas*) with a view to evolving a common basis for their appreciation of conceptions of 'Ultimate Reality' and 'Existence'. The famous Siddha treatise *Amrita-Kunda*, on *Hatha-Yoga* principles, was translated into Arabic and then into Persian as early as the thirteenth century.[5]

All this represented a deliberate Sufi intervention, not merely in society and the social order, but equally in politics, as an attempt at defining political directions. This is apparent from an episode reported by Barani from the period of Sultan Shams al-Din Iltutmish (r.1211–36). In Barani's account, Iltutmish did not reach the standards of his ideal of a Muslim sultan. As soon as he was free from challenges from within the Mu'izzi nobility and had reinforced his authority with an investiture from the caliph, Barani reports, a delegation of eminent theologians under the leadership of Qazi Wajih approached him with a demand to implement the *sharī'a* in his sultanate. The Hindus, according to the theologians' *sharī'a*, were to be given the option of *'imma'l islam, imma'l qatl'*, i.e. 'Islam or death'. Barani would like us to appreciate the sultan's quandary. The theologians' demand was clearly impossible to carry out. It was, however, also difficult to set it aside. His response was then evasive, in a measure. Iltutmish sought a reprieve, saying:

> But since at the moment, the land has just been conquered, the Hindus here are in such an [overwhelming] number that the Muslims in their midst are like salt [in a dish]. If this injunction is enforced they may unite and raise a commotion. The disturbance will be widespread, all around; we will be too weak to [suppress it]. However, after some years when in the capital and in the provinces and small towns, the Muslims and their army grow in strength, I shall then give the Hindus the choice of 'Islam or death'.[6]

---

*Politics in India during the Thirteenth Century*, reprint; Delhi, 1974, pp. 178–9, in particular for the significance and meanings of the circulation of *zanbīl*, and the *chilla-i ma'kūs* ('inverted' *chilla*).

[5] S.A.A. Rizvi, *History of Sufism in India*, vol. I, Delhi, 1978, p. 335.

[6] Ziya al-Din Barani, *Ṣaḥīfa-i Na't-i Muḥammadī*, MS. Raza Library, Rampur, cited and discussed by S. Nurul Hasan in *Medieval India Quarterly*, vol. I, nos 3–4, pp. 100–5.

In the inherited political theory from the originary Islamic lands, and also in the manner in which it was carried further in India, there was little to help the sultan. In Hanafi law, though, there is no such uncompromising position about infidels in an Islamic state;[7] but as yet no scholar of India had emerged with any significant interpretation suited to a new multi-religious society. The *akhlāqī* norms, of which we have written, were yet to be articulated. Iltutmish naturally feared losing the support of the *'ulamā'*. As a matter of fact, he instituted a full-fledged department, with *qāẓīs, muftīs* and *shaikh al-Islām*, to deal with religious matters. He built mosques and *madrasas* to strengthen the foundations of his rule.[8] But for our purposes what seems of equal significance is the fact that Barani, and before him Minhaj al-Siraj, would have asked the sultan to pay special attention to relations with the Sufis. The sultan is in fact portrayed as having looked for legitimacy from the Sufis, who had by then amply demonstrated that truth—the Islamic truth—was not confined to the pages of a book on *sharī'a*.

The sultan reportedly tried to establish his links with Sufis in a rather exaggerated way, as is illustrated by several anecdotes connected with his early life. Of many incidents from his past, he remembered and mentioned in public only those that included one or the other Sufi predictions of his acquiring a kingdom even while he was still a slave child.[9] He was hardly ten when he fell victim to the jealousy of his brothers, who brought him to the slave market of Bukhara and sold him to a kinsman of the *ṣadr-i jahān*. Here, on a certain occasion, certain members of his master's family gave him coins and asked him to go to the bazaar to buy some grapes. On the

[7] Cf. Johansen, *Contingency in a Sacred Law*, pp. 68, 223–4, 230; Y. Friedmann, *Tolerance and Coercion in Islam*, Cambridge, 2003, pp. 76–80.

[8] For a recent assessment of Iltutmish's relations with the '*ulamā*' and the *sharī'a*, see Sunil Kumar, 'The Emergence of the Delhi Sultanate' (forthcoming). See also his 'Qutb in Modern Memory', in *The Present in Delhi's Past*, New Delhi, 2002, pp. 1–61.

[9] For these stories, and others pertaining to Iltutmish, see K.A. Nizami, *Salāṭīn-i Dihlī ke Maẕhabī Rujḥānāt*, Delhi, 1958, pp. 102–8; Idem, *Studies in Medieval Indian History and Culture*, Allahabad, 1966, pp. 15–18.

way, Iltutmish lost the money and, being of young age, began to cry for fear. While he was crying a dervish came to him, and as he knew the reason for his weeping, took him by the hand, purchased some grapes, and gave them to him, taking in return a pledge from him by saying: 'When you obtain wealth and dominion, do show respect to dervishes and take care of their rights.'

The sultan did not simply relate this incident; he also said: 'The wealth and power that I am endowed with is all due to the blessing of that dervish.'[10]

Soon, Iltutmish managed to move on to Baghdad. The master of the house wherein he lived was religious-minded. Often, he vacated his house to facilitate the holding of music parties there by mystics. One night, in a grand music assembly arranged in this house, many eminent Sufis being present, the young Iltutmish stood devoted in their service through the night, clearing burnt wick from candles.[11]

Another story, related by the sultan about his Baghdad days, clearly shows the purpose of narrating these anecdotes. One day, he said, he went to the <u>kh</u>*ānqāh* of Shaikh Shihab al-Din Suhrawardi (d.1235) and presented him some coins. The shaikh accepted the money, recited the *fātiḥa*, and remarked: 'I see gleams of royal power (*salṭanat*) shining in the face of this person.' Another eminent Sufi, Shaikh Auhad al-Din Kirmani (d.1298), was present on this occasion. Looking at Iltutmish, he too remarked: 'Due to your grace, in his wordly kingdom religion too will be secure.'[12]

The last incident is reported in *Siyar al-'Ārifīn*, a Sufi *taẕkira*, which indicates the response Iltutmish received from the Sufis during his search for legitimacy, and this represents the manner in which Iltutmish's piety was recollected within the history of this Delhi sultan. Nizam al-Din Auliya also reports this, with some modification: 'he [Iltutmish] had obtained access to [and the bliss of] the service of Shaikh Shihab al-Din Suhrawardi and Shaikh

[10] Minhaj al-Siraj, *Ṭabaqāt-i Nāṣirī*, Calcutta, Bibliotheca Indica, 1863, p. 167.

[11] 'Isami, *Futūḥ al-Salāṭīn*, ed. A.S. Usha, Madras, 1948, p. 119.

[12] Nizami, *Studies in Medieval Indian History and Culture*, p. 17.

Auhad al-Din Kirmani. One of them had predicted, "you will become the king".'[13] And finally, in the popular (if apocryphal) Chishti *malfūẓ* text, Shaikh Mu'in al-Din (d.1236), the celebrated founder of the Chishti *silsila* in India, is mentioned among the dervishes who had forecast Iltutmish's ascension to the *salṭanat*. Qutb al-Din Bakhtiyar Kaki (d.1235) reports that, once, he was present in the company of his *pīr*, Khwaja Mu'in al-Din, in Baghdad, together with many other mystics. It so happened that a lad of twelve passed by with a bow in his hand. The mystic glanced at him, and prompt came these words from his mouth: 'This lad will be the king of Delhi.'[14] According to Chishti records, such cultural support or blessing for Iltutmish came also from the Chishti Sufis. Nizam al-Din says that, in his struggle against his rival Nasir al-Din Qabacha, Iltutmish had the full support of the eminent Suhrawardi Shaikh of Multan, Baha al-Din Zakariya.[15]

Sufi tradition in fact appropriates Iltutmish as one of the few Islamic heroes of India with mystical inclinations. In Sufi circles and Sufi memory he is projected as very pious, a devout Muslim regular in his observance of religious ritual. According to the author of *Khazīnat al-Aṣfiyā'*, a late medieval Sufi *taẕkira*, Qutb al-Din Bakhtiyar Kaki had willed that his funeral prayers be led by one who had never committed adultery, never missed the *sunnat* (supererogatory) prayers of the late afternoon (*'aṣr*), nor the opening announcement (*takbīr-i ūlā*) of congregational prayers. The report goes that Iltutmish, who was present at the saint's funeral, waited modestly a while, and as nobody came forth, at length stepped forward saying: 'I did not want to make a pedantic display of my piety, but the order of the Shaikh is at all cost to be obeyed.' He then led the prayers and carried the bier on his shoulder to the graveyard.[16]

Such stories arose from the image that this Delhi sultan had acquired by the thirteenth century, even in a text as important as the

[13] *Fawā'id al-Fu'ād*, p. 212.

[14] *Fawā'id al-Sālikīn* (Urdu transl. bound in *Hasht Bihisht*), Delhi, n.d., p. 15.

[15] *Fawā'id al-Fu'ād*, p. 120.

[16] *Khazīnat al-Aṣfiyā'*, p. 275.

*malfūz̤* ('table-talk') of Shaikh Nizam al-Din Auliya. Hasan Sijzi, compiler of the shaikh's conversations, says that while the sultan attended to the business of governance all day long, at night he stayed awake with his knees bent before God. If perchance he fell asleep, he arose startled and trembling, performed his ablutions, and continued his prayers.[17] All that the sultan did was in complete accord with tradition, and at the behest of the Prophet. He built the famous tank (*ḥauz̤-i Shamsī*) which the Prophet had wished him to do in a dream, it was constructed where he (the Prophet) had stood in the dream. In Nizam al-Din Auliya's *malfūz̤*, this tank has a special mention: after his death, the sultan appeared to a man in a dream to say that it was because he had constructed this tank that God had sent him to heaven.[18] This was the manner in which the sultan began building the capital of a new Islam in India. Indeed, Sufi support for Iltutmish is expressed with particular authority by Nizam al-Din Auliya when he says: 'The lamp of his [Iltutmish's] power was illumined with the light of Divine Support.'[19]

Noteworthy here are the conditions that prevailed at and around the time of the establishment of the Delhi Sultanate, both in India and Central Asia—from where the early Muslim conquerors had come. While on the one hand they were surrounded by a hostile population in India, on the other the Mongols had torn apart the fabric of Muslim power in Central Asia. Many members of ruined ruling dynasties—noblemen, saints and scholars—now looked to north India as the place where they might settle in peace. Rulers in such newly gained lands could not, thus, afford policies or actions which might reinforce opposition to their conquest. Even temporary strategic retreats to lands beyond the Indus were now unthinkable. In a bid to minimize local Hindu hostility, the new Islamic conquerors needed to emphasize that their conflict was only with those who challenged their paramount power and their authority to control revenue. With the rest of the local population, they maintained they

[17] *Fawā'id al-Fu'ād*, p. 213.

[18] Ibid., p. 119; see also *Fawā'id al-Sālikīn*, Urdu transl., pp. 28–30.

[19] *Siyar al-'Ārifīn*, p. 26.

had no quarrel. Delhi thus emerged as a sanctuary of Islam specifically for Muslims migrants. A liberal and tolerant attitude to the religious and social practices of local Hindus had to be adopted more or less out of compulsion. Barani's account of Jalal al-Din Khalji's reported comment is worth noting:

> Every day the Hindus . . . pass below my palace, beating cymbals and blowing conch shells to perform idol worship on the banks of the Jamuna . . . while my name is being read in the *khuṭba* as the defender of Islam, these enemies of God and his Prophet, under my very eyes, are proudly displaying their riches and live ostentatiously among the Muslims of my capital. They beat their drums and other musical instruments and perpetuate their practices.[20]

In this, he might well have added, they received support from many quarters of the Muslim intelligentsia, with the Sufis occupying the most significant place among such supporters. In a way, such Sufis promoted the interests of a stable state, even if in day-to-day governance the political authorities were helped by the *'ulamā'*, who are supposed to have held the opposite view.

Yet the Sufis, like the theologians, were also concerned, even if in more attractive ways, with the dissemination and consolidation of Islamic power in the newly conquered lands of the Muslims. In fact, as we shall see below, some of them, in projecting the absolute truth of their faith, militated against the general spirit of Sufi accommodation. This notwithstanding, there remained the basic difference in approach. As against the theologians, the Sufis made a plea for avenues of power through interaction and persuasion,[21] and these find an echo in Sultan Iltutmish's evasive answer to the theologians' purist demands.

A particularly remarkable development in Sufi circles was the popularity of Hindu themes in Hindi (or Hindavi) poetry (*maṣnawīs*)

[20] Ziya al-Din Barani, *Tārīkh-i Fīrūz Shāhī*, ed. Sayyid Ahmad Khan, W.N. Lees and Maulavi Kabir al-Din, Calcutta, 1862, p. 217.

[21] Cf. *Fawā'id al-Fu'ād*, pp. 65, 150 and 195–7; see also Muzaffar Alam, 'Competition and Co-existence: Indo-Islamic Interaction in Medieval North India', *Itinerario*, 1989, p. 2.

written by Sufis. Besides this, there are numerous verses (*dohās*) preserved in early Sufic literature. Even though most of these *dohās* and songs, recited at early *samā'* gatherings, have been lost, a few of the surviving verses have been ascribed to Sufis such as Shaikh Hamid al-Din Nagauri (d.1274) and Baba Farid (d.1265).[22] These *ma<u>s</u>nawīs* and *dohās*, which apparently excited the imagination of people from all classes, contributed a good deal to making Sufism popular. Among the celebrated early Hindavi *maṣnawīs*, verses from Mulla Da'ud's *Chandāyan*, compiled in 1379, have the distinction of being recited from the mosque pulpit of Delhi. According to the sixteenth-century chronicler Badauni, one Maulana Taqi al-Din strangely influenced people by integrating these verses into his sermons. The maulana believed that the whole of the *Chandāyan* was divine truth, and that it was compatible with the interpretations of some verses of the Qur'an.[23] Mulla Da'ud himself came from Dalmau (a town in modern Rae Bareli district, near Lucknow) and was a disciple and spiritual successor (*<u>kh</u>alīfa*) of Shaikh Zain al-Din, who in turn was the son of the sister of the great Chishti saint Nasir al-Din *Chirā<u>gh</u>-i Dihlī* (d.1356), and his uncle's *<u>kh</u>alīfa*. His work was composed in the latter half of the fourteenth century, under the patronage of the Tughlaq *wazīr* Khan-i Jahan Maqbul (d.1369).

The story of *Chandāyan* is wholly Indic. It revolves around the romance of a married Rajput princess, Chanda, with Lorik, an Ahir by caste, with whom she had to elope to escape the censure of her parents and the general public. Even if her marriage with Lorik is,

[22] *Surūr al-ṣudūr*, Aligarh Muslim University, Maulana Azad Library, Habibganj Collection, ff. 69, 74, 302; Baba Farid's compositions are also believed to have been incorporated by the fifth Sikh Guru Arjan in 1604 into the *Guru Granth Saheb*. For some other *dohās*, see *Maktūbāt-i Muẓaffar Shams Bal<u>kh</u>ī*, Khuda Bakhsh Library, Patna, MS., ff. 141b, 193a; cf. also *Patna University Journal*, vol. 12, 1958, for their English translations.

[23] Badauni, *Munta<u>kh</u>ab al-tawārī<u>kh</u>*, vol. I, ed. Ahmad Ali, Calcutta, 1868, p. 250; for an analysis of *Chandāyan*, cf. Savitri Chandra Shobha, *Social Life and Concepts in Medieval Hindi Bhakti Poetry: A Socio-Cultural Study*, Meerut and Delhi, 1983, pp. 21–34.

apparently, against the Brahmanical shastric injunctions, the society depicted in *Chandāyan* is fairly traditional, with Brahmans occupying the highest position within the framework of the fourfold division of society (*chaturvarna*). While Mulla Da'ud integrates his Sufic ideals allegorically into the story, much of the detail is heavily Indic. When Lorik, for example, is in despair after falling in love with Chanda—he has little hope of meeting her—he lives for a year as a Gorakhpanthi *yogī*. When Chanda is bitten by a snake after escaping from her father's city, Govar, Lorik says that his condition is worse than Ram's after the abduction of Sita, and he wants Ram and Hanuman to help him at this time, for he has no one else.[24]

Mulla Qutban of Jaunpur, the author of *Mrigāvatī*, and Manjhan, the author of *Madhumālatī*, and Malik Muhammad of Jayas, the author of *Padmāvat* (the best-known of the Muslim Hindi *maṣ̤nawīs*) also show full familiarity with Hindu mythology, Hindu manners, yogic rituals and Nath cults.[25]

At a more popular level, Sufism developed several offshoots, absorbing some local Hindu features. The Gurzmars, a branch of the Rifa'is, carried maces, and with them inflicted wounds upon themselves; the Jalalis took hashish, ate snakes and scorpions, and allowed their leaders sexual promiscuity with female members of the order. The Qalandars shaved their heads and facial hair, used intoxicants, and sometimes roamed naked; the Madaris consumed hashish, rubbed ash on their bodies, and wandered naked. The Haidaris adorned themselves with iron necklaces and bracelets and wore a ring attached to a lead bar piercing their sexual organs, thereby eliminating the possibility of sexual intercourse. Like a number of other heterodox orders that developed outside India, these locally

[24] Mulla Da'ud, *Chandāyan*, ed. Mataprasad Gupta, Agra, 1967, Introduction, pp. 16–36; Shobha, *Social Life and Concepts*, pp. 21–34.

[25] For some comments on these Sufi poets of Hindavi, cf. A. Rashid, *Society and Culture in Medieval India 1206–1556*, Calcutta, 1969, pp. 216–60; Mir Sayyid Manjhan Shattari Rajgiri, *Madhumālatī*, ed. and transl. Aditya Behl, Simon Weightman with Shyam Manohar Pandey, Delhi, 2000, Introduction, pp. xi–xlix.

influenced Sufi orders paid little care to regular Islamic rituals and prayers. The violation of Islamic norms and the absorption of the evidently anti-Islamic features were, however, glaringly blatant.[26]

## The Doctrine of *Waḥdat al-Wujūd*

It was the Sufic belief in unity in multiplicity, known as *waḥdat al-wujūd* (Unity of Being), which provided the doctrinal basis for all these developments in the process of religious synthesis and cultural amalgam. This Islamic doctrine had interesting parallels in India: it had no difficulty accommodating the various versions and interpretations of non-dualism given by Indian philosophers and saints.[27] The cultural ethos was at this level conducive to a greater interaction between different sects and the mutual appreciation of apparently divergent thoughts and practices, for all were believed to be 'one' in the ultimate analysis. This idea was also expressed in the Nirguna Bhakti assertion of the fundamental unity of Hindus and Turks. Kabir, for instance, saw no difference between Ram and Rahman. Notable in his poetry is the coalescence of Hari and Hazrat, Krishna and Karama, Muhammad and Mahadeva, Ram and

[26] Simon Digby, 'Qalanders and Related Groups: Elements of Social Deviance in the Religious Life of the Delhi Sultanate of the 13th and 14th Centuries', in Y. Friedmann, ed., *Islam in Asia, I, South Asia*, pp. 60–108; K.A. Nizami, 'Faḳīr', in *Encyclopaedia of Islam*, new edition, vol. 2, pp. 757–78; Ja'far Sharif, *Qanun-i Islam*, English transl. by G.A. Herklots, reprint, London, 1972, pp. 195–6, 289–92, 295–6; Aziz Ahmad, *An Intellectual History of Islam in India*, Edinburgh, 1969, pp. 44–5; Katherine Ewing, '*Malangs* of the Punjab: Intoxication or *Adab* as the Path to God', in Barbara D. Metcalf, ed., *Moral Conduct and Authority: The Place of 'Adab' in South Asian Islam*, Berkeley, 1984, pp. 357–71. See also Ahmet T. Karamustafa, *God's Unruly Friends: Dervish Groups in the Islamic Later Middle Period, 1200–1550*, Salt Lake City, 1994, for the development of heterodox Sufi orders in the larger world of Islam.

[27] Cf. Rizvi, *History of Sufism*, vol. I, pp. 322–96, for an abundance of details in this respect. Rizvi discusses Sankara's *advaita*, Ramanuja's *visishtadvaita*, Nimbarkar's *dvaitadvaita* and Chaitanya's *achinta-bhedabheda*, and shows similarities between these and the doctrine of *waḥdat al-wujūd*.

Rahim. This, in my view, represented a fact within the common man's religious ethos, and was much more than a verbal equation.[28]

In the sixteenth century, in fact, the influence of the ideology of *waḥdat al-wujud* was very strong in north India. Muhammad Ashraf Simnani, the ancestor of the famous saintly family of Kachhauchha (in the modern district of Faizabad) was, for example, an eloquent defender of the doctrine. Besides writing a number of treatises to explain it, Simnani popularized the use of the expression *Hama Ūst* (All is He), emphasizing the belief that anything other than God does not exist. Rudauli (in the modern district of Barabanki) was another major Sufi centre where the doctrine received unusual nourishment. The *k͟hānqāh* of Shaikh Ahmad 'Abd al-Haqq (d.1434) there has been mentioned as a 'clearing house' for Hindu *yogīs* and *sanyāsīs*. Shaikh 'Abd al-Quddus (1456–1537) was among the eminent Sufis associated with this *khānqāh*. His *Rushd Nāma*—a treatise on *tauḥīd* (monotheism), which consists of his own Hindavi verses and those of his preceptor (*pīr-i dastagīr*) together with the Persian and Hindavi verses of other saints (including the noted Iranian saint poet Shaikh Farid al-Din 'Attar)—identifies Sufi beliefs based on *waḥdat al-wujūd* with the philosophy and practices of the Hindu Shaivite Gorakhnath. The shaikh received his inspiration from the syncretic religious milieu of Rudauli. Some of his verses, with slight variations, appear in Nath poetry as well as in the *dohās* of Kabir. His aim in the compilation of the treatise was to discuss the origins of the universe and the purpose of the creation of man; to identify and define the 'path' or 'direction' (*naḥw, samt*) to the Truth; to discuss the real nature of life, as well as *samā'* or spiritual music; and finally to examine the Truth (*ḥaqq*) which manifests itself in the heart of man, and justifications for prostration (*sijda*) before one's spiritual master—all these as illustrations of *tauḥīd*.[29]

[28] For a different view, cf. Aziz Ahmad, *Studies in Islamic Culture in the Indian Environment*, reprint, Delhi, 1990, pp. 144–5.

[29] Compare *Rushd Nāma*, Staatsbibliothek, Berlin, Sprenger 827, ff. 2a, 35b, 39a–43a, 43b, 45b, and 49a, for instance. See also S.A.A. Rizvi, *History of Sufism*, vol. I, pp. 335–40; Simon Digby, 'Shaikh 'Abd al-Quddus Gangohi', *Medieval India—A Miscellany*, vol. III, Bombay, 1979, pp. 1–60.

This set of sentiments and philosophical approach found fascinating expression in the mid-sixteenth century in the *Ḥaqā'iq-i Hindī* of 'Abd al-Wahid Bilgrami (1510–1608), a work in which Bilgrami sought to reconcile Vaishnava symbols, as well as the terms and ideas used in Hindu devotional songs, with orthodox Muslim beliefs. According to Bilgrami, Krishna and other local names used in such verses symbolized the Prophet Muhammad, or 'Man', and even sometimes the reality of a human being (*ḥaqīqat-i insān*) in relation to the abstract notion of the oneness (*aḥadiyat*) of Divine Essence. *Gopīs* sometimes stood for angels, sometimes for the human race, and sometimes in relation to the relative unity (*wāḥidiyat*) of divine attributes. Braj and Gokul signified Sufi notions of the world (*'ālam*) in their different contexts, while the Yamuna and the Ganga rivers stood for the sea of unity (*waḥdat*) and the ocean of gnosis (*ma'rifat*); or else for the river of *ḥads̱* (origination) and *imkān* (contingent or potential existence). The *muralī* (Krishna's flute) represented the appearance of entity out of non-entity; and so on.[30]

There are unmistakeable imprints of these doctrines on the ideas of Abu'l Fazl, the most noted ideologue of Akbar's court.[31] While it is not necessary here to go into details of the influence of these mystic developments on Abu'l Fazl, in my understanding a number of Akbar's and Jahangir's measures and innovations could only have been inspired by this doctrine. Akbar showed keen interest in local cultures and mystic traditions. He invited Hindu scholars to his court and asked them about their religions and philosophy. In Agra, he is reported to have organized a separate quarter for *yogīs*

[30] Mir 'Abd al-Wahid Bilgrami, *Ḥaqā'iq-i Hindī*, Aligarh Muslim University, Maulana Azad Library, MS., Hindi transl. by S.A.A. Rizvi, Kashi, 1957/2014 VS; see also S.A.A. Rizvi, *Muslim Revivalist Movements in Northern India in the Sixteenth and the Seventeenth Centuries*, Agra, 1966, pp. 60–2. For Bilgrami's biography, see Mir Ghulam 'Ali 'Azad Bilgrami, *Ma'as̱ir al-Kirām*, II, Hyderabad, pp. 65–6.

[31] Cf. Rizvi, *Religious and Intellectual History of the Muslims in Akbar's Reign*, pp. 339–73; Azra Nizami, *Social and Religious Ideas of Abu'l Fazl*, Bombay, 1972; see also Irfan Habib, 'A Political Theory for the Mughal Empire: A Study of the Ideas of Abu'l Fazl', *Proceedings of the Indian History Congress*, 59th Session, Patiala, 1998.

which was called Jogipura.[32] Badauni informs us that Akbar would go to these *yogīs*, along with his close companions, and acquaint himself with Hindu beliefs, their methods of *murāqaba* (meditation), *mashāghils* (spiritual practices), *āsan* (postures), and preparation of *kīmiyā* (alchemy) and *sīmiyā* (the exercise of magical powers). Every year, on the occasion of Shivaratri, *yogīs* would assemble at the court in great numbers, having come from far and near. Following their practices, Akbar had strictly regulated his own lifestyle and food habits. He abstained from eating meat and had the centre of his head shaved. The disciples of *yogīs* were known as *chelās*: Akbar named his own household servants *chelās*.[33] Again from a certain Parshutam (purushottama) Brahman—who was appointed to translate a book, *Khirad Afzā*—Akbar reportedly learnt the secrets of idol-worship, and the worship of fire and the sun. The same Brahmin is also said to have taught the emperor to show respect to stars, and under his influence Akbar apparently began to believe in the idea of reincarnation.[34]

Such support for the doctrine of *waḥdat al-wujūd*, and associated philosophies which encouraged religious and cultural accommodation to local social beliefs and customs, continued through the seventeenth century. Following the example set by Akbar, Jahangir had close contacts with Hindu scholars and *yogīs*. One Sri Kant Kashmiri, a scholar of high repute with a profound knowledge of Hindu philosophy and religion,[35] was appointed by Jahangir as the *qāẓī* of Hindus.[36] Many a time, it is said, Jahangir held discussions

[32] Badauni, *Muntakhab al-tawārīkh*, II, pp. 324–5; Eng. transl., II, pp. 334–5.

[33] Ibid., pp. 324–6; Eng. transl., II, pp. 334–6.

[34] Ibid., pp. 257–8; Eng. transl., II, pp. 265–6. See also Titus, *Islam in India and Pakistan*, pp. 163–74.

[35] Mubad Kaikhusrau Isfandiyar, also known as Muhsin Fani, *Dabistān-i Maẓāhib*, ed. Rahim Rizazada Malik, Tehran, 1983/1362 *sh*., vol. I, p. 194, English transl. David Shea and Anthony Troyer, London, 1843, vol. II, pp. 164–5.

[36] Ibid., vol. I, p. 194; English transl. pp. 164–5. For a detailed account of the nature of discussions which Jahangir had with the Pandits, see *Tūzak-i Jahāngīrī*, p. 14; English transl., I, pp. 32–3.

on spiritual and religious matters with Jadurup, a noted Vaishnavite divine at Ujjain and Mathura. The result of all these discussions was the emperor's belief that the Vedantic philosophy of the Hindus, and the Sufi thoughts of Muslims, were more or less identical.[37] The influence of Jadurup on Jahangir was so great that the emperor's rebellious son, Khusrau, was released from prison upon his intercession.[38] Jahangir also visited Ghorkhatri with the desire to acquire knowledge of Hindu religion and mystic philosophy from the *yogīs* who lived there. According to a seventeenth-century text, *Dabistān-i Maz̤āhib*, Jahangir was also close to the noted Hindu saint Mehr Chand, a disciple of Akam Nath. The emperor's conversations with him included a discussion on monotheism.[39]

Mughal nobles and others among the elites were not slow in following the examples of their masters. Hakim Kamran Shirazi reportedly met Jadurup when the latter was staying at Benaras, and it was in his presence that one of the Muslim nobles came to Jadurup and sought his views regarding the Prophet Muhammad.[40] It is said that 'Abd al-Rahim Khan-i Khanan even offered *sijda* before Jadurup. The author of the *Dabistān-i Maz̤āhib* met the guru and learnt from him the *mantar sūraj* (*du'ā-i āftāb*), to be recited in praise of the sun. He also met other Hindu mystics, such as Kalyan Bharti at Kiratpur in Punjab; and Ishwargira, Badangar, Mahadev, Sadanand, Kohli Bairagi and Narayan Das. Another Mughal noble, Ahsanullah Khan, entitled Zafar Khan, was devoted to a certain Trilochan Pal.[41]

It is well known that Dara Shukoh's Sufi leanings led him to explore the depths of Hindu religion, and by his patronage as well as

[37] Nur al-Din Jahangir, *Tūzak-i Jahāngīrī*, ed. Sayyid Ahmad Khan, Aligarh, 1864, pp. 250–1, 252–3, 279, 280, 281; Eng. transl. Alexander Rogers and Henry Beveridge, reprint, Delhi, 1968, II, pp. 49, 52–3, 104, 105, 108. *Dabistān-i Maz̤āhib*, vol. I, pp. 184–6; English transl., vol. II, p. 159. Jadurup died in 1637.

[38] For details see Mirza Muhammad Mu'tamad Khan, *Iqbāl-Nāma-i Jahāngīrī*, ed. Abd al-Hai Ahmad Ali, and W.N. Lees, Calcutta, 1865, pp. 129–30.

[39] *Dabistān-i Maz̤āhib*, vol. I, p. 176; English transl., vol. II, p. 146.

[40] Ibid., vol. I, p. 186; English transl., vol. II, p. 145.

[41] Ibid., vol. I, pp. 186, 191, 192 and 203; English transl., vol. II, pp. 159, 194.

partly throught his own efforts, several Sanskrit works were translated into Persian.[42] These included *Bhagavadgīta, Yoga Vasishtha*, and *Prabodhachandrodaya*. Dara Shukoh himself translated the Upanishads, the translation being named *Sirr-i Akbar*. After a critical examination of Hindu religions he found that all religions are identical and lead to the same goal. His work *Majma' al-Baḥrain* is devoted to highlighting the similarity between the beliefs and practices prescribed in Islamic *taṣawwuf* and Hindu *yoga*.

The author of the *Dabistān-i Maẕāhib* prepared a new translation of *Amrita Kunda* and named it *Khawāṣṣ al-Ḥayāt*.[43] The celebrated seventeenth-century savant Chandra Bhan 'Brahman' compiled a treatise known as *Mukālma-i Dārā Shukoh wa Bābā Lāl*, around the discussions that Dara Shukoh had with the saint of that name. Apart from Dara Shukoh, Mulla Shah, Sarmad Shahid and many others emphasized the similarity between Islam and Hinduism.[44]

All this created a series of conditions whereby, in the seventeenth century, many Hindu Vedantists began to feel there were several points in the *maṡnawīs* of Maulana Rum, and in Islamic *taṣawwuf*, which they could call their own. Some Muslims likewise began to cherish the idea that, among the Hindus, there were not only idol worshippers and those who associated human qualities with idols, but also others who had a deep belief in pantheism and monotheist doctrines.

Among the best interpreters and defenders of this idea of religious closeness and subterranean cultural bonds during this century, were Shaikh Muhibb-Allah (d.1648) and Shaikh 'Abd al-Rahman Chishti (d.*c*.1683). The reputation of some of the treatises Shaikh Muhibb-Allah wrote to expose and elaborate on his doctrines brought him into close contact with Dara Shukoh. His *Risāla-i Taswiya* (Treatise on Equality) evoked a storm of opposition in orthodox

42 Compare Bikrama Jit Hasrat, *Dara Shikuh: Life and Works*, Calcutta, 1953, pp. 174–292; Kalika Ranjan Qanungo, *Dara Shukoh: Volume 1, Biography*, Calcutta, 1952, pp. 241–68.

43 *Dabistān-i Maẕāhib*, vol. I, p. 182.

44 *Ā'īn-i Akbarī*, III, pp. 125–7, Eng. transl., III, pp. 301–4; M. Ikram, *Rūd-i Kauṡar*, Lahore, p. 402.

circles, and later, under Aurangzeb—who is reported to have taken strong exception to its contents—it was ordered to be burnt in public. Shaikh Muhibb-Allah also laid emphasis on the acquisition of mystic knowledge from Hindu *yogīs*. One of his eminent disciples, Shaikh Muhammadi, undertook the study of and training in *yoga* from Brahmans after he had perfected his grounding in Islamic Sufism under Shaikh Muhibb-Allah.[45]

In another case, Shaikh ‘Abd al-Rahman Chishti, a descendant of Shaikh ‘Abd al-Haqq of Rudauli, translated and commented on an ancient Hindu text in a treatise he wrote under the title *Mir'āt al-Makhlūqat* (Mirror of the Creatures), framed as a conversation between Mahadev, Parvati, and the sage Vasishtha. ‘Abd al-Rahman sought to explain, at some length various Hindu legends; and, as Rizvi points out, he made a plea for them to be adapted to Muslim ideas and beliefs. He also prepared a recension in Persian of the *Gīta* entitled *Mir‘āt al-Haqā'iq* (Mirror of Realities), presenting it as an ideal exposition of the doctrine of *Hama Ūst*. It must be added, however, that ‘Abd al-Rahman's attitude in these texts is complex and somewhat inconsistent. If in *Mir‘āt al-Haqā'iq* he shows an appreciation for portions of the *Gīta* that he finds close to some Quranic verses and *ḥadīṣe*s as read by the proponents of *waḥdat al-wujūd*, the *Mir‘āt al-Makhlūqāt* reads like a polemic against Hindu beliefs and traditions. While the former begins with an invocation of the doctrine of *waḥdat al-wujūd*, the opening lines of the author's preface in the latter are as follows:

> This humble [writer] has read most of the Hindu history books written in the era of the '*jinns*'. Nowhere, however, is there found any mention of the birth of the father of the human species (Abu'l Bashar) Adam. Some stupid members of that community [Hindus] have removed the account of Adam from their books and as deficiency and defect predominate in their religion (*dīn*), they do not even mention it. After great search [this writer] got access to a book, utterances

[45] Rizvi, *Muslim Revivalist Movements*, p. 340. For an interesting discussion on the theme, see Shah Muhibb-Allah, *Maktūb Banām Mullā Maḥūd Jaunpurī*, Maulana Azad Library, Aligarh. *Zakhīra-i Aḥsan*, no. 297.7/37, *Fārsī Taṣawwuf*.

(*mulfūẓ*) of Bashist, that describes in detail the births and glories of Adam, the Prophet [Muhammad], and his descendants. Bashist was a '*mun*' [*muni*] of the '*jinns*'. In their language, a prophet (*rasūl*) is called *mun*. The great Bashist receives knowledge from Mahadev and communicates it to his community. Mahadev is the greatest prophet (*rasūl-i mursal*) of the community of the *jinns* and is regarded as their progenitor (Abu'l Jinn).

'Abd al-Rahman then proceeds to discuss various eras, including the 'Taratya', 'Dwapar', and 'Kaljug'. He describes Hindu gods as messengers of divine truth of the era of the *jinns*, much before the beginning of the human era in Kaljug, when the last prophet of mankind, Mahamat (Muhammad), was born. The eternal and divine truth, which had earlier manifested itself in Mahadev and Krishna, assumed finality in the personality and teachings of Muhammad. It was for Muhammad's message that Ali and Husain, the two noblest members of Muhammad's family, gave their lives.[46] There is no single voice, then, in 'Abd al-Rahman's writings.

## Integration and Identity: A Sufi Trajectory

In the early eighteenth century, the implications of these doctrines and the Sufi endeavour to define the larger political and social trajectory is well illustrated by the career of Shah 'Abd al-Razzaq Bansawi of the Awadh region. This was a region in which an atmosphere favouring the greater acceptability of Muslim orthodoxy, and the association of the Mughal state with it under Aurangzeb, had begun to strain the balance in the relationship between communities in the countryside. Rajput *zamīndārs*' clashes with Muslim revenue-grantees were a major source of tension. The keepers of the

[46] Or. 1883. For a description of this MS., see Charles Rieu, *Catalogue of the Persian Manuscripts in the British Museum*, vol. III, London, 1885, p. 1034. For *Mir'āt al-Haqā'iq's* translation, see Roderic Vassie, 'Persian Interpretations of the *Bhagvadgita* in the Mughal Period, with Special Reference to the version of Abd al-Rahman Chishti', unpublished Ph.D. thesis, School of Oriental and African Studies, University of London, 1988. See also Vassie, 'Abd al-Rahman Chishti and the *Bhagavadgita*: "Unity of Religion" Theory in Practice', in Leonard Lewisohn, ed., *The Heritage of Sufism*, vol. II, Oxford, 1999, pp. 367–77.

symbols of Islam (*sha'ā'ir-i Islām*) and the *shurafā'* encountered serious threat from 'infidels' surrounding their habitats. Strong-arm tactics in the handling of the 'rebel' *zamīndār*s further aggravated the problem.[47] This was later to be resolved by a policy of adjusting the claims of the dominant Rajputs on the one hand, and Muslims and non-Rajput Hindus on the other. This politics of balancing received strength from the prevailing Sufi ideology in the region, which, even where it had received a temporary setback in the seventeenth century, was reiterated with remarkable dexterity by Saiyid Shah 'Abd al-Razzaq Bansawi, the founder of a Qadiri Sufi centre in Bansa (a small town near modern Lucknow).

Shah 'Abd al-Razzaq is an important figure for our purposes. He was not merely eyewitness to the devastating implications of religious confrontations in his time, he had more personally inherited and experienced the suffering these brought to his family. His fascinating career, ideas and approach to the social and religious questions of the period are thus of considerable value, and we need to examine them in some detail.

Shah 'Abd al-Razzaq Bansawi came from a family of *zamīndārs* established in Awadh by the Muslim rulers of Delhi. The family was originally from Badakhshan and encountered untold hardships following Rajput raidson their *zamīndarī* and possessions in the seventeenth century. Bansawi's grandmother was one of only two women who survived these raids. She was pregnant with his father when she, along with her sister-in-law, was escorted to safety by one Rasul Khan, an old associate of the family, in a village of his *zamīndarī*, named Rasulpur after him, in the neighbourhood.[48] Bansawi's father, Saiyid 'Abd al-Rahim, who lived in the time of Jahangir (r.1605–27), Shahjahan (r.1628–58) and Aurangzeb (r.1658–1707),

[47] Muzaffar Alam, 'Assimilation from a Distance: Confrontation and Sufi Accommodation in Awadh Society', in S. Gopal and R. Champakalakshmi, eds, *Tradition, Dissent and Ideology: Essays in Honour of Romila Thapar*, Delhi, 1996, pp. 165–77.

[48] Mulla Nizam al-Din Farangi Mahalli, *Manāqib-i Razzāqiya*, Lucknow, 1896/1313 H, p. 4; Nawab Muhammad Khan Shahjahanpuri, *Malfūẓ-i Razzāqī*, Lucknow, 1896/1313 H, pp. 6–8. Francis Robinson, has a useful discussion on

was thus born in Rasulpur.[49] Sayyid 'Abd al-Rahim also had a difficult time with the powerful neighbouring Rajput *zamīndār* of Daryabad: the young Bansawi was made captive by kinsmen of this *zamīndār* when he was barely seven.

In their teens, the children of Awadh's *zamīndār*s mostly spent their time studying and training. But Bansawi had, at this age, to leave for the Deccan in search of a reasonable livelihood and a respectable position, apparently with the objective of reinstating his family to its earlier honour and dignity.[50] For about twelve years, Bansawi stayed in the Deccan. During this period he returned at least once to Awadh, to be married. As he had received no formal education, he failed to obtain a high position in state service and remained in its employ as an ordinary trooper. Later, his family responsibilities brought him back to Awadh, where too he served as a soldier, first under one Shah Muhammad Yusuf—a local shaikhzada in charge of troopers—and then under a Mughal military commander of the province. The Mughal paid him poorly, and irregularly to boot. Disgusted and tired, Bansawi decided to give up service and settle in Bansa, the village of his maternal grandfather 'Abd al-Malik Qidwa'i, in order to establish there what subsequently became one of the best-known Qadiri Sufi centres of eighteenth-century Awadh.[51]

Bansawi, it is reported, acquired a high Sufi position through exceptional means. He introduced and founded a branch of the Qadiri *silsila*, within which he had received *khilāfat* (legitimacy to initiate novices) from a little-known Sufi of the order, Mir 'Abd al-Samad

---

Bansawi's mysticism and on the scholarship of some of his eminent disciples. Cf. *idem*, *The Ulama of Farangi Mahall and Islamic Culture in South Asia*, Delhi, 2001, pp. 41–68.

[49] *Malfūẓ*, pp. 6–8.

[50] Cf. M.R. Ansari, *Tazkira-i Ḥaẓrat Sayyid Ṣaḥib Bansawī*, Lucknow, 1986, pp. 43–287. Ansari quotes from Mir Baqar 'Ali Razzaqi's unpublished *Manāqib-i Razzāqī*.

[51] *Malfūẓ*, p. 22; see also Nawab Muhammad Khan Shahjahanpuri, *Karāmāt-i Razzāqiya*, Hardoi, 1902/1319 H, p. 6.

*Khudā-Numā* of Ahmedabad. Later, according to his hagiographers, he obtained *khilāfat* in both the Nizamiya and Sabiriya branches of the Chishti *silsila* in a miraculous way, directly from the great Sufi masters, who had long passed away and had founded these orders.[52] Again, according to one tradition (spread obviously after he had acquired eminence), upon his birth a *majẕūb* had predicted that his fame would spread far and wide. Bansawi is reported to have had visions and performed miracles even as a boy. He set himself free, the tradition goes, from the clutches of the kinsmen of the Rajput *zamīndār* of Daryabad, unhurt and unnoticed, with the phenomenal help of ʻAli—the famous companion and cousin of the Prophet, who was also the fourth Pious Caliph, and who is believed to have been the fountainhead of nearly all the Sufi orders.

Bansawi's disinclination towards, or rather his being deprived of, formal learning has also been explained in Sufic terms. Bansawi himself related the story of a vision he had received, while still young, on the futility of formal education. The story goes that once, on his way from his village to a *madrasa* in Rudauli, he was left alone by his attendant, who had gone off to meet his relatives in a nearby hamlet in order to arrange food for Bansawi. In his absence, young and hungry, Bansawi felt lonely and depressed. A dervish then came mysteriously to his rescue: he gave him food, and with it a grand idea. Elated and enlightened, Bansawi now realized what he—and for that matter all young Muslims of his class and potential—ought to strive towards. The follow-up to this was, significantly, his decision to discontinue formal education and leave for the Deccan, not in search of employment but, according to tradition, to meet the same dervish. The dervish had apparently promised to meet him again, but only in the Deccan.[53]

[52] *Karāmāt*, p. 6; *Malfūẓ*, p. 28. This miraculous 'Uwaisi method of acquiring *rushd* and *khilāfat* was not so rare in the Islamic world. For a discussion on Uwaisis in India, see Meenakshi Khanna, 'Dreams and Visions in Northern Indian Sufi Tradition', Ph.D. thesis, Jawaharlal Nehru University, New Delhi, 2002.

[53] *Manāqib*, pp. 8–9; Muhammad 'Abdul Bari, *Fuyūẓ-i Ḥaẓrat-i Bānsa* (in Urdu) Lucknow, n.d., pp. 51–3.

Bansawi was a rather exceptional visionary. As he heard and then related stories of these unusual events surrounding his birth and childhood, he saw himself as one in possession of extraordinary social power and influence, as one with a mission to set in order the entire social scene of his time. He had risen too high to think now in terms of merely the interests of his own house, or narrowly of his community. He believed he existed to ameliorate the general predicaments of society at large. Education at a formal school or college (*maktab* or *madrasa*) appeared to him a sheer waste of his time and abilities.[54] A trip to the Deccan, the new Mughal power centre, and to the state service which had attracted many adventurers from his region, must have seemed like the promise of a fortune to help fulfil this extraordinary mission. Unluckily, the problems of Mughal rule in the Deccan, the uncertainty and plight of state service, and his own experience of unsuccess, all led him to a state wherein he found within extraordinary Sufic accomplishment a sure and guaranteed path to the world of his vision.

Details that are available of Bansawi's family history and personal life, the existing relations between ancient landholders on the one hand and the relatively new Muslim *zamīndār*s and holders of revenue grants of different denominations on the other, the persistent tension and threats to the *shurafā'* in the countryside even as they received support from the state—all indicate the helplessness of Muslim elites in this region at the time. However, the memory of unusual powers among the early saint-soldiers who had conquered the region remained strong, and also began to be recorded formally. Tales of a local Rajput raja's surrender to unarmed and unassuming Sufis nourished this memory. In the town and villages where descendants of these Sufis lived, such stories assuaged bruised souls. According to an eighteenth-century account, Malik Muhammad Jayasi, the oft-cited sixteenth-century Hindavi poet and author of the *Padmāvat*, had commanded immense respect in the court of the raja of Garh Amethi. Once, however, on the day of Lord Krishna's

[54] *Malfūẓ*, p. 22.

birthday, Jayasi was denied access to the raja on the plea that the latter, along with his Brahman priests, was busy with prayers relevant to the occasion. Infuriated and insulted, Jayasi protested that the time when he had sought an interview with the raja was in fact inauspicious for prayers, and claimed that the Brahmans who performed them had either no knowledge of astrology and had therefore miscalculated the time, or had knowingly misguided the raja. Disconcerted and embarrassed, the raja and the Brahmans eventually conceded Jayasi's claim and sought his forgiveness.[55]

Another story illustrating the companionable interaction of local Islam with Hindu practice details an encounter between the raja of Tiloi and a Chishti Ashrafi Sufi of *qaṣba* Jais. This tale is far more fanciful. In one of the Rajput raids, early in the seventeenth century, the raja of Tiloi, it is said, captured and made off with all the cattle of the residents of the *qaṣba* from their grazing grounds. The *shurafā'* of the *qaṣba*, who were particularly affected, appealed to Shah 'Inayat-ullah, an ancient Sufi and the *sajjāda-nashīn* of the *khānqāh* Chishtiya Ashrafiya, to intervene and recommend to the raja that he should release their cattle. The shah accordingly reached Tiloi to meet the raja. Sensing the purpose of his visit, the raja refused to meet him and instructed his attendants to tell him that he, the raja, was asleep, and that the shah could come to meet him some other time. Dejected, the shah returned. But when he visited Tiloi again, according to instructions, the same excuse was repeated. In a huff, the shah then cursed the raja and left for Jais, saying: 'as the raja has been sleeping so long, may his eyes remain closed.' Legend has it that the raja lost his eyesight; later, he thus repented and apologized to the shah for his misbehaviour. The shah then blessed him, praying that he be endowed with unusual bravery and the strength to overpower all other rajas of the area, even though blind. Tiloi then emerged, as the followers of the shah and many others believed, as the most powerful *rāj* in the region.[56]

[55] *Tārīkh-i Jā'is*, MS., Abdul 'Ali Collection, Nadwat-ul-'Ulama', Lucknow, pp. 15–16.

[56] *Tārīkh-i Jā'is*, pp. 53–6.

Besides providing a kind of consolation to the hapless descendants of these legendary 'triumphant' Sufis, such stories indicate the attempt to assert their social superiority. Bansawi may have known that through the Sufic way he could reinstate himself and his followers, to some degree, in their erstwhile 'high' position. But then if tradition is to be believed, Bansawi also had a much nobler mission before him. My aim here is not to establish that Bansawi made a cool and calculated assessment of the prevailing situation and planned his Sufi skills accordingly. My attempt is simply to see from the existing records the birth and growth of an individual's ideas within their surroundings; and more than this to highlight the context of the Sufi intervention in politics. It seems to me that Bansawi looked for a job commensurate with the reputation of his family with the intention of solving his worldly difficulties. Simultaneously, he also shows an anxiety to achieve something genuinely divine, inexplicable, and inaccessible to ordinary souls: this, according to tradition, was the real motive of his wanderings.

He searched for it everywhere, at Sufi hospices and at Hindu ascetic (*sādhū*) *mathas*, and he was delighted to get anywhere that seemed close to his destination—namely, the ability to provide remedies to human and social ailment. Again and again, he repeated to his disciples the story of the attitudes of an ascetic whom he had come across on a visit to Allahabad. A *sādhū*, went his story, while at his deathbed, called in his favourite *chelā* (disciple) to tell him the secrets of alchemy. The *chelā*, instead of being excited, refused to listen and said that he had not accepted the *sādhū* as his master for such inconsequential miraculous powers. He sought to learn and be a part of the *Ism-i A'ẓam* (The Great Name of Divinity).[57] With the *Ism-i A'ẓam*, it was believed, one could even turn the Wheel of the Universe. In his repeatedly expressed admiration for the ascetic *chelā*, Bansawi showed perhaps what he himself thought his destination was. This is evident from a perusal of his ideas and attitudes.

Bansawi's teachings and attitudes embodied, in large measure, the message of a pragmatic balance in social relationships. He tried

[57] *Manāqib*, p. 14.

to reduce to a minimum the conflicts between diverse groups and communities, without undermining their claims to their distinct individual slots in the whole. He throughout encouraged, both by his words and actions, a liberal and conciliatory approach to local Hindu religious rites and social practices. His stance towards the accommodation of these into the life of an average Muslim necessitated some obvious qualifications to orthodox Islam. Bansawi appreciated the necessity and importance of maintaining the great orthodox tradition of Islam: his catholicism notwithstanding, he remained in the end a protagonist of orthodox Sufism and saw to it that its dominance and supremacy were refurbished through his pronouncements and deeds. Yet to say this is not to deny the basic 'syncretic' impulse of his teaching.

In fact it is very clear, both from Bansawi's example and from others, that in Awadh many local non-*shar'ī* and non-Islamic customs, festivals and ceremonies had gradually, by this time, become a part of Muslim social life. Mulla Nizam al-Din mentions *sehra* (bridal wreath) for the bride and bridegroom approvingly. A number of other exclusively local and regional rituals had come to be tolerated at various levels in the life of average Muslims. The *bhakti-bāz* song and dance sequence, which depicted the life of the Narasimha Avatar and Lord Krishna,[58] was one such local ceremony commonly patronized and staged both by Hindu and Muslim upper classes at celebrations and festivities. At no stage did Bansawi discourage this practice. Two of his major disciples (*khalīfas*), who had his permission to initiate novices into the order and train them—namely Mir Muhammad Isma'il and Shah Muhammad Ishaq Khan, as well as his son Shah Ghulam Dost Muhammad—had a special liking for this sequence. And it was in the full knowledge of their preceptor, Bansawi himself, that they once watched, apparently with avid interest, *bhaktiyas* performing the life of Krishna in a wedding at the residence of one of Bansawi's disciples (*murīds*). As this was an occasion for joy and merriment, Bansawi allowed it to

[58] Cf. Masud Husain Rizvi Adeeb, *Lakhnau Kā Shāhī Stage*, Lucknow, 1968, pp. 46–50.

go on, even though the senior host wanted his family members and friends to stop, in deference to his *pīr*.[59]

The plea for tolerance is implicit in this: Bansawi tolerated and showed interest in a social practice which was violative of the *sharīʻa*. He did this on the strength of his own assessment of existing social realities. In Sufi terms, he had a justification for this: *mushāhada* (observation, contemplation) and *ilhām* (divine inspiration) provided such justification. But since Bansawi was an orthodox (*bā-sharʻa*) Sufi, he appreciated the limits of his authority. According to established Sufic norms, the act of a Sufi, based on *ilhām*, was not necessarily to be followed by others, in particular when it was overtly in contravention of the dictates of *sharīʻa*. Bansawi intended only to emphasize the exigent need for tolerance; he never insisted upon his disciples acting or thinking as he did. Far from this, he showed due regard for the strict observance of *sharīʻa*. In one way he conceded the argument of his famous theologian disciple Mulla Nizam al-Din (founder of the eighteenth-century *madrasa* curriculum *dars-i Niẓāmī*), who had accompanied him to the above-mentioned wedding: he kept the Mulla away from the spectacle of the Krishna performance, and he also—as this same theologian in his account of the saint would have us believe—reasoned that he wanted the Mulla nowhere near the scene 'lest the common Muslim should take his presence as a *sanad* [allowed in the *sharīʻa*].' On another occasion, while watching an animal fight between a buffalo and a pig—which the Ahirs used to organize as part of their Diwali celebrations—Bansawi advised the Mulla and his nephew Mulla Kamal al-Din, also an illustrious theologian and jurist, to stay away from the other viewers.[60]

It seems from this that, with reference to the *sharīʻa*, Bansawi advocated a difference in attitudes and actions between an *ʻālim* (theologian) and a Sufi. He shrewdly recognized the limits of the law-oriented worldview of a theologian, while seeing himself as a

[59] *Malfūẓ*, pp. 145–7; *Karāmāt*, p. 21; Ansari, *Tazkira*, pp. 271–3.

[60] *Malfūẓ*, pp. 52–3.

Sufi who, guided by his own observations, had the power to act at variance with such law. Indeed, he suggests that a Sufi can appear, on occasion, as violating the dictates of Islamic law. Bansawi thus preferred a measure of ambiguity. He also realized that any argument over the legality of his actions could eventually weaken his position. The theologians' association with him may have been to their spiritual benefit, but, by his refusal to implicate them with his own position, Bansawi ensured their silence over his position, and this certainly guaranteed its acceptability among literate Muslims. A straightforward resistance to *sharī'a* would have been self-defeating; it would have antagonized many of those otherwise prepared to concede an equivocal stance. This was how a Sufi often defined the *sharī'a*, and the boundaries of its enforcement. He approved an apparently anti-*sharī'a* social practice promoted by *zamīndār*s and the laity and, like a local power-monger, he extended legitimacy by his own participation while keeping the theologian and purist at a distance. This represents yet another contestation of the juridical meaning of *sharī'a*.

It was not for this, though, that Bansawi was any less concerned with either the destiny of the Faith or the integrity and cohesion of his own community. While watching and participating in Hindu religious festivals, this Sufi was motivated not only by an urge to establish rapport with the followers of local cults, but also by the truth of his own faith. This is borne out by various other examples: for instance, of *Sufi–yogī* encounters, some of which we will look at in some detail.[61] At this point we note the evidence available in a *malfūẓ* (conversation) collection of another eighteenth-century Sufi, Khwaja 'Ali Akbar Maududi Chishti. To the question of whether a Muslim could attend a Hindu *melā* (fair), Maududi's reply was in the negative. He then elaborated on this to the effect that several Sufis, including Bansawi, had visited Hindu fairs and places of worship to see for themselves the mortality and transience of this

[61] Compare Simon Digby, 'Hawk and Dove in Sufi Combat', *Pembroke Papers*, I, 1990, pp. 7–25; and Alam, 'Competition and Co-existence'.

world, and to experience a sort of specimen of the Day of Judgement. Maududi then related the Qur'anic story of the Prophet Moses' encounter with the Pharaoh's magicians, which took place on a day of festivities (*yaum al-zīnat*) among the infidels. Moses participated in the festival with the aim of defeating the magicians and establishing the truth of his own message.[62] This provided legitimacy to later missionaries for visits to places of idol worship and to gatherings of infidels. As sceptics of the Marxists put it in an analogous context, it is sometimes necessary to study the bourgeois in his own habitat.

The meanings of the true faith, its achievements, and the cohesion of the community were, however, completely different from orthodox Islam in Bansawi. The closer a Muslim's contact with his non-Muslim neighbours, the greater his ability to show care and concern for them, the greater the glory to Islam. We have here echoes of the terms in which Shaikh Abd al-Rahman Chishti appreciated Mughal liberal and non-sectarian policies. Religion, to Bansawi, signified bliss for all. Bansawi demonstrated this through his *Bairāgī* friends, Chait Ram and Paras Ram. These *Bairāgī*s had become almost his formal disciples.[63] At a Krishna *bhakti* dance-drama, organized by Chait Ram at his residence to celebrate the appointment of one of the *chelās* as his successor, Bansawi reportedly fell into a trance, claimed the Lord was present, and thereby moved his entire audience—which obviously consisted mostly of Hindu followers of the *Bairāgī*. After the play was over, Bansawi retired to rest under the shadow of a nearby banyan tree. Some of the *chelās* then asked their *Bairāgī* master if they too could have vision of the Lord. The master replied: 'We can give you all that we have got from our gurus. But we have no power to show you the Lord. Only if that gentleman, who has just left this place, wishes, can you have the Lord's *darshan*.' The *chelās* then approached Bansawi and were thus blessed by the Sufi to have Lord Krishna's vision.[64] This Sufi's Islam did not,

[62] *Tazkira*, p. 205, Ansari cites *Laṭā'if-i Maudūdī*, compiled by Maududi's disciple Khwaja Hasan Maududi (d.1835).

[63] *Malfūẓ*, pp. 74–8.

[64] *Karāmāt*, pp. 20–1; *Malfūẓ*, pp. 74–5.

thus, prevent him being the most blessed *bhakta* (devotee) of a Hindu Lord. What is equally significant is that the*Bairāgī*s' religion did not stand in the way of their seeking their Lord's *darshan* through a Muslim. Bansawi's life illustrates a remarkable achievement in eighteenth-century Awadh culture.

In another instance, Bansawi's eminent theologian disciples—Mulla Nizam al-Din, his brother Mulla Muhammad Raza, and their nephew Mulla Kamal al-Din—were blessed by their Bansawi*pir* to see the Lord with his*gopī*s when they were on their way from Lucknow to Bansa. Initially, the mullas mistook Lord Krishna and his *gopī*s for an ordinary man and his womenfolk. But as they came close, the Lord approached them and said: 'Convey our *salām* (greetings) to your *pīr.*' The mullas were dismayed by this, and also unhappy at the man's open flirtation with his women. Only later, when they related their experience to Bansawi, did they learn that the man and his women were not ordinary souls. They had actually been favoured with a *darshan* of Lord Krishna and his *gopīs*.[65]

In another case, Bansawi is reported to have had a vision of Lord Ram and his brother Lakshman. Bansawi himself narrates this: during his stay in the Deccan, late one evening he lost his way in a jungle. As it became dark and he was getting jittery, he saw a tall and handsome man approach. The man came near and asked Bansawi the name of his home town. To Bansawi's reply that he was from Lucknow, the man exclaimed, 'Our Lachhnau', adding, 'then you are my guest.' He disappeared, and in a few moments two handsome gentlemen emerged, bearing sweetmeats (*ḥalwa sohan*). They instructed the bears and the lions of the jungle to keep watch over their guest that night. They left after a while, promising to come again in the morning to lead Bansawi home. Bansawi spent the night comfortably, protected, as the gentlemen had instructed, by the beasts of the jungle. The following day, two young cowherds led him safely back home.[66]

In all these instances, regardless of whether they actually happened and were narrated by Bansawi, or whether they were ascribed

[65] *Malfūẓ*, p. 126.

[66] Ansari, *Tazkira*, p. 298.

to him later in the eighteenth century by hagiographers, there is repeated evidence of the Sufi effort to maintain social order. Bansawi accepted, in considerable measure, the religious beliefs of Hindus, and supported their myths and memories. Strictly and theologically speaking this was un-Islamic; yet it had, nonetheless, a noble purpose, justifiable as being in consonance with the spirit of Islam, if not its letter. Bansawi tried to drive home the message that Ram, Lakshman and Krishna, protectors of Hindus, were also his friends, and thereby the well-wishers of his disciples and followers. The implication is that while no two individuals experience truth the same way, they must show due regard to each other's beliefs, despite all disagreement.

It is difficult to say if Bansawi believed in this multiplicity of religious truth, but he certainly continuously emphasized multiple manifestations of the same truth and regularly made a plea to blend conflicting phenomena. The famous line by Kabir: '*Kabira bali wah murakh ke jo mātī mahjid jāi*' (O Kabir: May I sacrifice my life to the fool who visits the mosque in a state of intoxication)—often sent Bansawi into a trance.[67] In this line the poet, according to Bansawi, makes a plea for the acceptance of what, to the average soul, seems incompatible. Saying prayers in a state of intoxication was unlawful, according to the theologians; but the Sufi, believing in reconciling the irreconcilable, sees in Kabir the ideal. If this proved unattainable, or incomprehensible, his advice was to remain engrossed in prayer. Here again Bansawi sought support in Kabir's '*tū Rām Rām Bhaj, jag jhagṛan de*' (you keep repeating the name of Ram, even as the world quarrells).[68] Ram *bhakti* would eventually end the world of hatred.

Of the final value of his own tradition, however, the Sufi had no doubt. His aim was to serve humanity with it. At a feast on the occasion of Janmashtami (Lord Krishna's birthday) at Paras Ram's house, the host got panicky when he realized the food was insufficient

[67] *Karāmāt*, pp. 15–16.
[68] Ibid., pp. 24–7.

for those invited. He approached Bansawi for help. The latter directed his son to inscribe the name *Ghauṣ-i A'ẓam*, i.e. Shaikh Abd al-Qadir Jilani, the eponymous founder of the Qadiri *silsila*, at the door of the kitchen, and this Muslim ritual, far from polluting a Hindu kitchen, is reported to have averted the crisis.[69]

Treading a sane middle path, Bansawi disapproved of anything that might imply an insult to the *sharī'a*: such was his attitude to the *bī-shar'a* (*malāmatī, majẕūb, qalandar*, etc.). But since this too had come to stay within medieval Indian Islam, Bansawi, unlike the ordinary orthodox Muslim, did not declare it anti-Islamic. Instead, he tried to integrate *bī-shar'a* Sufism into his own brand of orthodox Sufism in a bid to bring the former under the hegemony of the latter. This is illustrated by his dealings and relations with Shah Dosi and Shah Daula, the two best-known *majẕūbs* of Awadh. Shah Dosi lived in Lucknow with considerable command, popularity and fame attached to his supernatural power and miracles. Bansawi made special efforts to win his friendship and bring him under his influence, even as he showed due respect to his ego and claims to miraculous power. He accepted a piece of limestone as an auspicious gift from Shah Dosi and willed it to remain as part of his legacy at his *khānqāh*. He saw to it that he and the *majẕūb* should remain a model for Sufi Islam in the region. In another case, over a brief meeting, he made Shah Daula of Rudauli declare, 'the secrets which Raghav [Ram] declined to reveal have now been divulged to him by Rajak [Razzaq].'[70]

The specific mystic path that Bansawi traversed, and how sublime was his intended destination, are not my concern. I wish to note that apart from his yearnings for the ultimate Sufic communion with divinity, he was no less anxious that mundane things exist in harmony with each other. The Sufi in Bansawi did not live beyond this world; he was fully sensitive to the politics around. It would not be wide off the mark to say that he, like other members of the elite,

[69] *Manāqib* (MS. Mir Baqer 'Ali).

[70] *Malfūẓ*, p. 128.

had no small role in late-seventeenth- and early-eighteenth-century political configurations. Interestingly, he tried to discipline, whenever possible, even the *majẕūbs*, who would otherwise roam unfettered, pronouncing rewards and punishments upon all they encountered. Once a *majẕūb* disciple of his, in a state of intoxication, promised to give the imperial throne of Delhi to anyone who would prepare the *chillum* (tobacco) of his *ḥuqqa* (hubble-bubble). When this was reported to Bansawi, he remarked: 'With little control over one's ancestral *zamīndārī*, it is easy to claim to reward someone with the kingdom of Delhi!'[71] Exposing the hollow claims of the *majẕūb*, Bansawi's sarcasm suggests the necessity of managing immediate surroundings. Within the existing conditions, if a Sufi claimed power he needed first to manage the *zamīndārī* and the immediate resources of his followers.

Bansawi was not enthusiastic about politics; yet he was not completely detached either. In this sense Bansawi was no aberration. At almost every stage in the history of Islam in India, Sufis showed concern for, even if they did not directly interfere in, the country's political vicissitudes. Early in the thirteenth century, the position of the Turkish rulers, as we saw, followed upon the support of Sufis. If, on the one hand, they prayed for the stability of the Sultanate and recommended their followers and disciples for political favour, Sufis also, on the other hand, entered into open conflict with various sultans and thus had a role in the rise and fall of one or other. If Iltutmish earned laurels from the Chishtis, Ghiyas al-Din Tughlaq had serious differences with Shaikh Nizam al-Din Auliya, principally because the shaikh refused to return the money he had accepted from his predecessor, Khusrau Khan. The shaikh had distributed this money to the poor, to whom, he asserted, it rightfully belonged. The shaikh's illustrious disciple Khwaja Nasir al-Din *Chirāgh-i Dihlī* openly clashed with Muhammad bin Tughlaq, but had no hesitation in blessing the coronation of his successor, Firuz Tughlaq.[72]

[71] *Karāmāt*, p. 31.

[72] See, for instance, Simon Digby, 'The Sufi Shaykh and the Sultan: A Conflict of Claims to Authority in Medieval India', *Iran*, XXVIII, 1990, pp. 71–81; I.A. Zilli, 'Early Chishtis and the State', Anup Taneja, ed., *Sufi Cults and the*

There is ample evidence of Sufi involvement in power politics in the Deccan under the Bahmanis and their successors.[73] Later, under the Mughals, the Naqshbandis arguably, and the Raushanayis, indisputably, had an overt role in political matters.

Certainly Sufis, unlike the political elite, were not motivated by any immediate overt ideology of personal material gain or glorification.[74] Often with their own vision of power and authority, they assessed the prevailing situation and took firm positions. Their vision and judgement varied in specific contexts, and over the centuries. There were serious differences among them from one order (*silsila*) to another, and sometimes even within an order. A very powerful section of them sought to promote a healthy and positive interaction between the diverse and sometimes conflicting traditions and social practices. They had their own vision of the *sharī'a* too—which, as we have noted, was not always in conformity with the views of jurists.

How *taṣawwuf* influenced or interacted with medieval Indian politics as a totality requires a fresh, detailed and careful examination.[75] We cannot ignore the fact that the *bā-shar'a* Sufis, like the theologians, also eventually highlighted the finality and truth of their own faith.[76] And this was not confined to any one Sufi *silsila*.[77]

---

*Evolution of Medieval Indian Culture*, Delhi, 2003, pp. 54–108. For an opposite view, see K.A. Nizami, 'Early Indo-Muslim Mystics and their Attitude Towards the State', *Islamic Culture*, vol. XXII, no. 4, 1948, and vol. XXIII, no. 2, 1949.

[73] Compare Richard M. Eaton, *Sufis of Bijapur: Social Roles of Sufis in Medieval India, 1300–1700*, Princeton, 1978; Muhammad Suleman Siddiqi, *The Bahmani Sufis*, Delhi, 1989, and also the review by Muzaffar Alam, 'The Sufis in History in the Bahmani Deccan', *Islam and the Modern Age*, Delhi, 1990, pp. 207–13.

[74] But, on occasion, material considerations could also influence Sufi attitudes. For one such discussion, see Iqtidar Alam Khan, 'Shaikh Abd al-Quddus Gangohi's Relations with Political Authorities: A Reappraisal', *Medieval India: A Miscellany*, IV, Bombay, 1977, pp. 73–90.

[75] For some discussion around this question, see Muzaffar Alam, 'Sufis and Mughal Politics' (forthcoming).

[76] Alam, 'Competition and Co-existence'.

[77] We may recall that Naqshbandis apart, 'Abd al-Rahman Chishti also ended

This is an aspect of Sufism we will examine in a later chapter: for the moment, I submit that this dimension of Sufism was neutralized, in no small measure, by the fact that by the time the Mughals came to power, the images and the metaphors from the world of Persian poetry had come to influence the lifestyle of the political elites in a major way.

It is, hence, to this dimension of Indo-Islamic interaction that we must turn in the chapter that follows, and from there return to issues of contestation and reaffirmation by Sufis and other social actors of the eighteenth century.

---

his translation of an ancient text on the creation of the world with the arrival of the Prophet of Islam, Muhammad, his grandson Imam Husain, the martyr of Karbala, and the triumph of their mission. See his *Mir'āt al-Ma<u>kh</u>lūqāt*, MS., British Library, OIOC.

CHAPTER 4

# Language and Power

In the preceding chapters our main concern has been the language and idioms of power in the Indo-Islamic context, and our main focus has been on various extensions of *sharī'a* outside its narrowly juridical context. Beginning with an examination of various traditions and their treatises on statecraft, our endeavour was to ask how Sufis approached the problem of the relationship between power and religion in a context within which the religion of the ruler and the ruled were seldom the same. The language of the bulk of the materials that I have used in support of my argument, whether from the time of the Delhi Sultanate or the later era of the Mughals, has been Persian. This naturally takes us to the question of how Persian came to assume the role it did in medieval India. In order to address this issue, our focus cannot remain exclusively on the syntax and language of power; it must equally be the vexed question of the power of language in a context within which several languages were competing for favour at various levels of society—including in the highest echelons of power.

## Persian in Medieval India

India came into contact with an emergent New Persian culture some time around the third quarter of the ninth century, when Sind was integrated into the Saffarid kingdom by Ya'qub bin Abi Lais. Persian was still evolving at this time as a language of literary expression in the Islamic East. Towards the end of the tenth century the presence of Persian in Sind, Multan and Punjab was strengthened in the wake of the growing importance of the Isma'ili presence there.[1] A more formal relationship between this language and the subcontinent was established somewhat later, in the wake of the founding of Ghaznavid power in Punjab in the eleventh century. In the area around his capital of Ghazna, Sultan Mahmud and his *wazīr*, Khwaja Abu'l Qasim Ahmad Maimandi, created a major centre of Persian culture which was the successor to Samanid Bukhara. This was the context within which Firdausi composed his famous *Shāh-nāma*, and it also led to the development of a particular literary form, the *qaṣīda*—a long poem in the nature of an ode or elegy.[2] Mahmud of Ghazna was also responsible for an institutional innovation in the form of the position of *malik al-shu'arā'* (poet laureate), which, after him, was absorbed into the court traditions of Timurid Herat, and which eventually reached its height in Mughal India. (It was only far later, in the nineteenth century, that the Qajars on the Iranian plateau took on board this innovation.) To our mind, the post of *malik al-shu'arā'* was crucial for the development of a certain style of royal and courtly patronage of literature. From Ghazna the new Persian literary culture eventually spread further east to Lahore, a major staging post for Ghaznavid ventures into Hindustan. In its first phase the Muslim presence in that city seems to have been dominated by plunder-seeking frontier warriors (or *g͟hāzīs*), but over time large numbers of Persian-speaking people are reported to have settled around Lahore. This city, which had emerged as an important political centre of the eastern Ghaznavids, gradually attracted scholars and literary figures from Iran, Khurasan, and Mawara-an-nahr.[3] Punjab thus witnessed the beginning and efflorescence of a high Persian literary tradition. By the time of the first

[1] Abdul Ghani, *Pre-Mughal Persian Poetry in Hindustan*, Allaḥabad, 1941, pp. 74–5; Abdul Majid Salik, *Muslim S̤aqāfat Hindustān Mein*, Lahore, 1957, p. 523.

[2] C.E. Bosworth, *The Ghaznavids*, Edinburgh, 1963, pp. 131–4; *idem*, 'The Development of Persian Culture under the Early Ghaznavids', *Iran*, vol. 6, 1968, p. 37.

[3] S.M. Latif, *Lahore: Its History, Architectural Remains and Antiquities*, Lahore, 1981.

Ghurid ruler, 'Ala al-Din Jahansoz, Persian texts of the period suggested that among the areas where Persian verse had cast its shadow, and was appreciated, was 'the periphery of the land of Hind' (*atrāf-i bilād-i Hind*), which was another way of referring to Punjab.[4] Among the poets associated with this region and its vicinity were the great Abu'l Faraj Runi and Mas'ud Sa'd Salman, acclaimed by Persian literary critics as innovators and masters of a new diction.

Later, Persian came to flourish further east, in Delhi and beyond, in the wake of the Turkish conquest of north India. In its first phase here, in the thirteenth century, Persian speakers were part and parcel of the new political developments in the region, among these being soldiers and adventurers from the Khurasan and Mawara-an-nahr regions. The sultans of Delhi of the thirteenth, fourteenth and fifteenth centuries extended generous patronage to Persian scribes, writers and poets. The shortlived kingdom of Nasir al-Din Qabacha (r.1205–28) in Uchch played host to some of the best Persian poets and writers. The first major *taẕkira* of Persian poets and a critical anthology of Persian poetry, *Lubāb al-albāb* of Sadid al-Din Muhammad 'Aufi (d. *c.*1252), was compiled at Qabacha's court.[5] When Chengiz Khan invaded the Perso-Islamic world, this trickle of scribes, savants, and holy men became a flow of some importance, and a truly significant elite migration then began into north India. The migrants at this time included members of distinguished ruling families, alongside men of learning (*'ulamā'*), and Sufis. The Persianized traditions of these groups came to be implanted deeper in the north Indian milieu, aided by the activities of men of piety. The Sultanate of Delhi patronized these men of learning and piety by revenue grants (*imlāk, auqāf, idrārāt, waẓā'if*, etc.) of lands that

[4] Sadid al-Din Muhammad 'Aufi, *Lubāb al-Albāb*, reprint, Tehran, 1982/1361 *sh.*, 1982, p. 89.

[5] Mumtaz Ali Khan, *Some Important Persian Prose Writings of the Thirteenth Century A.D. in India*, Aligarh, 1970, pp. 96–7; Sunil Kumar, 'The Emergence of the Delhi Sultanate, 1190–1290', Ph.D. thesis, Duke University, 1992, pp. 76–234.

were often located in the countryside. A gradual penetration of the small towns and rural centres began via this class of migrants, who were the beneficiaries of state largesse. While specific quarters in several north Indian cities came to acquire the names of towns and ethnic groups located elsewhere in the Persian-speaking world—as for instance Atabaki, Khwarazmshahi, Samarqandi, Khata'i, etc.—rural centres too were often named anew, or, when freshly founded, given names that emerged from a new Persian vocabulary. Later waves of migration accompanied the political and social turmoil in Central and South Central Asia. Thus, in the wake of the empire building of Timur in the late fourteenth century, additional groups sought refuge in north India, while in the fifteenth century the Afghan sultans of Delhi and Jaunpur encouraged their clansmen to settle in the Gangetic plain as far as Bengal and Bihar.[6]

From one perspective, then, India became a part of the Perso-Islamic world, in precisely the same way as Transoxiana, Ghazna, and Ghur. Just as Bukhara, Tirmiz, Nishapur, Isfarain, Sabzawar, and Herat had an importance in this cultural landscape, so too Delhi and Lahore acquired an analogous place and reputation. In this manner the life of north India became considerably marked, in various aspects, by the influence of Persian language and culture. Similarly, Persian itself was influenced by its interaction with north Indian languages. This is reflected first in the smattering of Hindavi words, concepts and metaphors that appeared in Persian: examples are the use of Hindavi words in verses by the early Persian poets of India. In the Persian poetry of Mas'ud Sa'd Salman of Lahore, for instance, the rainy season in India is called *bahār* (i.e. spring).[7]

Sufi hospices also contributed to this Indian-Persian tradition. These hospices become common meeting-grounds for a wide range of people who learnt methods of devotional practice in Persian. Sufi

[6] K.A. Nizami, *Some Aspects of Religion and Politics in India during the Thirteenth Century*, reprint, Delhi, 1974, pp. 75–8; Rashid, *Society and Culture in Medieval India*, pp. 2–14.

[7] Mas'ud Sa'd Salman, *Dīwān*, pp. 11, 39, 562. For an excellent study of Salman's poetry, see Sunil Sharma, *Persian Poetry at the Indian Frontier: Mas'ud Sa'd Salman of Lahore*, Delhi, 2001.

conversations (*malfūẓ*), letters, and discourses on religious practice were all written in Persian. As a matter of fact, the genre of *malfūẓ* developed almost entirely, at least to begin with, in India.[8]

Persian was further enriched by the contributions of several pre-Mughal poets in India, in particular Amir Khusrau and Hasan Sijzi of Delhi, who were both closely associated with the Chishti Sufi hospice of Shaikh Nizam al-Din Auliya, of whom we have already spoken in earlier chapters. Their poetry is noted, among other things, for its sense of the universal Sufi message, transcending religious and sectarian differences, as we see from these lines of Amir Khusrau.[9]

*Raftam ba kalīsa-i Tarsā wa Yahūd*
*Tarsā wa Yahūd jumlagī rū batū būd*
*Baryād-i wiṣal-i tū ba butkhāna shudam*
*Tasbīḥ-i butān zamzama-i 'ishq-i tū būd.*

(I went to the church of the Christian and of the Jew
And saw that both were facing You
The desire to meet You took me to the temple of idols
And I heard the idols singing your love songs.)

Khusrau's verse echoes an early Sufi message in the verses of Abū Sa'īd Abu'l Khair:

*Nazdi-i ahl-i bīnish kūrast o kūr bīshak*
*'Āshiq ki pīsh-i chashmash zangī ṣanam na bāshad.*

(Men of insight know that man is blind and undoubtedly blind
[the man who calls himself] a lover and does not regard a black worth
his love and devotion.)

[8] For a recent discussion of *malfūẓ*, see Ishtiaq Ahmad Zilli, 'The Production of Early *Malfūẓāt*: Fact and Fiction', paper presented at the conference on Patronage in Indo-Persian Culture, Paris, Centre d'Etudes de l'Inde et de l'Asie du Sud, March 21–3, 2001. See also Carl W. Ernst, *Eternal Garden: Mysticism, History and Politics at a South Asian Sufi Center*, Albany, 1992, pp. 62–84.

[9] Compare M. Safdar Ali Baig, 'Amir Khusrau: His Beliefs and the Sufi Tradition', in *Life, Times, and Works of Amir Khusrau Dehlavi: Commemoration Volume*, Delhi, 1975, pp. 201–2.

And again:

*Mā wa'ishq-i yār agar dar qibla gar dar butkada.*
*'Āshiqān-i dost rā az kufr-o-īmān kār nīst.*

(We, and love of the beloved, are in Ka'ba or in the house of idols.
Lovers of the Friend [God] are not concerned with infidelity and Faith.)

Amir Khusrau's message is summed up in his celebrated phrase '*har qaum rāst rāhī dīnī wa qibla gāhī*' (each community has a way, religion, and sacred place to worship). Hasan Sijzi, on the other hand, found excellent expression for this universal religion in the love story of a Hindu, which he describes in his famous *maṡnawī* entitled *'Ishq Nāma*. Addressing objections from an orthodox Muslim challenger, Sijzi legitimizes the Sufi understanding of divine love as follows.[10]

*Agar gū'ī ki īn guftan chirā būd*
*Bayān-i 'ishq-i bīdīnān khaṭā būd*
*Bayān-i 'ishq kār-i har zabān nīst*
*Chū qā'il zinda dil bāshad ziyān nīst*
*Tawān kardan ba ṣad chashma zabāntar*
*Walekin 'ishq daryā-'īst dīgar*
*Ki kār-i 'āshiqī kārīst jānī*
*Ze kufr-o-dīn birūnast ān ma'ānī.*

(If you say: 'Why did you tell this story?—
For such narration [identifying the love of a Hindu as divine] is an error.'
[I say] the description of love is not everyone's job [lit. 'every tongue']
There's no harm—if the narrator possesses a live heart.
It is possible to quench the thirst of your tongue with the water of hundreds of springs.
Love is, however, an altogether different river.
The work of a lover concerns the heart.
Its soul is beyond [the realm of] Faith and infidelity.

[10] Hasan Sijzi Dihlawi, *Dīwān*, ed. Mas'ud 'Ali Mahvi, Hyderabad, 1934/1352 H, pp. 590–618. Also see Muhammad Shakil Ahmad Siddiqi, *Amīr Ḥasan Sijzī Dihlawī: Ḥayāt Aur Adabī Khidmāt*, Lucknow, 1979, pp. 335–48.

The echoes of this message, like the one in the following verse of 'Urfi Shirazi, gain force in Mughal Persian poetry (which we will discuss in greater detail):

*'Ārif ham az Islām k͟harābast-o-ham az kufr*
*Parwāna chirāg͟h-i-ḥaram o dair nadānad*

(The mystic is in ruins, both because of Islam and infidelity.
The moth doesn't distinguish between the candle in a mosque and a lamp in a temple.)

All these referents and metaphors became crucial constituents within an Indian-Persian diction, better known to literary critics today as *sabk-i Hindī*.[11] We should be clear at the outset that *sabk-i Hindī*, as this notion has been developed in Muhammad Taqi Bahar's classic nineteenth-century account of Persian titled *Sabk Shenāsī*, and as it has generally been understood, does not simply denote a Mughal poetic style. The shaping of *sabk-i Hindī* in fact signified a dialogue between the Persian language and the Indian cultural ethos. It developed as a result of constant interaction between the literary matrices of India, on the one hand, and of Iran, Afghanistan and Central Asia on the other. It implied the use of words and phrases as well as the appropriation and integration of ideas from the Indian world into Persian. This process, which began with Mas'ud Sa'd Salman and Amir Khusrau and showed signs of stability first in fifteenth-century Timurid Herat, combined in its idiom what may be termed the best of the 'culture of 'Ajam'—that is to say the non-Arab world of eastern Islam. This style, mentioned in our sources sometimes as *ṭarz-i Hindūstāniyāna*, matured and scaled new heights in the late-sixteenth and seventeenth-century movement of *tāza-gū'ī* (fresh diction) among Mughal poets.

*Īhām*, which is to say 'ambivalence' or 'deliberate ambiguity'—yet another feature of *sabk-i Hindī*—was largely developed in its initial stages by Amir Khusrau, and soon became a distinctive

[11] The following discussion draws on Muzaffar Alam, 'The Culture and Politics of Persian in Pre-Colonial Hindustan', in Sheldon Pollock, ed., *Literary Cultures in History: Reconstructions from South Asia*, Berkeley, 2003.

aspect of Indian Persian poetics and aesthetics. *Īhām* was, as a rhetorical device, not really new in Persian poetry. Early Persian writers like 'Arūẓī Samarqandi, Rashīd al-Dīn Waṯwāt and Shams al-Dīn Qais al-Rāzī, had all discussed it as a form of literary artifice. To Waṯwāt and Rāzī it meant the creation of doubt by the employment of a word with different meanings, one direct and immediate (*qarīb*), the other remote and strange (*gharīb*). The newness of Amir Khusrau's *īhām* lay in the suggestion that a poet could use a word, or a combination of words, in as many senses as he wished (*ẕu'l wujūh*), and that all these could be simultaneously intended—each direct, equally true (*durust*), logical and sensible. Khusrau rejected the idea that *īhām* meant deception; for Khusrau, the meanings in poetry are all discernible and radiant, clearer and brighter than a mirror. The reader has only to concentrate, to think on, and around, the verse.

This new meaning of *īhām* was received with favour in Sufi circles in India. The Sufi saint from Delhi (and later the Deccan), Sayyid Muhammad Gisudaraz (d.1422), is reported to have compiled a treatise in which he discussed the true meanings of select *īhām* verses. It was this *īhām* which supported, as we saw above, Mir 'Abd al-Wahid Bilgrami's interpretative endeavour to find Islamic meanings in Vaishnava Hindavi songs.

## Persian under the Mughals

The Mughals, who succeeded the Afghan sultans of north India in the sixteenth century, showed unprecedented interest in patronizing Persian literary culture during their rule. Mughal India has been particularly noted for its extraordinary achievements in poetry and wide range of prose writings in Persian. In terms of sheer profusion and variety of themes, this literary output probably exceeded that produced under every other Muslim dynasty. The Mughals were Chaghatay Turks by origin, and we know that, unlike them, Turkic rulers outside Iran—such as the Ottomans in Asia Minor and the Uzbeks in Central Asia—were not quite so enthusiastic about Persian. Indeed, in India too, Persian did not occupy such a position of dominance in the courts of the early Mughals. Babur's *Bābur-Nāma*, the story of his exploits in Turkish, and Turkish poetry, enjoyed a considerable audience at his son Humayun's court even after Humayun's return from Iran.[12]

Nonetheless, it was not Turkish but Persian which came to symbolize Mughal triumph in India. One may conjecture that, in matters of language, the Mughals had no other choice, and that they simply inherited a legacy and continued with it. In some measure, this conjecture seems plausible. Persian had established itself in a large part of north India as the language of the Mughal elite.[13] The famous line of Hafiz of Shiraz (d.1398)—'All the Indian parrots will turn to crunching sugar with this Persian candy which goes to Bengal'[14]—was testimony of a receptive audience for Persian poetry in north India. However, subsequently, there seems to have been a setback to the literature of the language here. There is hardly a notable Persian writer to be found in the fifteenth and early sixteenth centuries,[15] even while Hindavi texts such as Malik Muhammad Jayasi's *Padmāvat* represent the best expression of Muslim Sufi ideas at this time. Persian does not appear to be very strong under the Afghans either, from whom the Mughals took over the reins of power. Most of the Afghans, Babur tells us, could not speak Persian. Hindavi was recognized as a semi-official language by the Sur Sultans (1540–55), and their chancellery scripts even bore transcriptions in the Devanagari script. The practice is said to have been introduced by the Lodi sultans, immediate predecessors to the Mughals.[16] For

[12] Sidi 'Ali Reis, *The Travels and Adventures of Turkish Admiral Sidi Ali Reis*, transl. A. Vambéry, repr. Lahore, 1975, pp. 47, 40–51 and 52–3.

[13] M.A. Ghani, *Pre-Mughal Persian in Hindustan*, Allahabad, 1941, pp. 152–233, and 381–485, for Persian literature under the Ghaznavids, Khaljis and Tughlaqs.

[14] Hafiz Shirazi, *Dīwān*, ed. Qazi Sajjad Husain, Delhi, 1972, p. 172. (My translation.)

[15] For the history of Persian in the period, see S.B.F. Husaini, *A Critical Study of Indo-Persian Literature during the Sayyid and Lodi Period, 1414–1526*, Delhi, 1988; Annemarie Schimmel, *Islamic Literature in India*, in vol. VII of Jan Gonda, ed., *A History of Indian Literature*, Wiesbaden, 1973, p. 21.

[16] Momin Mohiuddin, *The Chancellery and Persian Epistolography under the Mughals: From Babur to Shahjahan, 1526–1658*, Calcutta, 1971, p. 28. Mohiuddin

the extraordinary rise of Persian under the Mughals, the explanation may then be sought more in a convergence of factors within the Mughal regime than within the Indo-Persian heritage of preceding Muslim regimes. We can list a number of these factors.

A large number of Iranians accompanied Humayun on his return from Iran, where he had taken refuge following his defeat against the Afghans in 1540. They assisted him in reconquering Hindustan in 1555. Later, in the 1560s, Akbar needed Iranian help too, and encouraged them to join his imperial service to overcome the difficulties he faced from ambitious Chaghatay nobles. Before Humayun, the Iranians had helped Babur in 1511, during his fight against the Uzbeks, following the destruction of Timurid power in Herat.[17] All of this Iranian help to the Mughals contributed to the expansion of the frontiers of Persian in Mughal India.

Then there is Akbar's unusual interest in promoting social, cultural and intellectual contacts with Iran.[18] The emperor's success on this account was far from superficial. A very large number of Persian writers and poets came in to India, many of them in search of better fortune, others fleeing religious and political persecution in the sectarian Safavid regime.[19] Akbar's India earned the distinction of being termed the place of refuge and the abode of peace (*dār*

---

cites from Maulavi Muhammad Shafi's article in *Oriental College Magazine*, (Lahore) May, 1933, for a reference to a UP State Archives Document No. 318, for an edict of Sher Shah dated 947H. For Babur's remark about the Persian of the Afghans, see Zahir-ud-Din Muhammad Babur, *Bābur-Nāma*, translated by A.S. Beveridge, reprint, Delhi, 1970, pp. 459–60.

[17] J.F. Richards, *The Mughal Empire: The New Cambridge History of India*, 1.5, Cambridge, 1933, pp. 11 and 19.

[18] Abu'l Fath Gilani, *Ruq'āt-i Abu'l Fatḥ Gīlānī*, ed. Muhammad Bashir Husain, Lahore, 1968, pp. 116–20; Riazul Islam, *A Calendar of Documents on Indo-Persian Relations, 1500–1750*, Karachi, 1979, vol.I, pp. 106–7 and 117–20; Abu'l Fazl, *Akbar-Nāma*, ed. Agha Ahmad 'Ali and 'Abdur Rahim, vol. III, Calcutta, 1886, p. 747; Mulla Qati' Herawi, *Tazkira Majma'al-Shu'ārā'-i Jahāngīr Shāhī*, ed. Saleem Akhtar, Karachi, 1979, pp. 35, 203.

[19] Aziz Ahmad, 'Safavid Poets and India', *Iran*, vol. 14, 1976, pp. 117–32; see also Hadi Hasan, *Mughal Poetry: Its Culture and Historical Value*, Madras, 1952, *passim*, and Zabihullah Safa, *Tārīkh-i Adabiyāt-i Irān*, Tehran, 1961/1363 *sh.*, pt 1, for some Iranian poets in India.

*al-amān*) where the wise and the learned would receive encouragement.[20] Migration to India at this time promised material comforts and honoured positions, Iran under the Safavids having turned Shi'ite in a very narrow sense of the term. In Mughal India, on the other hand, the space for accommodating opposition and conflict was widening, subsequent to the Mughal policy of *ṣulḥ-i kull* (peace with all). Growing numbers of nonconformist and dissident Iranians thus found a natural refuge in India.[21] As an ambitious ruler in obvious competition with the Iranian shah, Akbar tried to exploit this situation, extending the frontiers of his authority, at least symbolically, over the Safavid domain. His intention was to neutralize the awe that the Iranian shah exercised over the Mughal household because of the Iranian help to Babur and Humayun.

The extent to which Iranian scholars in Akbar's court served as his agents in extending his influence within Iran is a moot question. His invitation to such people landed many of them in trouble; some of those he chose to invite in person, and who were among the noted nonconformists, faced drastic punishment and several were even executed by the shah.[22] However, the Mughal emperor's desire to bring 'the exalted [Iranian] community close to him spiritually and materially' prepared the ground for many of them to make India their second home. Iranian talents in the arts, it began to seem, could flourish more in Mughal India than at home. As a consequence, Mughal India drew close to Iran culturally, and Persian attained its status as the first language of the Mughal king and his court.

Among the first literary works in the reign of Akbar—at a time when he was consolidating Mughal power in India—was the preparation of a Persian translation of his grandfather's *Bābur-Nāma*.

[20] 'Abd al-Nabi Qazwini, *Tazkira-i Maikhāna*, ed. Ahmad Golchin Ma'ani, Tehran, 1961/1340 *sh.*, p. 809.

[21] 'Abd al-Qadir Badauni, *Muntakhab al-Tawārīkh*, transl. W.H. Lowe, reprints, Delhi, 1973, II, p. 253; Riazul Islam, *Calendar*, vol. I, pp. 101–2; see also his 'Akbar's Intellectual Contacts with Iran', in Milton Israel and N.K. Wagle, eds, *Islamic Culture and Society: Essays in Honour of Aziz Ahmad*, Delhi, 1983, pp. 351–73.

[22] Israel and Wagle, *Islamic Culture*, p. 356.

Ironically, the translator was 'Abd al-Rahim Khan, Khan-i Khanan, the son of Bairam Khan, who had been a poet in Turkish. But it was not just Babur's memoir that was rendered into Persian; the emperor also desired that the sources of the new court history recording Mughal achievements be compiled in Persian. Then, a work by Humayun's sister, Gulbadan Begum, titled *Humāyūn-Nāma*, was written in Persian, even though Turkish was the native tongue of the princess and of her husband Khizr Khwaja Khan. (Antoinette Beveridge, who translated Gulbadan's work into English, suspects that the book was originally composed in Turkish.[23]) Similar was the case of two other accounts of Humayun's time, *Tazkira-i Humāyūn wa Akbar* and *Tazkirat al-Wāqi'āt*: both were meant to serve as sources for Abu'l Fazl's mammoth history, *Akbar-Nāma*; it was well known that their authors, Bayazid Bayat and Jauhar Aftabchi, respectively, could manage little beyond a 'shaky and rustic' spoken Persian. Jauhar, in fact, got the language of his account revised and improved by the noted writer and lexicographer Ilahdad Faizi Sirhindi before presenting it to the emperor.[24]

Akbar had no formal education. Important books were therefore read out to him regularly, in his assembly hall. His library consisted, indeed, of hundreds of prose books and poetical works in Arabic, Persian, Hindi, Greek and Kashmiri, but the books that the emperor heard repeatedly were all in Persian.[25] Akbar, according to one report, could also compose verses in Persian and Hindi; but Mughal sources generally record only his Persian couplets, and we have to wade through these to find the few Hindi verses that are attributed to him. We also know that only Persian poets had the privilege of enjoying extensive royal patronage at Akbar's court.

[23] Gulbadan Begum, *Humayūn-Nāma*, transl. A.S. Beveridge, London, 1902, p. 79.

[24] Compare H. Ethé, *Catalogue of the Persian Manuscripts in the Library of the India Office*, vol. I, Oxford, 1903, no. 222, ff. 2. Sirhindi was a reputed litterateur and philologist; cf. his *Madār al-Afāzil*, 4 vols, ed. Muhammad Baqar, Lahore, 1959–70.

[25] Abu'l Fazl, *Akbar-Nāma*, vol. I, Calcutta, 1873, p. 271.

Among the Muslim rulers of north India, Akbar was probably the first to institute the formal position of *malik al-shu'arā'* (poet laureate) at a royal court. To be awarded to a Persian poet only, this position continued until Shahjahan's time (1628–58). The *malik al-shu'arā'*, during these Mughal years, were Ghazali Mashhadi, Husain Sana'i, Talib Amuli, Kalim Kashani and Qudsi Mashhadi—all Iranians; Abu'l Faiz 'Faizi' (1547–95) was the sole exception. Only nine out of the fifty-nine rated in Akbar's court as the best among the thousand poets in Persian who had completed a *dīwān* or written a *maṡnawī*, were identified as non-Iranians.[26] Again, a large number of other Persian poets and writers—81 according to Nizam al-Din Bakhshi and 168 according to Badauni—received the patronage of the emperor or his nobles.[27] Over a 100 poets and 31 scholars were associated with the establishment of 'Abd al-Rahim Khan-i Khanan alone.[28]

Persian thus emerged as the language of the king, the royal household and the high Mughal élite. Akbar's son and successor Jahangir (1605–27) was not particularly accomplished in Turkish, but he cultivated his own style in Persian and wrote his memoirs in elegant prose. He was also a good critic of Persian poetry and composed several verses and *ghazals*.[29] It was for him that Jayasi's *Padmāvat* was translated into Persian, though the work was

[26] Abu'l Fazl, *Ā'īn-i Akbarī*, ed. H. Blochmann, vol. I, Calcutta, 1872, pp. 617–80.

[27] Badauni, *Muntakhab al-tawārīkh*, vol. III, pp. 171–388; Khwaja Nizam-ud-Din Ahmad, *Ṭabaqāt-i Akbarī*, ed. B. De, II, Calcutta, pp. 484–520.

[28] 'Abd al-Baqi Nihawandi, *Ma'āṡir-i Raḥīmī*, ed. H. Hosain, vol. III, Calcutta, 1931, pp. 9–114 and 115–57. Evidently many of these poets were also from Central Asia, but only a few of them could earn a coveted place in Mughal courts. Mutribi Samarqandi also notes some Central Asian Persian poets in his report on his meetings and conversations with Jahangir; cf. *Khaṭirāt-i Muṭribī Samarqandī*, ed. A.G. Mirzoyef, Karachi, 1977.

[29] Cf. Nur al-Din Jahangir, *Tūzak-i Jahāngīrī*, ed. Syud Ahmad, Allygurh (Aligarh), 1863–4, pp. 103, 245, 303, 316 and 341; *Tazkirat al-shu'arā'*, ed. Abdul Ghani Mirzoyef, Karachi, 1976, *passim*; Mutribi Samarqandi, *Khaṭirāt*, ed. Abdul Ghani Mirzoyef, Karachi, 1977, pp. 44, 48–9, 56–61, 66; see also Shibli Numani, *Shi'r al-'Ajam*, vol. III, Azamgarh, 1945, pp. 5 and 148.

recognized only as an Indian fable (*afsāna-i Hindī*) and not as one on Islamic mysticism in Hindi.[30] Still later, with volumes of letters and edicts, Aurangzeb (1658–1707) established himself as an accomplished prose writer of his time.[31] The formal abolition of the institution of *malik al-shu'arā'* only slightly affected the supreme status of Persian. Indeed, late-seventeenth-century northern India witnessed the emergence of numerous native poets of high standard in Persian, including the great Mirza 'Abd al-Qadir Bedil (d.1720) and Nasir 'Ali Sirhindi (d.1694).

## The Language of Empire

The frontiers of Persian came to extend far beyond the narrow circle of the emperor, the princes, and high nobles. Akbar was the first among the Indo-Islamic kings of north India to formally declare Persian as the language of administration at all levels. The proclamation to this effect was issued by his famous Khatri Hindu revenue minister, Todal Mal. It was accompanied by a reorganization of the revenue department as well as the other administrative departments by the equally famous Iranian noble Mir Fath-Allah Shirazi. How an eighteenth-century historian, Ghulam Husain Tabataba'i, remembered and recorded this change is worth quoting:

> Earlier in India the government accounts were written in Hindi according to the Hindu rule. Raja Todar Mal acquired new regulations (*ẓawābiṭ*) from the scribes (*nawīsindagān*) of Iran, and the government offices then were reorganized as they were there in *wilāyat* [Iran].[32]

[30] Compare 'Abd al-Shakur Bazmi, *Dāstān-i Padmāvat*, ed. A.H. Abidi, Tehran, 1350 *sh*. See also the editor's Introduction for twelve other renderings of *Padmāvat*, pp. 16–26.

[31] Compare recently edited published volumes of Aurangzeb's writings, e.g. Shaikh Abu'l Fath Qabil Khan, *Ādāb-i 'Ālamgīrī*, ed. Abdul Ghafur Chaudhuri, 2 vols, Lahore, 1971; 'Inayatullah Khan Kashmiri, *Kalimāt-i Ṭayyibāt*, ed. S. 'Azizuddin Husain, Delhi, 1982; Ashraf Khan Husaini, *Raqā'im-i Karā'im*, ed. S. 'Azizuddin Husain, Delhi, 1990; see also Najib Ashraf Nadvi, *Muqaddima-i Ruq'āt-i 'Ālamgīr*, Azamgarh, 1981.

[32] Ghulam Husain Tabataba'i, *Siyar al-Muta'akhkhirīn*, vol. I, Lucknow, p. 200.

Thus, it was not simply the royal household and the court which bore the Iranian impress. As *mutaṣaddīs* and minor functionaries, Iranians could be seen everywhere in government offices, even though they were not in exclusive control of these positions. A substantial part of the administration was still carried out by members of the indigenous Hindu communities which had hitherto worked in Hindavi; this was of great consequence, for our purpose, for these communities soon learnt Persian and joined the Iranians as clerks, scribes and secretaries (*muḥarrirs* and *munshīs*). Their achievements in the new language were soon extraordinary. To this development Akbar's reform in the prevailing *madrasa* education—planned and executed again by the Iranian Mir Fath-Allah Shirazi—contributed considerably. Hindus had already begun to learn Persian in Sikandar Lodi's time, and Badauni even mentions a specific Brahman as an Arabic and Persian teacher of this period.[33] Akbar's enlightened policy and the introduction of 'secular' themes in the syllabi at middle levels 'stimulated a wide application to Persian studies'. Hindus—Kayasthas and Khatris in particular—joined *madrasas* in large numbers to acquire excellence in Persian language and literature, which now promised a good career in the imperial service.[34]

From the middle of the seventeenth century, the departments of accountancy (*siyāq*), draftsmanship (*inshā'*), and the office of revenue minister (*dīwān*) were mostly filled by Hindu *munshīs* and *muḥarrirs*. Harkaran Das Kambuh of Multan is the first known Hindu *munshī* whose writings were taken as models by later *munshīs*.[35] Chandra Bhan 'Brahman' and Bhimsen were other influential members of this group. Chandra Bhan was rated second only to Abu'l Fazl. He also wrote poetry of high merit.[36] There followed a

[33] Badauni, *Muntakhab al-Tawārīkh*, vol. III.

[34] Balkrishan, *'Arẓadāsht*, British Library, London, Addn. MS. 16859, cited in Mohiuddin, *Chancellery*, p. 41; see also Syed Muhammad 'Abdullah, *Adabiyāt-i Fārsī meiñ Hindūwoñ kā Ḥiṣṣa*, Lahore, 1967, pp. 240–3.

[35] For an analysis, see Mohiuddin, *Chancellery*, pp. 215–20.

[36] Muhammad 'Abdul Hamid Faruqui, *Chandra Bhan Brahman: Life and Works with a Critical Edition of his Dīwān*, Ahmedabad, 1966; for his prose, see Mohiuddin, *Chancellery*, pp. 228–34. For Bhimsen, see J.F. Richards, 'Norms of

large number of other Kayastha and Khatri *munshīs*, including the well known Madho Ram, Sujan Rai, Malikzadah, Bhupat Rai, Khushhal Chand, Anand Ram 'Mukhlis', Bindraban 'Khwushgu', and a motley crew which made substantive contributions to Indian-Persian language and literature. Selections and specimens of their writings formed part of the syllabi of Persian studies at *madrasas*. Certain areas hitherto unexplored or neglected found skilled investigators, chiefly among Kayasthas and Khatris. They produced excellent works, in the eighteenth century, in the philological sciences. The *Mir'āt al-Iṣṭilāḥ* of Anand Ram 'Mukhlis', the *Bahār-i 'Ajam* of Tek Chand 'Bahar', and the *Muṣṭalaḥāt al-Shu'arā'* of Siyalkoti Mal 'Warasta' are among the most exhaustive lexicons compiled in India. These Persian grammars and commentaries on idioms, phrases, and poetic proverbs show their authors' keen interest, admirable research, and unprecedented engagement in the development of Persian in India.[37] A passage from a celebrated letter written by Chandra Bhan 'Brahman' to his son Khwaja Tej Bhan is worth quoting to illustrate the spread of Persian in Mughal India:

> Initially, it is necessary for one to acquire a training in *a<u>kh</u>lāq* [the system of norms]. It is appropriate to listen always to the advice of elders and act accordingly. By studying the *A<u>kh</u>lāq-i Nāsirī, A<u>kh</u>lāq-i Jalālī, Gulistān*, and *Būstān*, one should accumulate one's own capital and gain the virtue of knowledge. When you practice what you have learnt, your code of conduct too will become firm. The main thing is to be able to draft in a coherent manner, but at the same time good calligraphy possesses its own virtues and it earns you a place in the assembly of those of high stature. O dear son! Try to excel in these skills. And together with this, if you manage to learn accountancy (*siyāq*), and scribal skills (*nawīsindagī*), that would be even better. For scribes who know accountancy as well are rare. A man who knows how to write good prose as well as accountancy is

---

Comportment among Imperial Mughal Officials', in Metcalf, *Moral Conduct and Authority*, pp. 255–89.

[37] Abdullah, *Adabiyāt*, pp. 121–68.

a bright light even among lights. Besides, a *munshī* should be discreet and virtuous. I, who am among the *munshīs* of the court that is the symbol of the caliphate, even though I am subject to the usual errors, am still as an unopened bud though possessing hundreds of tongues.

Although the science of Persian is vast, and almost beyond human grasp, in order to open the gates of language one should read the *Gulistān, Būstān*, and the letters of Mulla Jami, to start with. When one has advanced somewhat, one should read key books on norms and ethics, as well as history books such as the *Habīb al-Siyar, Rauẓat al-Ṣafā, Rauẓat al-Salāṭīn, Tārīkh-i Guzīda, Tārīkh-i Ṭabarī, Ẓafar-Nāma, Akbar-Nāma*, and some books like these that are absolutely necessary. The benefits of these will be to render your language elegant, also to provide you knowledge of the world and its inhabitants. These will be of use when you are in the assemblies of the learned. Of the master-poets, here are some whose collections I read in my youth, and the names of which I am writing down. When you have some leisure, read them, and they will give you both pleasure and relief, increase your abilities, and improve your language. They are Hakim Sana'i, Mulla Rum, Shams Tabriz, Shaikh Farid al-Din 'Attar, Shaikh Sa'di, Khwaja Hafiz, Shaikh Kirmani, Mulla Jami, and Unsuri, Fardausi, Jamal al-Din 'Abd al-Razzaq, Kamal Isma'il, Khaqani, Anwari, Amir Khusrau, Hasan Dehlavi, Zahir Faryabi, Kamal Khujandi, Amiq Bukhari, Nizami Aruzi Samarqandi, 'Abd al-Wasi Jabali, Rukn Sa'in, Muhyi al-Din, Mas'ud Bek, Farid al-Din 'Usman Mukhtari, Nasir Bukhari, Ibn Yamin, Hakim Suzani, Farid Katib, Abu'l 'Ala Ganjawi, Azraqi, Falaki, Sauda'i, Baba Fighani, Khwaja Kirmani, Asfi, Mulla Bana'i, Mulla 'Imad Khwaja, Ubaid Zakani, Bisati, Lutf-Allah Halawi, Rashid Watwat, Asir Akhshikati, and Asir Umami. May my good and virtuous son understand that, when I had finished reading these earlier works, I then desired to turn my attention to the later poets and writers and started collecting their poems and *masnawīs*. I acquired several copies of their works, and when I had finished them I gave some of them to some of my disciples. Some of these are as follows: Ahli, Hilali, Muhtasham, Wahshi, Qazi Nur, Nargis, Makhfi Ummidi, Mirza Qasim Gunai, Partawi, Jabrani, Hisabi, Sabri, Zamiri Rasikhi, Hasani, Halaki, Naziri, Nau'i, Nazim Yaghma, Mir Haidar, Mir

> Ma'sum, Nazir, Mashhadi, Wali Dasht Bayazi, and many others who had their collections (*dīwāns*) and *maṣnawīs*, and whose names are too numerous to be listed in this succinct letter.[38]

The masters of the Iranian classics thus found an increasingly appreciative audience even among the middle-order literati in big and small towns, as well as among village-based revenue officials and other hereditary functionaries and intermediaries. All Mughal government papers, from imperial orders (*farmāns*) to bonds and acceptance letters (*muchalka, tamassuk qabūliyat*) that a village intermediary (*chaudhurī*) wrote, were in Persian.[39] Likewise, there was no bookseller in the bazaars and streets of Agra, Delhi and Lahore who did not sell anthologies of Persian poetry. *Madrasa* pupils were in general familiar with the Persian classics.[40] Persian, then, had practically become the first language of north India. Its users appropriated and used Perso-Islamic expressions such as *Bismillāh* (in the name of Allah), *lab-bagūr* (at the door of the grave), and *bajahannam rasīd* (damned in hell) just as much as their Iranian and non-Iranian Muslim counterparts did. They would also now look for, and appreciate, Persian renderings of local texts and traditions. Lest they be forgotten, the religious scriptures were rendered in full into Persian by various Hindu translators.[41]

If, on the one hand, the prospects of a good career and direct access to the ancient scriptures now available in Persian provided incentives for learning Persian to Hindus, on the other, this language acquired a kind of religious sanctity among Muslims. Jamal al-Din Inju, author of *Farhang-i Jahāngīrī*, the first comprehensive

[38] 'Abdullah, *Adabiyāt*, pp. 241–3, cites the passage from Chandra Bhan's letter.

[39] Even in Bengal, administrative papers prepared and issued in the name of the local Hindu intermediaries were in Persian. Persian *inshā'*, indeed, even succeeded in influencing Bengali prose; cf. Promesh Acharya, 'Pedagogy and Social Learning: *Tol* and *Pathsala* in Bengal', *Studies in History* (New Series), vol. 10, no. 2, July-December 1994, pp. 255–72.

[40] Badauni, *Muntakhab al-tawārīkh*, vol. II, p. 285.

[41] Compare Gopal bin Govind's preface to his Persian translation of the *Rāmāyana*, BN, Paris, MS. Blochet, I, 22.

Persian lexicon, dwells at length on the point that Persian, together with Arabic, is the language of Islam. The Prophet of Islam, he reports from various sources, knew and spoke Persian. The prophets, according to Inju, spoke highly of the merits of the people of Pars; he cites verses from the Qur'an in appreciation of the people of Pars for their bravery and courage in fighting for a noble cause. Faith (*īmān*), according to Inju, is integral to their (the people of Pars') character, to the point that they would have acquired the true faith even if it were far from them up in the sky.[42] Inju began to compile the *Farhang* at Akbar's instance, and, since it was completed after the emperor's death, it was dedicated to his son Jahangir.[43]

The work's message was possibly intended to be communicated to Indian converts, whose native language was largely some form of Hindavi. There was certainly a wide application of Persian studies among the *shurafā'*—Muslim landed magnates, revenue-free landholders in the rural areas and those who had a daily allowance (*a'imma, waẓīfa*) in towns, and petty officials. Even ordinary literate Muslims—soldiers, for instance—were now expected to read simple Persian.[44]

## Persian and Political Culture

Learning, knowledge and high culture began to be associated with Persian at many levels of Mughal society. Command over good Persian was a matter of pride, and deficiency in elegant expression in Persian meant cultural failure. For Mirza Muhammad Bakhsh 'Ahshub', a noted poet and writer of the later Mughal era, the major failure in Samsam al-Daulah, Khan-i Dauran—the well-known early-eighteenth-century noble—was his inability to speak good Persian: Khan-i Dauran generally spoke in 'Hindi'. On occasion, he would embellish his conversation with Persian couplets and remark

[42] Mir Jamal al-Din Husain Inju Shirazi, *Farhang-i Jahāngīrī*, ed. Rahim Afifi, 3 vols, Mashhad, 1972, vol. I, pp. 14–22; Siraj al-Din 'Ali Khan Arzu, *Muthmir*, ed. Rehana Khatoon, Karachi, 1991, pp. 6, 7 and 14–17.

[43] *Farhang-i Jahāngīrī*, vol. I, pp. 6, 7 and 14–17.

[44] *Ḥujjat al-Hind*, British Library, London, Addn. MS. 5602, f. 11.

that 'to speak in Persian for an Indian is to make oneself a butt of ridicule.'[45]

Khan-i Dauran was an exception. In general, Persian was held to be the only effective language in which to express cultural accomplishment, and it came to be recognized as the language of politics in nearly the whole of the subcontinent.[46] This status received nourishment from the Mughal power which sustained it, and the Mughal belief in Persian as the most functional, pragmatic and accomplished vehicle of communication remained unshaken among north Indian populations long after the demise of the Mughal empire.[47] The long association of the Mughals, and of their supporters and successors, with Persian in the fields of political and military management created a memory of the language as an instrument of conquest. Persian facilitated Mughal triumph. The intrinsic strengths of the language, combined with the emperor's decision supporting it, prepared the grounds for forging links between the court and remote villages.

The Mughals were not content with establishing a merely paramount and imperial authority over numerous local and regional power groups. They aspired also to evolve a political culture—as we have seen in earlier chapters—arching over diverse Indian religious and cultural identities. Persian, in the existing circumstances, promised to be the most appropriate vehicle to communicate and sustain such an ideal. Persian was known to literate Indians from the banks of the Indus to the Bay of Bengal. If Amir Khusrau is to be believed, as early as in the fourteenth century 'Persian

[45] Mirza Muhammad Bakhsh 'Ashub', *Tārīkh-i Shahādat-i Farrukh Siyar wa Julūs-i Muḥammad Shāh*, British Library, London, MS. Or. 1832, f. 726.

[46] For the position of Persian in the East India Company territories in the late eighteenth century, see Bernard Cohn, 'The Command of Language and the Language of Command', in Ranajit Guha, ed., *Subaltern Studies IV: Writings on South Asian History and Society*, Delhi, 1985, pp. 284–95.

[47] Mirza Asad-Allah Khan Ghalib, for instance, insisted that the depth and variety of ideas could be conveyed through Persian alone. *Kulliyāt-i Ghālib*, ed. Syed Murtaza Husain, vol. I, Lahore, 1967, p. 161; S.M. Kamal, *Hyderābād mein Urdū kā Irtiqā*, Hyderabad, 1990, p. 102.

parlance enjoyed uniformity of idiom throughout the length of four thousand leagues, unlike the Hindavi tongue, which had no settled idiom and varied after every hundred miles and with every group of people.'[48] As late as the eighteenth century, Hindavi had not evolved a uniform idiom even in north India. Siraj al-Din 'Ali Khan Arzu (d.1756), a noted eighteenth-century poet, writer and lexicographer, mentions Gwaliyari, Braj, Rajputi, Kashmiri, Haryanavi, Hindi, and Punjabi as diverse authentic forms of Hindavi, besides the dialects of Shahjahanabad Delhi and Akbarabad Agra.[49] Sanskrit, or *Hindī-yi kitābī* (Hindi of the Book)—as Khan-i Arzu calls it—could have served in place of Persian as the language of the empire. But Sanskrit, as Mirza Khan (the author of *Tuḥfat al-Hind*) noted in Aurangzeb's time, was not taken as an ordinary human tongue; it was seen as a *deva-bānī* (language of the gods) and *ākāsh-bānī* (language of the upper firmament). Sanskrit was, in short, seen as too sacred, too divine. No *mlechha* could have been allowed to pollute it by choosing it as the symbol and vehicle of his power. The *mlechha* could not have used it to create the world of his vision. Prakrit, on the other hand, was a *pātāl-bānī*—the language of the underground and of snakes—and thus considered too low by the Mughals to be appropriated for lofty imperial ideals. Braj or Bhakha, the language of the normal world, was also a rather regional dialect. And Bhakha, in the Mughal view, was suitable only for music and love poetry.[50]

Again, Persian was valorized because its poetry had integrated many elements from pre-Islamic Persia. It had already served as an important vehicle of liberalism in the medieval Muslim world—as illustrated by the verses of Amir Khusrau and Hasan Sijzi Dihlawi. These factors helped significantly in encouraging and promoting conditions that would accommodate diverse religious and cultural

[48] Compare Amir Khusrau, *Nuh Sipihr*, ed. Wahid Mirza, Oxford, 1950, preface and p. 173.

[49] Siraj al-Din 'Ali Khan Arzu, *Nawādir al-Alfāẓ*, preface cited in Syed Muhammad Abdullah, *Mabāḥis̱*, Delhi, 1968, pt I, p. 75.

[50] Mirza Khan bin Fakhr al-Din Muhammad, *Tuḥfat al-Hind*, vol. I, ed. Nurul Hasan Ansari, Tehran, 1977/1356 *sh.*, pp. 51–2.

traditions. Among the Persian books which Akbar had read aloud to him every night was the *Masnawī* of Jalal al-Din Rumi. The emperor's non-sectarianism could have been inspired by Rumi's verses, such as the following.

*Tū barā-i waṣl kardan āmdī*
*na barā-i faṣl kardan āmdī*
*Hindiyān rā iṣṭilāḥ-i Hind madḥ*
*Sindiyān rā iṣṭilāḥ-i Sind madḥ*[51]

(Thou hast come to unite,
not to separate.
The people of Hind worship in the idiom of Hindi.
The people of Sind do so in their own.)

Echoes of these messages, and the general suspicion of the mere 'formalism' of their faith in orthodox Islam, are unmistakeable in Mughal Persian poetry as well. The Mughal poet Faizi had the ambition of building 'a new Ka'ba' with stones from the Sinai.

*Biyā ki rū ba miḥrāb-gāh-i nau ba-nihīm*
*Binā-i Ka'ba-i dīgar ze sang-i Tūr nihīm*[52]

(Come, let us turn our face towards a new altar
We shall take stones from the Sinai and build a new Ka'ba.)

Mughal poets, like their predecessors, portrayed the pious (*zāhid*) and the shaikh as hypocrites. It was with the master of a wine-house (*mughān*), and in the temple, rather than in the mosque, they believed, that eternal and divine secrets were to be sought.

*Shi'ār-i millat-i Islāmiyān ba-guzar agar khwāhī*
*ki dar dair-i mughān ā'ī wa asrār-i nihān bīnī*[53]

[51] Jalal al-Din Rumi, *Masanawī-yi Maulānā Rūm*, ed. Qazi Sajjad Husain, vol. II, Delhi, 1976, p. 173. (My translation.) For Akbar's administration and fondness for the *masnawī* of Maulana Rum, see Abu'l Fazl, *Akbar-Nāma*, vol. I, p. 271.

[52] Abu'l Faiz 'Faizi Fayyazi', *Dīwān*, ed. A.D. Arshad, Lahore, 1962, p. 470. (My translation.)

[53] Muhammad Jamal al-Din 'Urfi Shirazi, *Kulliyāt*, ed. Jawahiri Wajdi, Tehran, 3rd reprint, 1990/1369 *sh.*, p. 152.

(Give up the path of the Muslims, come to the temple,
to the master of the wine-house
so that you may see divine secrets.)

The idol (*but*) was to them the symbol of divine beauty; idolatory (*but-parastī*) represented love of the Absolute; and, significantly, they emphasized that the brahman should be held in high esteem because of his sincerity, devotion and faithfulness to the idol. To Faizi, it seems a matter of privilege that his love for an idol led him to embrace the religion of the Brahman.

*Shukr-i Khudā ki 'ishq-i butān ast rāhbaram*
*bar millat-i brahmān-o bar dīn-i Āẕaram*[54]

(Thank God, that the love of idols is my guide,
I follow the religion of the Brahman and Azar.)

To 'Urfi the temple (*dair, but-kada*) and the wine house (*mai-khāna*) meant the same as the mosque and Ka'ba: the divine spirit pervaded all.

*Chirāgh-i Somnāt ast ātish-i Ṭūr*
*buwad zān har jihat rā nūr dar nūr*[55]

(The lamp of Somnath is [the same as] the fire at Sinai,
from which light spreads all around.)

This feature of Persian poetry was not diluted even when Aurangzeb tried to associate the Mughal state with Sunni orthodoxy. Nasir 'Ali Sirhindi (d.1696), a major poet of his time, echoed 'Urfi's message with real enthusiasm.

*Nīst ghair az yak ṣanam dar parda-i dair-o-ḥaram*
*kai shawad ātish du rang az ikhtilāf-i sang-hā*[56]

(In the temple or in the Ka'ba, the image is the same behind the veil.
With a change of flints, does the colour of fire change?)

[54] Faizi, *Dīwān*, p. 53.
[55] 'Urfi Shirazi, *Dīwān*, Kanpur, 1915, p. 445.
[56] Nasir 'Ali Sirhindi, *Dīwān*, Lucknow, 1872, p. 15.

In fact, at other times, neither mosque nor temple seem illumined by divine beauty: the heart (*dil*) of the true lover is its abode. The message was therefore, at times, that man should aspire to the high place that lovers occupy.

Another poet, Talib Amuli, called for transcending the differences in attitude that emerge because of people's names.

*Na malāmat-gar-i kufr am na ta'aṣṣub-kash-i dīn*
*khanda-hā bar jadl-i Shaikh-o Barhaman dāram*[57]

(I do not condemn infidelity, I am not a bigoted believer,
I laugh at both, the Shaikh and the Brahman.)

In all these varied ways Persian made a plea for conquest and dominance without staining the victor's apparel with the blood of the vanquished.

*Zakhm-hā bardāshtīm o-fatḥ-hā kardīm lek*
*hargiz as khūn-i kas-i rangīn nashud dāmān-i mā*[58]

(We have suffered wounds, we have scored victories,
but our skirts were never stained with anyone's blood.)

The desire to build an empire in which both shaikh and brahman might live with minimal conflict also necessitated the generation of information about diverse local traditions. Akbar's historian Abu'l Fazl is not content in his *Akbar-Nāma* with a mere description of the heroic achievements of his master; he concludes his account with what he calls the *Ā'īn* (institutes) of Akbar. Of particular note here is the third book of the *Ā'īn*, which contains a survey of the land, the revenues, and the peoples or the castes in control thereof. Above all, the fourth book 'treats of the social conditions and literary activity especially in philosophy and law, of the Hindus, who form the bulk of the population, and in whose political advancement the emperor

[57] Talib Amuli, *Kulliyāt-i Ash'ār-i Malik al-Shu'rā Ṭālib Amulī*, ed. Tahiri Sihab, Tehran, 1967, p. 688.

[58] 'Urfi Shirazi, *Dīwān*, p. 3.

saw the guarantee of the stability of his realm.'[59] As we have noted earlier, in order to make the major local texts accessible and thus to dispel the ignorance about local traditions, Akbar took special care to render Indian scriptures into Persian. The translations of these religious texts were followed in Akbar's own time, and later in the seventeenth and eighteenth centuries, by Persian renderings of a large number of texts on 'Hindu' religion, law, ethics, mathematics, medicine, astronomy, romance, moral fables and music.[60]

Persian thus promoted the conditions in which the Mughals could build a class of allies out of heterogeneous social and religious groups. While this class cherished universalist human values and visions, the emperor was seen, in the words of the noted Braj poet Keshav Das, as *dūhū dīn ko sahib* (the master of both religions), possessing the attributes of the Hindu god Vishnu.[61] *Dīn*, in this atmosphere, assumed a new meaning: the king could blend Hindu social practices and Rajput court rituals with Islam at the Mughal court. These practices ranged from applying *tīka* (the vermilion mark) on the foreheads of political subordinates, to *tūladān* (the royal weighing ceremony) and *jharoka darshan* (the early morning appearance of the emperor on the palace balcony), to the public worship of the sun by Akbar—and this entailing prostration facing the east before a sacrificial fire and the recitation of the sun's names in Sanskrit.[62] The influence of the illuminationist philosophy of Shihab al-Din Suhrawardi Maqtul apart,[63] it was perhaps in

[59] H. Blochmann's Preface to his translation of the *Ā'īn-i Akbarī*, vol. I, reprint, Delhi, 1965.

[60] S.A.A. Rizvi, *Religious and Intellectual History of the Muslims in Akbar's Reign*, Delhi, 1975, pp. 203–22; F. Mujtabai, *Aspects of Hindu-Muslim Cultural Relations*, Delhi, 1978, pp. 70–91, for a brief description of the Persian translation of religious texts.

[61] Keshavdas, *Keshavgranthāvalī*, part 3, ed. V.P. Misra, Allahabad, 1958, pp. 620–1.

[62] Sri Ram Sharma, *The Religious Policy of the Mughal Emperors*, revised edn, London, 1972, pp. 40–4 and 48; Ishtiaq Husain Qureshi, *Akbar: The Architect of the Mughal Empire*, Kanpur, 1978.

[63] J.F. Richards, 'The Formulation of Imperial Authority under Akbar and

order to highlight their affinity with the Rajputs—in whose legends fire and light had special position—that Abu'l Fazl emphasized the legendary origins from light of the Mughals themselves.[64] Mughals married Rajput princesses and allowed them to observe their rituals, ceremoniously, in their palaces. Such alliances entailing cross-practices were reciprocated by local Hindu culture in Rajputana and within Rajput society. Rajputs often considered the Mughals as a sub-category of their own *jāti*. The Mughal emperor, in their traditions, held high rank and was esteemed sufficiently to be equated with Ram,[65] the Kshatriya cultural hero and exemplary Hindu king. The Rajputs identified themselves with the house of the Mughal to the extent that they believed it should be defended in the same way as their own families and royal houses.[66]

Taken together, all the varied religious, cultural and literary developments and innovations that were a consequence of Islam's contact with Hinduism echoed the Mughal concern for ensuring 'justice' and 'peace' for all. In terms of their theory of social equipoise (*i'tidāl*) and non-sectarian approach to matters of faith, these made political sense, even as they diverged from orthodox Islam. In these attempts at social stability, language played no small role. Persian became a crucial vehicle for the mode and idiom of politics that Mughal rule attempted to propagate. It was perhaps inevitable that such a liberal policy would not go unchallenged by other forces in medieval society: and it is to the nature and extent of such challenges—as well as responses to them—that we shall now turn.

---

Jahangir', in Muzaffar Alam and Sanjay Subrahmanyam, eds, *The Mughal State, 1526–1750*, Delhi, 1998, pp. 126–67.

[64] Compare *Akbar-Nāma*, vol. I, p. 122.

[65] Norman P. Zeigler, 'Some Notes on Rajput Loyalties during the Mughal Period', in Alam and Subrahmanyam, *The Mughal State*, pp. 168–210.

[66] This is best illustrated in Raja Ram Singh Hara's reported response to the anxiety expressed by Prince Muhammad A'zam's wife (a Safavid princess), who asked what the raja was planning to defend her with against the Marathas, who were threatening her party. Jadunath Sarkar, *History of Aurangzeb*, vol. IV, Calcutta, 1919, p. 302, cited in M. Athar Ali, *The Mughal Nobility under Aurangzeb*, revised edn., Delhi, 1997, p. 25.

CHAPTER 5

# Opposition and Reaffirmation

## The Problems of Persian and *Akhlāq* Texts

We have followed the making of the medieval Indo-Islamic state specifically in relation to political and cultural developments in India as well as in the larger Islamic world. We have seen how processes of state and identity formation derived from a tradition of appropriating and assimilating different cultural strands which appeared to be and, on occasion, were indeed incompatible with the received textual tradition of Islam. Islam's interaction with the area of 'Ajam (a large part of the eastern non-Arab cultures), and 'Ajam's cultural domination over a good part of the Islamic world, were manifest both in the accumulative character of the meanings of *sharī'a* as well as in the substitution of the 'sacred' Arabic language by a relatively 'secular' Persian. In brief, *sharī'a* came to acquire more than one meaning in the course of this encounter between Arab and non-Arab; the language of the Islamic East moved towards a syncretic mix; a legacy of cooperation and assimilation developed from the days of the Sultanate to the end of Mughal rule; and conflictual situations tended to be resolved along a pattern informed by this strong political tradition of accommodation within medieval Islam.

This does not mean that forces contesting the assimilative tradition were not active. While Jahangir, unlike Iltutmish and 'Ala al-Din Khalji, did not have to contend with the views of a Nizam al-Mulk Junaidi or a Qazi Mughis, the strength of such views in the community still carried considerable weight. These views expressed themselves, in a measure, in the compilation of the *Fatāwā-i 'Alamgīrī* under Aurangzeb and, again, in the early eighteenth century, in the demand from some quarters of Muslim orthodoxy to earmark all Mughal revenues for the maintenance of the *'ulamā'* and Muslim religious establishments.[1] We shall examine, here, some of the features that militated against the tradition of tolerance of which we have earlier spoken.

We can see, first of all, that while Persian and Persianization acted as a potent agent of assimilation, it also encouraged a kind of anti-tolerant worldview at elite levels. The Ghaznavid period (1062–1186), when Muslims from Central Asia and Iran began to settle in north India, marked the first zenith of Persian revival in the non-Arab Islamic East. The origins of the Persian revival lay in the almost constant struggle of Persians, beginning from about the end of the ninth century,[2] to assert their political and national identity against that of their Arab conquerors. Though arrested temporarily by the Mongol invasions, this process culminated in the practically complete Persianization of rulers and intellectuals in almost the whole of the non-Arab areas of the eastern caliphate. Persian thus came to symbolize high culture in politics as well as in literature and art. As we saw earlier, Firdausi, the famous Persian poet, composed his *Shāh-Nāma* at the court of Mahmud of Ghazna, rendering in epic poetry the history of the heroic deeds of pre-Islamic Sasanid kings

[1] Muzaffar Alam, *The Crisis of Empire in Mughal North India: Awadh and the Punjab, 1707–1748*, Delhi, 1986, pp. 114–17; Zafarul Islam, 'Nature of Landed Property in India: Views of an Eighteenth Century Jurists', *Proceedings of the Indian History Congress*, 36th Session, Aligarh, 1975, pp. 301–9.

[2] Even though Tahirids established the first Persian dynasty in Khurasan, the Saffarids (867–892), the Samanids (874–999) and the Buyids (934–1055) were the first consciously Persian principalities. The Samanids claimed to be descendants of the pre-Islamic Sasanid nobleman Saman, while the Buyids mentioned Yezdgerd, a Sasanid king, as their ancestor. Rudaki and Daqiqi, the first Persian poets, were patronized by the Samanids. Later, the Turks, the Ghaznavids, the Seljuqs and Khwarizmshahis became enthusiastic patrons of Persian language and culture. Cf. Edward G. Browne, *A Literary History of Persia*, vol. II, Cambridge, 1964, in particular pp. 339–480.

up until the conquest of Iran by Arabs. The process of narrating pre-Islamic Iranian history in this 'New Persian' poetry had begun with the Samanid poet Daqiqi, and in the *Shāh-Nāma* Firdausi resurrected 'Ajam with his Persian.[3]

North Indian Muslim rulers remained under the hegemony of this resurrected 'Ajam. The court of the Delhi sultans imitated the ancient Sasanid culture wholesale, and rulers looked upon Iranian heroes as their models. This was, as we noted, certainly a secular feature of the Islamic polity and showed Islam's capacity to assimilate non-Islamic culture, though obviously only in the context of Persian-speaking lands. But pre-Mughal Muslim rulers in north India did not show the same interest in India's pre-Islamic past, as such rulers had done, for instance, in Khurasan and Iran. True, there appeared certain Sanskrit legends on some early Ghaznavid coins,[4] and there is also evidence, as we saw, of Hindavi official records from the Afghan regime. These, however, were exceptions which hardly had much bearing on the fact of a dominant Persian culture. In north India, rulers generally patronized not only Persian language, literature and art, but also the process of Persianization. This process encouraged a composite culture at the higher levels, but equally it bred tensions that surfaced in the days of political decline and decentralization.

A final factor in this dominant Persian influence, which went against the tradition of accommodation at northern Indian courts, was the continued flow into India of immigrant princes, noblemen

[3] Cf. *Shahnama: The Epic of the Kings*, English tr. by Reuben Levy, revised by Amin Banani, London, 1967, particularly the last sections. The poet's support to the notion of 'Ajam is illustrated, among other things, in the letter he mentions as written by Rustam, the Iranian hero, to Sa'd ibn Wiqas, the Companion of the Prophet of Islam, who led the Arab campaigns. See also Alam, 'The Culture and Politics of Persian in Pre-Colonial Hindustan', in Pollock, ed., *Literary Cultures in History*, pp. 131–48.

[4] Compare Dines Chandra Sircar, ed., *Select Inscriptions Bearing on Indian History and Civilization: From the Sixth to the Eighteenth Century A.D.*, Delhi, 1983, pp. 650–64; Parmeshwari Lal Gupta, *Coins*, New Delhi, 1969, pp. 204–5, nos 215–18. I am grateful to my colleague B.D. Chattopadhyaya for these references.

and men of learning from Iran and Central Asia. As we noted earlier every time there was a political upheaval in Turkestan, Iran or Afghanistan, or when disaster struck those regions, various elites moved to north India, seeking shelter or in quest of livelihood. These regular incursions from the original lands of north Indian rulers lent strength to the local Perso-Turkic culture at the higher levels; immigrations of this type also caused a kind of inferiority complex among non-immigrant Indians close to the royal courts. Sultans and courtiers were so completely in the grip of this complex that they were keen to establish their Iranian or Central Asian lineage. The ideal within the high culture of north Indian Muslims, irrespective of their class and position, in this sense remained Perso-Turkic.

This process gets accentuated with the unprecedented rise of the Persian language and Iranian emigres under the Mughals. Persian, being an alien language, also drove, in some ways, a wedge between the Mughals and their subjects. Persian, under the Mughals, was not entirely sensitive to local languages and local usage. The choice of Persian as the language of empire was, in very large measure, the outcome of specific Indian conditions inasmuch as the non-sectarian and liberal features of Persian idiom and expression made it an ideal vehicle through which the Mughals could effectively negotiate the diversities of Indian society. The culture and ethos of Persian matched more closely their vision of a diverse yet overarching empire: the language was a particularly useful instrument for political manoeuvrability. Yet Persian was not an Indian language, and even though it had begun to assume an identity of autonomous Indian proportions in pre-Mughal India, the Iranian idiom remained the favoured reference point among the Mughals.

Amir Khusrau, with whose poetry and writings Indian diction assumed a distinct personality of its own, had disapproved of the 'Khurasani' idiom of his day and had noted that, in India, Persian was written and pronounced according to the standard of Turan.[5]

[5] Amir Khusrau, *Dībācha-i Dīwān-i <u>Gh</u>urrat al-Kamāl*, ed. Sharif Husain Qasemi in *Majalla-i Taḥqīqāt-i Fārsī*, Delhi, 1988, pp. 161–2; Wahid Mirza, *The Life and Works of Amir Khusrau*, Calcutta, 1935, p. 160.

The models, in particular for prose, were the authors of Transoxiana. The writings of Rashid al-Din Watwat and Baha al-Din of Khwarizm, for instance, were read and imitated by Indian Persian writers. Khusrau then innovated a new Indo-Persian style.[6] For pre-Mughal lexicographers, however, the languages spoken in Shiraz, Mawara-an-nahr and Farghana were dialects of the same Persian tongue. They incorporated within their lexicons words used in 'Fars, Samarqand, Mawara-an-nahr and Turkistan', and they also gave their Hindavi synonyms as a matter of routine.[7]

The Mughal court, in contrast, was concerned with the purification of Persian (*taṭhīr-i Fārsī*). The objective of the lexicon that Akbar asked Jamal al-Din Husain Inju to prepare in his name was to cleanse Persian in India of non-Persian words and expressions.[8] The drive at purification continued later. Inju's *Farhang*, together with the *Majma' al-Furs Surūrī*, were accepted as the sole and standard lexicons of the first half of the seventeenth century. By the middle of the century, Mulla 'Abd al-Rashid Thattawi felt the necessity of compiling a new dictionary (among other things) because, first, in the two major existing dictionaries (*Jahāngīrī* and *Surūrī*) certain Arabic and Turkish words were listed without clarifying that they were not Persian; and, second, because many words were 'wrongly' pronounced by Inju and Sururi.[9]

In the late sixteenth and seventeenth centuries the most sublime and finest Persian poetry of the time was produced in India, and the eighteenth century was the richest in terms of the number and varieties of prose and poetic works in Indian Persian. Take for instance, the case of poetry. Seventy-seven of the Persian poets who lived during the earlier half of that century found a place of honour in the great *tazkira* titled *Majma' al-Nafā'is* by Siraj al-Din 'Ali Khan Arzu, who was the best and the most revered scholar-poet and

[6] Mohiuddin, *Chancellery*, p. 23. Later, however, Watwat's *Ḥadā'iq al-Siḥr* inspired Warasta's *Maṭla' al-Sa'dain*. Cf. Abdullah, *Adabiyāt*, p. 144.

[7] Husaini, *Indo-Persian Literature*, pp. 201–26.

[8] Inju Shirazi, *Farhang-i Jahāngīrī*, Preface, p. 4.

[9] Zahuruddin Ahmad, *Pakistān mein Fārsī Adab kī Tārīkh* (*Jahangir to Aurangzeb*), Lahore, 1974, p. 542.

critic of the period.[10] Many *tazkiras* were written in this period. Among these, Ali Ibrahim Khalil's (d.1793) *Ṣuḥuf-i Ibrāhīm*, which was among the most comprehensive at least for north Indian poets, noted no less than 460 poets from among those who lived in the eighteenth century, and whose works he considered of some worth.[11] No less than 56 of these were non-Muslims.[12]

Of greater significance was the development of Persian literary sensibilities. Poetry was marked by an outspoken spirit of innovation and experimentation, while showing due regard to the past literary heritage of Iran as well as Central Asia. Mughal poetry signified a fine blending of forms of rhetorical excellence. Thought was to occupy a distinct and uncontested superior position, and while Abu'l Fazl had emphasized the splendour of ideas,[13] his poet-brother Faizi advocated their sublime quality and emotional texture.

*Gar durd nīst dar sukhan-i man 'ajab madār*
*kīn bāda rā ba parda-i dil ṣāf karda-īm*[14]

(Don't be surprised if there are no dregs in my poetry,
for I've refined this wine through the filter of the heart.)

Still, it was the Iranians who were enabled to dictate terms for literary culture in Mughal India, as much as in their own home. Despite the incomparable accomplishments of hundreds of Indian-Persian writers and poets, and the enthusiasm of thousands in their audiences, the Iranians generally rejected Indian usages (*isti'māl-i Hind, taṣarruf-i Hind*), disregarding the centuries-old local contact with and command over Persian. This was the case not simply with Indian words and phrases: even Indian ideas translated into Persian, and Indian pronunciation and the spellings of certain words,

10 For a selection (*intikhāb*) of his work, see British Library, London, OIOC, MS., I.O. 4015.

11 Cf. *Ṣuḥuf-i Ibrāhīm* (Portion dealing with the accounts of the twelfth century AH), ed. A.R. Bedar, Patna, 1981.

12 Abdullah, *Adabiyāt*, pp. 169–84.

13 Abu'l Fazl, *Akbar-Nāmā*, vol. II, Calcutta, 1879, p. 381.

14 Faizi, *Dīwān*, p. 405.

were made to seem unacceptable. The principal Persian philological works of the period, including *Sirāj al-Lug̱hat* of Arzu, *Mirā't al-Iṣṭilāḥ* of Anand Ram 'Mukhlis', *Muṣṭalaḥāt al-Shu'arā'* of Siyalkoti Mal 'Warasta', and *Bahār-i 'Ajam* of Munshi Tek Chand 'Bahar', were all oriented towards updating the language as used in India in the light of usages current in Iran.[15]

In terms of Persian language and literature, Mughal India thus virtually emerged as a kind of Iranian colony. Abu'l Barakat Munir Lahori (d.1645) even hesitated to comment favourably on the new poetry of his time for he apprehended that no one would listen to his plea: he believed it was one's Iranian origins more than one's ability and knowledge that carried weight.[16] Local Iranian anthologists and *taẕkira* writers dismissed the achievements of hundreds of Indian-Persian poets with perfunctory praise. Muhammad Tahir Nasrabadi (d.1781) dispatched the entire history of Indian-Persian poetry in seven or eight pages, while Lutf 'Ali Beg Azar (d.1780), in his list of over 850 poets from Iran, Turan (Central Asia) and India, identified only twenty or so as Indian. In Azar's account of Amir Khusrau all the positive adjectives, which earlier anthologists such as Daulat Shah Samarqandi had employed, disappeared. He considered the new ideas, with which Indian poets had enriched Persian poetry, outlandish, and a factor in the decline of classical Persian poetry. Shaikh 'Ali 'Hazin' (d.1766), who left Iran, and lived and died in India in Benares, derided Indian poets as mere 'crows'. Only Faizi Faiyazi (d.1595) and his historian brother, he said, were of any consequence, but even they were treated ultimately as crows rather than 'nightingales'. The writings of 'Abd al-Qadir Bedil and Nasir 'Ali Sirhindi were good enough only as comic gifts for the delectation of his friends in Iran.

There were some debates in the eighteenth century on what constituted the principal components of good poetry, and whether an

[15] H. Blochmann, 'Contributions to Persian Lexicography', *Journal of the Royal Asiatic Society of Bengal (JRASB)*, vol. 37, pt ɪ, 1868–69, pp. 1–72.

[16] Abu'l Barakat Munir Lahori, *Kārnāma-i Munīr*, ed. S.M.A. Ikram, Islamabad, 1977, p. 36 and Editor's Introduction.

Indian could really master the language of Persian poetry.[17] Persian in Mughal India was, or was rather reborn as, a foreign language. Rarely was there a poet able to boast like Amir Khusrau and write:

> *Shakkar-i Miṣrī na dāram kaz 'Arab gūyam jawāb*
> *Turk-i Hindustāniyam dar Hindawī gūyam jawāb*[18]
>
> (I have no Egyptian sugar with which to talk to an Arab,
> I am an Indian Turk, I respond in Hindavi.)

Moreover, the Mughals also failed to give meaningful patronage to any of the other languages of the land. It was only in the late seventeenth century, when the regions began to assert their autonomy, that there seems to have been a kind of Mughal policy to learn and encourage Hindavi. But there is little in our sources to suggest that Hindavi, at any stage in the seventeenth century, was regarded as a language of the Mughal court or administration.[19] Besides his excellent command over Persian, the language which he used most often in his conversations, Aurangzeb had good knowledge of Turkish and Hindavi. But he used Hindavi only when he talked with an Indian who knew no Persian, or who had poor knowledge of the language—and even this only when it was unavoidable.[20] Thus when Laldas, a Nijananda Sampradaya religious leader, sought an audience with Aurangzeb for a discussion around issues of religion, the emperor preferred to speak in Persian. The tradition goes that when this Nijananda guru arrived in Delhi, he directed his attendant, Dayaram, to look for and hire a 'mulla' who knew good Persian to act as an interpreter during his dialogue with the emperor.[21]

All this was in sharp contrast to the developments in regional

[17] See Alam, 'The Culture and Politics of Persian in Pre-Colonial Hindustan', in Pollock, ed., *Literary Cultures in History*.

[18] Mohiuddin, *Chancellery*, pp. 23 and 26.

[19] Some historians of the Urdu language, however, claim that already in Shahjahan's time a familiarity with Urdu (Hindavi) was essential requirement for state service. Cf. Jamil Jalibi, *Tārīkh-i Adab-i Urdū*, vol. I, reprint, Delhi, 1989, pp. 69–70.

[20] Muhammad Kazim, *'Alamgir-Nāma*, Calcutta, 1867, p. 1095.

[21] *Lāldās kā Bītak*, Allahabad, 1966/2023 VS, p. 213.

sultanates. Ibrahim ʻAdil Shah, who ascended the throne in Bijapur in the Deccan in 1535–6, is reported to have proclaimed Hindavi (in this case Dakkani) as the language of his government, entrusting all the important administrative and financial offices to the Brahmans.[22] Later, in the time of ʻAli ʻAdil Shah II in seventeenth-century Bijapur, there seems to have been a widespread craze for writing and listening to poetry in Dakkani. The king had a special liking for the language (*lughat-i khaṣṣ-i khwesh*) and, because 'people follow the religion of their kings', everyone attempted to compose verses in 'Hindi' (or Dakkani).[23]

From the Barid Shahi Sultanate of Bidar (1503–1619) we have some inscriptions in both Persian and Marathi,[24] while the local language had the honour of being the language of the sultan in Golkunda. Ibrahim Qutb Shah encouraged the growth of Telugu, and his successor Muhammad Quli Qutb Shah patronized, and himself wrote, poetry in Telugu and Dakkani.[25] Later, ʻAbdullah Qutb Shah instituted a special office to prepare royal edicts in Telugu (*dabīrī-yi farāmīn-i Hindawī*); administrative and revenue papers at local levels in the Qutb Shahi sultanate were prepared largely in Telugu, while royal edicts were often bilingual.[26] The last Qutb Shahi sultan, Abu'l Hasan 'Tana Shah', sometimes issued his orders only in Telugu, with a Persian summary given on the back of his *farmāns*.[27]

[22] Muhammad Qasim Firishta, *Tārīkh-i Firishta*, Lucknow, 1864/1281 H, vol. II, p. 49; see also Muhammad Hashim Khafi Khan, *Muntakhab al-Lubāb*, ed. K.D. Ahmad and Wolseley Haig, Calcutta, 1925, vol. III, pp. 206–7.

[23] *Basātīn al-Salāṭīn*, cited in ʻAbd al-Haqq, *Malik al-Shuʻarā' Nuṣratī Bijāpūri ke Ḥālāt aur Kalām par Tabṣira*, Delhi, 1988, p. 9.

[24] G. Yazdani, *Bidar: Its History and Monuments*, pp. 140–203, cited in P.M. Joshi and H.K. Sherwani, eds, *History of Medieval Deccan*, vol. I, Hyderabad, 1973, pp. 395–6.

[25] H.K. Sherwani, *Muhammad Quli Qutb Shah: Founder of Haidarabad*, Bombay, 1967, pp. 44–55.

[26] Mirza Nizam al-Din Ahmad al-Saʻidi al-Shirazi, *Ḥadīqat al-Salāṭīn*, ed. S. Asghar ʻAli Bilgrami, Hyderabad, 1931, pp. 36 and 41; see also Joshi and Sherwani, *History of Medieval Deccan*, vol. I, pp. 40 and 48.

[27] Andhra Pradesh State Archives, Hyderabad, *farmāns* dated (i) 1677/1088 *sh.* concerning a land grant; (ii) 1679/1090 *sh.* pertaining to the weekly marts

Earlier, in the east, the rulers of Arakan had encouraged translations of Sanskrit, Arabic and Persian works into Bengali. The first translation of the *Mahābhārat* was undertaken at the order of Nasir Shah, the king of Gaur in Bengal (who ruled for forty years, till 1325). Yasoraj Khan, who lived in the second half of the fifteenth century, was among the first prominent poets and writers in Bengali. He was an officer of the court of Sultan Husain Shah (r.1493–1518). Yasoraj's *Krishna-Mangal* is regarded as among the earliest instances of a Muslim poet using a Hindu theme. Poets helped by court patronage also enriched the language with Islamic ideas and themes, examples being Hatim Ta'i, Laila Majnun and Yusuf Zulaikha. Sayyid Ala'ul was another major poet, patronized by the Arakan ruler in the seventeenth century, who produced a version in Bengali of the *Padmāvat* as well as a *Sikandar-Nāma*.[28]

In contrast with this, memory of the Great Mughals in the regions has it that they discouraged the local languages. The legend goes that when Akbar conquered Gujarat, all the poets and writers of the local languages of the province fled to, and took shelter in, the courts of the Deccani sultans.[29]

Turning to another sphere of writing, we find that texts with legal, juristic and religious material circulated as *a<u>kh</u>lāq* digests, and often offset the impact of Nasirean ethics. These texts followed the tradition of early Arabic treatises such as the work of Abu Bakr bin Abi'l Dunya (d.894) entitled *Makārim al-A<u>kh</u>lāq*, and Mawardi's *Ādāb al-Dunyā wa'l-Dīn* on 'religious ethics'.[30] The *A<u>kh</u>lāq-i Ḥakīmī* and *A<u>kh</u>lāq-i Jahāngīrī*, discussed earlier, could also be counted among such texts. Later, in Aurangzeb's reign, a certain

of Wanipur, Ibrahimpattan; (iii) 1682/1093 *sh*. concerning a land grant; and (iv) 1676/1087 *sh*. regarding the construction of a temple at Wanipur, Ibrahimpattan.

[28] Compare D.C. Sen, *History of Bengali Language and Literature*, Calcutta, 1954, pp. 12, 13–15 and 38–40; J.C. Ghosh, *Bengali Literature*, London, 1948, pp. 46, 82, 83 and 526.

[29] Cf. 'Abd al-Majid Siddiqi, *Tārī<u>kh</u>-i Golconda*, Hyderabad, 1964, p. 395.

[30] For a discussion on some such *a<u>kh</u>lāq* texts, see Majid Fakhry, *Ethical Theories in Islam*, second expanded edition, Leiden, 1994, pp. 151–83.

Hafiz Muhammad Sa'id and then one 'Aqil Khan compiled similar digests—*Risāla-i Muḥammad Sa'īd* and *Wājib al-Ḥifẓ* respectively, in 1690 and 1693. Again, in 1721, one Mir Ahmad 'Ali Khan wrote a text entitled *Akhlāq-i Muḥammad Shāhī* at the behest of the *wazīr* Amin al-Daulah, which bore resemblance more to Hamadani's *Zakhīrat* than Tusi's *Akhlāq*. Ahmad 'Ali Khan began his *Akhlāq* with an adulation of reason (*'aql*), invoked the names of Aristotle, Buzurchmehr and Bu 'Ali Ibn Sina (Avicenna), but throughout this book showed a rather exaggerated concern for Islam and Muslims. Islam, for Ahmad 'Ali Khan, should constitute the strongest bond within a community (*rābiṭa dar birādarī*); the faithful (*mūminīn*) were to act in unison, as a single soul; and the community (*birādarī*) deserved special rights and honours.[31] Even in digests based on Tusi's *Akh-lāq*, the exclusivity of the *sharī'a* is sometimes highlighted. Jalal al-Din Dawwani's *Akhlāq-i Jalālī*, we know, is not the same as Tusi's *Akhlāq*. Even Ikhtiyar al-Husaini sometimes exaggerated the import of the *sharī'a-i Islāmiya*—the rights of Muslims (*ḥuqūq-i ahl-i Islām*)—and unlike Tusi, who ended his book with a passage containing Plato's advice, he closed by pleading with rulers to pursue the *sharī'a* of Muhammad and strengthen the community of Ahmad (*mutāba'at-i sharī'at-i Muḥammadī wa taqwīyat-i millat-i Aḥmadī*).

A significant section of Muslim elites still regarded these treatises—as well as books such as Hamadani's *Zakhīrat al-Mulūk*—as comprising the true principles of state management. The political culture that received nourishment from the tradition of Nasirean ethics and Persian poetry had thus to contend with several forces which debilitated its vitality.

## The Limits of Sufi Assimilation

As the doctrine of *waḥdat al-wujūd* evolved and encouraged assimilation, it also posed a serious threat to orthodoxy. The *'ulamā'* as

[31] Mir Ahmad 'Ali Khan, *Akhlāq-i Muḥammad Shāhī*, Bodleian Library, Oxford, MS., Elliot 6, f. 41b.

well as a section of the political elite thus spared no effort to counteract its impact. The growth and expansion of centres of Islamic learning (*madrasas*) under 'Ala al-Din Khalji and the Tughlaq sultans (1320–1413); efforts to popularize classical Arabic texts on *fiqh* (Islamic jurisprudence) and commentaries (in Arabic or Persian) on them written in India; the compilation of the *Fatāwā*;[32] and the narrow sectarian policies of Firuz Tughlaq and Sikandar Lodi—these were all indicative of an endeavour by the orthodoxy to reinforce the Perso-Arabic fabric of theological Islam.

To counter the heterodox or *bī-shar'a* Sufi orders some of the *'ulamā'* later emphasized that the *sharī'a* was more a set of moral ideals manifested in the life of the Prophet than a mere system of law.[33] At a popular level, Sufism developed several offshoots, absorbing evidently anti-Islamic features: we have noted many of these, specially in relation to the heightened interest in sexual practices—either promiscuity or its opposite, total denial—among orders like the Qalandars and the Madaris and the Haidaris. With these went a cavalier attitude towards regular Islamic rituals and prayers in many heterodox Sufi milieux.[34] Support for their behaviour and activities was sought in the doctrine of *waḥdat al-wujūd* and its extended implications, sometimes even within circles of relatively 'orthodox' Sufis. To the celebrated sixteenth-century saint Shaikh 'Abd al-Quddus Gangohi, for instance, neglect of the injunctions of the *sharī'a* by the Qalandars and the other such Sufis was only 'apparent'; he argued the paradox that the destruction of external aspects of religion sometimes becomes essential, and that it is for this reason that some true men of God shave their beards, put on sacred

[32] K.A. Nizami, 'Some Religious and Cultural Trends of the Tughluq Period', and also his 'A Medieval Indian Madrasah', both in Nizami, *Studies in Medieval Indian History and Culture*, pp. 54–64 and 73–9.

[33] M. Mujeeb, *The Indian Muslims*, London, 1966, pp. 272–6, for such an attempt by Shaikh 'Abd al-Wahhab Muttaqi, 'Ali Muttaqi and Shaikh Husam al-Din.

[34] Ja'far Sharif, *Qanūn-i Islām*, English transl. by G.A. Herklots, reprint, London, 1972, pp. 195–6, 289–92, 295–6; Aziz Ahmad, *An Intellectual History of Islam in India*, pp. 44–5.

threads, and pray in temples. It is reported that when queried regarding the neglect of prayers by a Qalandar called Shaikh Husain, Shaikh Fakhr al-Din responded by saying: 'A Qalandar could appear to be neglecting prayers in one bodily form and be offering them elsewhere, in another embodiment. The Qalandars prefer one way; the [orthodox] Sufis another.'[35]

On the other hand, *'ulamā'* like Shaikh Husam al-Din of Multan, and the celebrated Muttaqis Shaikh 'Ali and Shaikh 'Abd al-Wahab of Burhanpur, despite their association with the Chishti *silsila*, advocated the rejection of such a doctrine and called for the *sharī'a* to be taken as an exalted way of living—as illustrated exclusively by the acts and sayings of the Prophet and his Pious Companions. Shaikh Husam al-Din illustrated his message with an exaggerated emphasis on personal piety, self-denial and asceticism, while Muttaqis revived and reinforced *ḥadīs̤* learning. Even some of the protagonists of *waḥdat al-wujūd* (so-called *wujūdīs*) tended to reject the unqualified *waḥdat* (oneness) of being. Shaikh Nizam al-Din of Amethi (d.1517), a Chishti Sufi, is said to have snatched away from his pupil the *Fuṣūṣ al-Ḥikam* by the Iberian Muslim propounder of the doctrine, Ibn al-'Arabi. The shaikh gave his pupil another book and advised him, and other pupils, to limit their readings to recognized theological and orthodox Sufi treatises.[36]

Equally significant are the records, or at least the memory, of certain sayings and activities of some of the eminent early Sufis of the same orders that propounded *waḥdat al-wujūd*. They, like the orthodox *'ulamā'*, appear in these records as having highlighted the difference between faiths, with a plea for discrimination on religious grounds. They are also portrayed as possessing a heightened sense of superiority, and of the finality of the truth of their faith. While they believed that an infidel or non-believer (*kāfir*) could be a monotheist and a Unitarian (*muwaḥḥid*), and that all religions

[35] Shaikh 'Abd al-Quddus Gangohi, *Maktūbāt-i Quddūsiya*, Delhi, 1870/1287 H, p. 205; Shaikh Rukn al-Din, *Laṭā'if-i Quddūsiya*, Delhi, 1893/1311 H, pp. 21–2.

[36] Compare Mujeeb, *Indian Muslims*, pp. 274–5 and 306–7.

were in essence the same, they deemed it their duty to show others the path of Islam which, in their view, was the straightest, smoothest and safest way to the truth. Sometimes, as missionaries, they also offered armed resistance to propagate their faith.

Notable in this connection are the stories of the performance of miracles by early Sufis and of their 'competitive spirituality' with Hindu *yogīs*. Many such stories appeared first in the fifteenth- and sixteenth-century hagiographical literature, which, even though not always correctly ascribed to these Sufis,[37] showed the nature of the emerging legends about them. Legends surrounding Khwaja Mu'in al-Din Chisthti (1142–1234), founder of the Chishti *silsila*—the best acclimatized and most popular Sufi order in north India—are a case in point. According to an early-seventeenth-century hagiographical account, the khwaja's arrival in the 1190s in Ajmer (where he settled finally) had been prophesied by the mother of its ruler, Rai Pithaura, who was a soothsayer and magician. She had even prepared a portrait of the saint, which was handed over to officials and commandants at the borders to prevent his entry into Pithaura's territory. Still, the khwaja managed to reach Ajmer. He settled or camped near the Ana Sagar and Pansela lakes with a handful of his disciples, who killed a cow and cooked *kabābs* for him. The Brahmans, who looked after a thousand temples in the surroundings, however, stopped the khwaja's disciples from performing their ablutions with the water of these lakes. The khwaja thereupon sent

[37] For an assessment of some of these stories cf. Muhammad Habib, 'Chishti Mystic Records of the Sultanate Period', in K.A. Nizami, ed., *Politics and Society during the Early Medieval Period*, Delhi, 1974, pp. 385–433. It is not unlikely that these legends gained wider currency in the fifteenth and sixteenth centuries in the face of increasingly effective resistance to the authority of the sultans by local landed chiefs. The central Muslim authorities may have aimed at reinforcing their positions by popularizing these legends. Richard M. Eaton also notes such legends in his *Sufis of Bijapur*, pp. 110–13 and 166. Susan Bayly makes some perceptive observations on the political significance of some such similar legends in the eighteenth-century South Indian context; cf. Bayly, 'Islam and State Power in Pre-Colonial South India', *Itinerario*, vol. 12, no. 1, 1988, pp. 143–64.

his servant to bring water for him in an ewer, and as soon as the ewer touched the lake it sucked in the water of all the lakes, tanks and wells around. Thereafter the khwaja went to the Āna Sagar Lake temple, turned the idol (called Sawai Deva) into a human being, made him speak and recite the *kalima* (confession of faith), and gave him a new Islamic name, Sadi. This caused a sensation in the town. Pithaura asked his minister, Jaipal, who was also a magician, to contain the khwaja. Jaipal proceeded to fight him, accompanied by his 700 disciplines, 700 magical dragons, and 1500 magical discs. The khwaja killed or destroyed them all, advising his men to remain within a circle that he drew for their defence. Jaipal then decided to compete with the khwaja in the performance of miracles. In this too he was completely outplayed. When he flew to the heavens sitting on his deerskin, the khwaja ordered his slippers to fly and beat him, and thereby forced him back to earth. Pithaura and Jaipal then begged the khwaja's forgiveness, and he on their plea restored water to the lakes, tanks and wells. Jaipal and a large number of others then accepted Islam.[38]

Another story of miracles performed by the khwaja, which concerned not only proselytization but also the Islamic conquest of the town, is related by an authentic Chishti hagiographer with reference to that most liberal and catholic-minded Chishti Sufi, Nizam al-Din Auliya. According to the *Siyar al-Auliyā'*, Pithaura and his high officials resented the khwaja's presence in Ajmer, but because of the latter's eminence and power to perform miracles, they could take no action against him. A disciple of the khwaja was in Pithaura's service, to whom the raja was very hostile. When the khwaja sent a message to the raja in favour of this disciple, the raja not only rejected his recommendation but also expressed indignation over the former's spiritual claims. On hearing of this response, the khwaja prophesied: 'we will seize Pithaura alive and hand him over to the army of Islam.' About the same time Muhammad Ghuri's army marched from Ghazna, attacked the forces of Pithaura, and defeated

[38] 'Ali Asghar bin Shaikh Maudud, *Jawāhir-i Farīdī*, Lahore, 1883–4/1301 H, pp. 155–60.

them. Pithaura was captured alive and thus the khwaja's prophesy was fulfilled.[39] An early-seventeenth-century *tazkira* adds: 'and from the same date Islam spread in this country, uprooting the foundations of infidelity.'[40]

To illustrate this conflictual or contestatory aspect further, we need also to consider one or two cases of conversion in the valley of Kashmir. In Kashmir, the establishment of the Rishi Sufic order was a result of interaction between Islamic Sufism and Hindu mystic ideas and teachings as these were expressed, in particular, in the *Lalla-Vakyani* (the wise sayings of Lalla Yogeshwari or Laleshwari, a fourteenth-century Shaivite *yoginī* and poet). The Kashmiri verses of its founder, Shaikh Nur al-Din (1378–1439), echoed Lalla's ideas and her teachings. Shaikh Nur al-Din and his disciples preferred for themselves the Shaivite Hindu term 'rishis' instead of 'Sufis'. Stories of Nur al-Din's spiritual attainments portray him as a preceptor of both Muslims and Hindus. Like Hindu ascetics, he lived in a cave, and on a vegetarian diet. He is reported to have admitted that, for him, meat-eating, even though permitted by the *sharī'a*, was cruelty to animals.[41] Yet, he was a dedicated proselytizer. Of his many disciples, Bam al-Din, Zain al-Din, and Latif al-Din were Brahmans by birth who converted to Islam through his efforts. Before converting, Bam al-Din (Bam Dev or Bhum Sidha) was a most revered Brahman divine in Kashmir. Shaikh Nur al-Din therefore intended to make him a Muslim as well as his disciple. Accordingly, he came to meet him, wearing a cow-skin, at the temple where he lived, had a seven-day-long discourse with him to highlight the excellence of the message of the Prophet of Islam, and finally, on Bam Dev's demand, convinced him of its superiority by making the idols recite the *kalima*. Further, the idols set Bam Dev's

[39] Mir Khwurd, *Siyar al-Auliyā'*, pp. 45–7.

[40] 'Abd al-Haq Muhaddis Dihlawi, *Akhbār al-Akhyār*, reprint, Deoband, n.d., pp. 28–9.

[41] Compare M. Ishaq Khan, 'The Impact of Islam on Kashmir in the Sultanate Period (1320–1586)', *Indian Economic and Social History Review*, vol. 23, no. 2, 1986.

doubts at rest by proclaiming: 'We were mere stone, and we will again be so. It is owing to the greatness and miraculous power of this saint [Shaikh Nur al-Din] that we could speak out. You will indeed be fortunate to recite the *kalima* right now and become a Muslim.'[42]

The story of another Kashmiri ascetic's conversion at the hands of Sayyid 'Ali Hamadani, the legendary fourteenth-century propagator of Islam in the valley, is reminiscent of Khwaja Mu'in al-Din Chishti's miracles at Ajmer, with some minor differences. In 'Ali Hamadani's case, the saint broke a very big idol into four pieces. From its inside he took out a bark which he folded and tied tightly with a wire. Then he asked those present to untie the knot, and on doing this they found to their dismay the *kalima* written on the bark.[43]

Again, there were memories and traditions of bloodshed and bitter Hindu–Muslim fights, associated ironically with the very tombs and graves around which there emerged 'syncretic' beliefs and practices. Some such graves were of those 'martyrs' who, according to legend, had lost their lives for Islam in a missionary struggle to penetrate into inhospitable Hindu regions. The famous shrine of Ghazi Miyan or Salar Mas'ud Ghazi in eastern Uttar Pradesh, remembered both by Hindus and Muslims as Bale Miyan, Bale Pir and Hateli Pir, has been a centre of popular pilgrimages since the fourteenth century. Haji Ilyas of Bengal, Sultan Muhammad bin Tughlaq, and his successor Firuz, are all reported to have visited his (alleged) tomb in Bahraich. Several graves in modern Uttar Pradesh, associated with Ghazi Miyan, are worshipped both by Hindus and Muslims. At Bahraich, Hindu mendicants and Muslim Qalandars, together with their followers, dance and sing around a long bamboo pole wrapped in coloured rags with horse-hair tied on its top. Sikandar Lodi reportedly tried in vain to stop these un-Islamic practices.

[42] Baba Nasib Kashmiri, *Nūr-Nāma*, MS., Research and Publication Department, Srinagar, ACC, no. 795.

[43] Sayyid 'Ali Magray, *Tārīkh-i Kashmīr*, MS., Research and Publication Department, Srinagar, ACC, no. 739. For this reference and for the one to the *Nūr-Nāma*, I am indebted to Mr A. Hamid Rather of Kashmir University.

Later, Muslim and Hindu puritanical and revivalist movements failed to undermine their popularity. However, the legends—recorded and verbal—show that Ghazi Miyan was a Ghaznavid army commander who fought several successful *jihāds* against the Hindu rajas before he was struck down at Bahraich by an arrow from one Raja Hardu or Sahdev.[44]

In another case, in North Bihar, there used to be a huge fair attracting a very large number of Hindus and Muslims at the tomb of Makhdum 'Owais Shuttari at Basarha, near Vaishali. The grave of Makhdum, who was killed by a Cheru chief while attempting to build a mosque, was worshipped by Hindus and Muslims alike.[45] In yet another case, in Bengal, Shaikh Jalal Suhrawardi, whose miracles made him tremendously popular with local Hindus, Buddhists and animists, pursued according to legend a long career of warfare against infidelity and finally fought and defeated the raja of Sylhet to propagate Islam in eastern Bengal.[46]

Thus the Sufis too, at times and in their own way, asserted the finality and supremacy of their faith. Their discourses with Hindu ascetics and mendicants seem to have signified a kind of religious disputation in a spirit of competition. Through these discourses they tried to establish how their faith was superior, giving them the power to cleanse souls of all impurity, and thus subjugate both the microcosm and the macrocosm (*'ālam-i aṣg͟har* and *'ālam-i akbar*). Their appreciation of the spiritual attainments of *yogīs* was, hence, real but qualified. Shaikh Sharaf al-Din of Maner is reported to have spoken highly of *yogīs* who had acquired exceptional inner power

[44] Sharif, *Qānūn-i Islām*, pp. 201–2. For a recent study of the memory of Ghazi Miyan, see Shahid Amin, 'On Retelling the Muslim Conquest of North India', in Partha Chatterjee and Anjan Ghosh, eds, *History and the Present*, New Delhi, 2002, pp. 24–43.

[45] Rashid, *Society and Culture in Medieval India*, p. 233; Reports of the Archaeological Survey of India 16, 90.

[46] Muhammad Ghaus Gwaliyari, *Gulz̤ār-i Abrār*, f. 75; for some *g͟hāzī* and *shahīd* legends from Bengal, see Dinesh Chandra Sen, *The Folk Literature of Bengal*, reprint, Delhi, 1982, pp. 123–52. See also Eaton, *Sufis of Bijapur*, pp. 19–44, for a useful account of 'Sufis as Warriors'.

by their severe austerities. But when a visitor to his *khānqāh* told him that he had seen clouds appearing and showering the place where a Hindu ascetic was offering prayers, the shaikh set his mind at rest by explaining the incident in terms of the creation of illusion.[47] According to Sufi hagiographical traditions, a *yogī* could perform miracles merely on the strength of his austerity, but only to a limited extent; and those among them who had achieved spiritual purity were certain to accept the Muslim faith. At the very first sight of the shaikh, a *yogī* visitor to the *khānqāh* of Shaikh Sharaf al-Din of Maner turned back saying: 'He looks like Kartar Rup and I dare not go before him.' Later, following the shaikh's direction, the *yogī* came and sat in the *majlis* for long and accepted Islam.[48]

The nature of the Sufi approach to Hindu religious cults becomes even clearer in later hagiographic literature. Certain Sufis showed an interest in and tried to understand Hindu philosophy. This interest was stimulated by the availability in later times of Persian translations of the Sanskrit classics, and continued until the end of our period. Sufis also wrote and commented upon Hindu religious texts. But it should be noted that an underlying aim of such works was at times to reiterate the finality of Islam. The work of the seventeenth-century Chishti mystic 'Abd al-Rahman on creation could be counted among such attempts.[49] Again, in a number of stories and incidents reported in Sufic literature—which have generally been taken as illustrative of 'syncretism'—the underlying objective seems to be to highlight the extraordinary spiritual power of Sufis. In a measure, these represent cases of 'competitive spirituality'.

[47] S.H. Askari and Q. Ahmad, eds, *A Comprehensive History of Bihar*, vol. II, Patna, 1984, p. 407.

[48] Rashid, *Society and Culture in Medieval India*, pp. 192–3.

[49] Rizvi, *History of Sufism*, vol. I, p. 14. For a brief account of Persian translations of the Hindu scriptures, see Mujtabai, *Aspects of Hindu-Muslim Cultural Relations*, Delhi, 1978, pp. 61–91. See also Roderic Vassie, 'Abd al-Rahman Chishti and the *Bhagavadgita*: "Unity of Religion" Theory in Practice', in Leonard Lewisohn, ed., *The Heritage of Sufism, Volume II: The Legacy of Medieval Persian Sufism*, Oxford, 1999, pp. 367–77.

As we have seen, it was not the Hindu *bairāgīs* but Shah 'Abd al-Razzaq Bansawi who had the power of inspiring a vision of Ram, Lakshman and Krishna. In Mathura, one Abu Salih was greeted by Krishna at the end of the day—when he was at his *tahajjud* (late-night prayer)—to laud the Prophet, his religion and those who followed this religion.[50] In Delhi, in 1751, it is reported that a blind woman had a vision of the goddess Bhawani, who told her that Shaikh Nizam al-Din Chishti could restore her eyesight.[51]

In this connection, it is also interesting to note an effort to establish the Central and West Asian origins of, or to Islamicize, the indigenous features of Sufism. A seventeenth- and early-eighteenth-century Chishti luminary, Shah Kalim-Allah of Delhi (1650–1729), asserted that yogic practices like *ḥabs-i nafs*, adopted by the Sufis of India, were actually taught first by the legendary Khwaja Khizr to Khwaja 'Abd al-Khaliq Ghujdwani (d.1220) in Bukhara.[52] This statement not only underplayed the local Indian influence on Sufism but was the opposite of the earlier Sufic approach. Hindu *yoga*, as we saw above, was seen as a very significant method of acquiring ascetic and spiritual power.

In a letter to Babur, Shaikh 'Abd al-Quddus Gangohi made a plea that only pious Muslims be appointed government officials. He wanted Hindus to be excluded from high offices, particularly from those of the department of revenue, and suggested that their dress be different from that of Muslims, and that their activities be confined to their traditional professions and trades. He wanted them to receive no financial assistance from the government, which ought to recognize that they were inferior to Muslims. Later, Gangohi also wrote to Humayun, recommending a particularly honourable status

[50] *Maqāmāt-i Maẓharī*, pp. 23–4.

[51] Rizvi, *History of Sufism in India*, vol. II, p. 305.

[52] *Kashkūl-i Kalīmī*, Delhi, 1890/1307 *sh.*, p. 10. In his letters to his disciples, Shah Kalim-Allah and following him, his *khalīfas* Shaikh Nizam al-Din and Shaikh Fakhr al-Din, laid special emphasis on the lives of the Prophet and his Companions as models for Muslims and on spreading, preaching and glorifying the 'word of Allah'. Cf. K.A. Nizami, *Tārīkh-i Mashā'ikh-i Chisht* (in Urdu), vol. 5, Delhi, 1984, pp. 105–6, 161–2, 215–16.

to theologians and Muslims divines.[53] It is not without significance that this plea was made to a ruler who, in a way, re-established the political dominance of Muslims in India, specially when he defeated Rana Sanga and thereby ended the possibility of the re-emergence of Rajput hegemony in north India.

Gangohi's demands were, in terms of their severity, comparable only with those made later by fanatics among the orthodox. It has been suggested that Gangohi's plea was motivated by the desire to secure pecuniary advantages for his ilk. He wanted the *'ulamā'* and Sufis to retain their landed property, completely free of cess. The ruler, however, claimed *'ushr* on these lands, which prompted him towards such an extreme attitude by way of reaction.[54]

The accommodativeness of Sufis thus suffered from serious limits: they could not completely free themselves from the hegemony of orthodox, juristic Islam. Until about the end of the seventeenth century, Sufism could not fully integrate other such efforts, nor did it extend the circle of Islam to include within itself even the radical but 'non-Muslim' monotheists. To the Sufi, Kabir, for example, was only a *muwaḥḥid* (monotheist); and to the question 'was a *muwaḥḥid* a Muslim?' their answer was ambivalent.[55]

Against this background, one can register the intensity as well as the acceptability in certain circles of Sunni revivalism, in particular

[53] *Maktūbāt-i Quddūsiya*, Letter 169, pp. 336–7; Cf. also K.A. Nizami, *Tārīkh-i Mashā'kh-i Chisht*, 1957, pp. 219–21; *idem*, *Salāṭīn-i Dihlī ke Mazhabī Rujḥānāt*, pp. 466–8.

[54] Iqtidar Alam Khan, 'Shaikh Abd-ul-Quddus Gangohi's Relations with Political Authorities: A Reappraisal', *Medieval India: A Miscellany*, vol. IV, Delhi, 1977, pp. 73–93. In this view, however, there is little consideration of the fact that Gangohi was the *pīr* of the Afghan elite, and was thus seen by Babur and Humayun as an ally of their foes, who were still to be fully subjugated. Gangohi's over-enthusiastic sectarian approach may have been intended just to dispel the apprehensions of the Mughals. These letters were meant to show that his concern was with the interest of Islam and not the support of one or the other group.

[55] *Akhbār al-Akhyār*, p. 306. Kashmir, however, presents a different case. The Rishis there claimed the Shaivite poetess, Lal Ded, as 'Rabi'a the Second', incorporating her message in their compositions in the local language. Cf. Ishaq Khan, 'The Impact of Islam on Kashmir'.

as this was expressed in the writings of Shaikh Ahmad Sirhindi (1564–1624)—the proponent of the rival Sufi doctrine of *waḥdat al-shuhūd*—and the theological studies of Shaikh Abd al-Haqq Muhaddis of Delhi (1551–1642) in the late sixteenth and seventeenth centuries. The writings of Shaikh Ahmad Sirhindi, in the times of Akbar and Jahangir, which reverberated with the claim that Islam had failed against Hinduism, and which expressed a fear of dominance by Hindus, were then at least partly an outcome of the Sufi tradition itself. Sirhindi emphasized difference and advocated a social distance between Hindus and Muslims. Some of his letters express outright hostility towards Hindus—their religion as well as their social practices—and, ironically, contain apprehensions about the fate of Muslims and Islam at a time when Muslim political power was at its zenith. He feared that if Hindus shared political power, as was the case under the Mughals, they [the Hindus] would capture it, ultimately, and would not then be satisfied merely by promulgating laws of infidelity: they would wish to obliterate Islamic laws, the Muslim community, and Islam. Sirhindi emphasized the Hindu concept of *ḥulūl* (incarnation) in order to dispel illusions of similarity between Islamic and Hindu beliefs in Ultimate Reality. He said that though particular Hindu gods acknowledged the existence of a Supreme Creator, they had invited people to worship them instead, asserting that the Supreme Being was infused into and united within them. This idea of divine infusion and incarnation or *ḥulūl*, he said, was incompatible with the basic tenets of Islam. He asserted that no Sufi should ever be prepared to accept the theory regarding the limitation (*ta'ayyun*) of the Absolute in any specific form.[56]

Sirhindi's major contribution was that he developed his philosophy in purely Sufic terms. He asserted that the claims of similarity

[56] Cf. Yohanan Friedmann, *Shaykh Ahmad Sirhindi: An Outline of His Thought and a Study of His Image in the Eyes of Posterity*, Montreal and London, 1971, pp. 69–75; Rizvi, *Muslim Revivalist Movements in Northern India in the Sixteenth and Seventeenth Centuries*, pp. 148–75 and 246–60. See also Nizami, *Ḥayāt-i Shaikh 'Abd al-Ḥaqq Muḥaddis̤ Dihlawī*, Delhi, 1953.

between the two were based on immature Sufi experiences and observations in states within which a Sufi made no distinction between truth and falsehood. In this state, the Sufi sought a perception of the beauty of the Divine and, as he drew nearer it, he was so lost that he failed to see the distinction between creation and the Creator. All this was mere illusion, arising from a state of unity. The unity (*waḥdat*) was simply in the Sufi's perception (*shuhūd*), but not in actual being (*wujūd*).[57]

*Waḥdat al-shuhūd* did not originate with Sirhindi, nor was he the first to introduce it in India. But he was certainly among those who gave a highly sophisticated and elaborate exposition of the doctrine, and this at a time when it was difficult, even for his opponents, to repudiate it outright. *Waḥdat al-shuhūd* could never replace *waḥdat-ul-wujūd*, which also received a new lease of life at the Qadiri *k͟hān-qāhs*, through some of the powerful Chishti writings, as well as at the hands of the descendants of none other than Sirhindi's *pīr*, Khwaja Baqi-billah, in the seventeenth and eighteenth centuries.[58] Still, the generally accepted form of the doctrine in the latter period was what the famous Naqshbandi scholar-saint Shah Wali-Allah presented in the eighteenth century.[59] *Waḥdat al-shuhūd* thus endeavoured to modify *waḥdat al-wujūd*, allowing it to act only marginally as a basis for Muslim 'syncretic' beliefs. An average literate Muslim was expected to believe that Islam and Hinduism belonged to two radically diverse traditions, and that the twain would never meet.

We can perhaps explain the competitive and combative attitude of the Sufis, the *wujūdī*s in particular, in terms of changes in their relations with the political authorities. Sultan 'Ala al-Din Khalji, for

[57] Friedmann, *Shaikh Ahmad Sirhindi*, pp. 59–68; J.G. ter Haar, *Follower and Heir of the Prophet: Shaykh Ahmad Sirhindi (1564–1624) as a Mystic*, Leiden, 1992, pp. 117–36.

[58] Rizvi, *Revivalist Movements*, pp. 331–75.

[59] Cf. Burhan Ahmad Faruqi, *The Mujaddid's Conceptions of Tauhid*, Lahore, 1940, pp. 95–100.

instance, sought to visit the hospice of Shaikh Nizam al-Din Auliya for an audience and to seek his blessings; and while his nobles approached the shaikh with a request to allow one of his disciples to accompany them on their campaigns in difficult areas, 'Ala al-Din's successor Qutb al-Din Khalji insisted that the shaikh come over to his court regularly, to offer the sultan his respects. Later, Ghiyas al-Din Tughlaq had an almost direct confrontation with the shaikh. This was on account of the sultan's insistence that the shaikh return to the royal coffers certain sums which he had accepted from the earlier neo-Muslim ruler, Khusrau Khan.[60] The shaikh's association with Khusrau Khan, who has generally been portrayed in contemporary Persian accounts as a usurper out to re-establish Hindu rule, may have also impaired the Sufi's image, and that of other Chishtis, in some circles. By way of overcompensation, it is not unlikely that hagiographers sought to highlight the Sufi role in the establishment of Muslim power in India, a role even greater, in their view, than the military victories achieved by Muslim soldiers and their Turkish commanders in battlefields. Thus, we see that a major Hindu ruler is shown not simply being captured by Khwaja Mu'in al-Din, the founder of the Chishti order in India, but actually handed over to Sultan Mu'izz al-Din of Ghur. This Sufi act is also projected as the start of the uninterrupted triumphant march of Islam in India.

The first such image of Khwaja Mu'in al-Din as pioneering Islamizer comes from Amir Khwurd Kirmani's *Siyar al-Auliyā'*, compiled in the second half of the fourteenth century. Later in the seventeenth century, when the Chishtis seemed to lose favour with

[60] For details, see Simon Digby, 'The Sufi Shaykh and the Sultan: A Conflict of Claims to Authority in Medieval India', *Iran*, vol. 28, 1990, pp. 71–81; *idem*, 'The Sufi Shaykh as a Source of Authority in Medieval India', in Marc Gaborieau, ed., *Islam et Société dans l'Asie du Sud,* Paris, Collection Purusartha, no. 9, 1986, pp. 57–77. I.A. Zilli, 'Chishtis and the State: A Case Study of the Relations of Shaikh Nizamuddin with the Khaljis', in I.H. Siddiqui, ed., *Islamic Heritage in South Asian Subcontinent*, Jaipur, 2000, pp. 46–59; Raziuddin Aquil, 'Sufi Cults, Politics and Conversion: The Chishtis of the Sultanate Period', *Indian Historical Review*, vol. XXII, nos 1–2, 1995–6, pp. 190–7.

the political elites following the coming of the Naqshbandis from the erstwhile homeland of the Mughals, and when it appeared that the new Central Asian shaikhs and their Indian disciples would head the most powerful Sufi order in Mughal India—dislodging all others, including the Chishtis—Khwaja Mu'in al-Din began to be projected as the *only* prophet-like figure in Indian Islam (even if not a full-fledged prophet, the term used being *Nabī-yi Hind*). Almost the entire religious world of north Indian Muslims now began revolving around spiritual feats and miracles performed by him. Shaikh 'Abd al-Rahman Chishti, who assessed anew the biographies of Sufis of various orders in a voluminous *tazkira* titled *Mir'āt al-Asrār*,[61] wrote at length on the achievements of the early Chishtis, in particular of Khwaja Mu'in al-Din, who occupied a most special position here. He also wrote—or rather invented—the biographies of two popular legendary figures, namely, Sayyid Salar Mas'ud Ghazi, as a nephew of Mahmud Ghaznavi (r.998–1030) and a commander of his army in Hindustan; and of Shaikh Badi' al-Din Madar, a Jew converted to Islam in the fifteenth century. All this was in a bid to integrate and associate the legends that had developed around these figures with the life and work of Khwaja Mu'in al-Din.

Madar's mission begins in India with the blessings of the shaikh, which he receives when he visits Ajmer (where the Sufi saint had built his hospice after his victory over a Hindu *yogī* and the raja). Madar visits Ajmer following an instruction from the Prophet during meditation and prayers at his grave in Medina; Madar's first task in India is to offer prayers at the grave of the khwaja. Since Salar Mas'ud lived before the time of the khwaja, the town of Ajmer was made to figure in a significant way within his career. His mother conceived him, it was said, in Ajmer—the city destined to

[61] See the preface and other relevant sections of the text in the British Library, London, MS. Or. 216, *Mir'āt al-Asrār*, ff. 225a–37a, in particular 226a; also Staatsbibliothek, Berlin, MS. Orient. Quart. 1903. For an analysis of the text, see Bruce Lawrence, 'An Indo-Persian Perspective on the Significance of Early Persian Sufi Masters', in Leonard Lewisohn, ed., *Classical Persian Sufism from its Origins to Rumi*, London, 1993, pp. 19–32.

be the Medina of India—when she was invited to live there for a while by her husband, who was commandant of a Ghaznavid military camp in the city.[62]

In regions like Kashmir, too, there seems to have been a kind of competitiveness between the different Sufi orders, such as the Suhrawardi, the Kubrawi, and the Rishi, for providing the best device on subjugating the local population and adjusting to local conditions. In one case, conversion was advised through the state machinery; in another, it was advised through dialogue, as a process of disputation and argument spread over centuries.[63]

The narrative tradition of the combat between Muslim Sufi and Hindu *yogī* seems then to have been a part of the Sufis' struggle to refurbish their image *vis-à-vis* other influential groups within the community of Muslims. In this connection, it seems relevant that between the late fifteenth and seventeenth centuries the Mahdawis, the Chishtis, the Naqshbandis and the Isna 'Asharis endeavoured to demonstrate the finality of their understanding of the Islamic tradition, and to establish the supremacy of their spiritual and religious practices—all with reference to other Muslim religious and Sufi orders.[64] It is not unlikely that, in the early part of this period, when Muslim political power disintegrated into separate units, Sufis tried all this with the aim of providing a secure and stable centre for Islam. When the Mughals fulfilled this purpose, Sufi orders competed with each other to show their contributions to this process of consolidation and stability.

62 Compare *Mir'āt-i Madāriya*, British Library, London, MS. Add.16858; *Mir'āt-i Mas'ūdī*, British Library, MS. Or. 1837.

63 See Aziz Ahmad, 'Conversion to Islam in the Valley of Kashmir'; A.Q. Rafiqi, *History of Sufism in Kashmir*, pp. 80ff; M. Ishaq Khan, *Kashmir's Transition to Islam*, pp. 177–98.

64 Derryl N. MacLean, 'Real Men and False Men at the Court of Akbar: The Majalis of Shaykh Mustafa Gujarati', in David Gilmartin and Bruce B. Lawrence, eds, *Beyond Turk and Hindu: Rethinking Religious Identities in Islamicate South Asia*, Gainesville, 2000, pp. 199–215; Qamaruddin, *The Mahdawi Movement in India*, Delhi, 1985, pp. 50–78; S.A.A. Rizvi, *A Socio-Intellectual History of the Isna 'Ashari Shi'as in India*, vol. I, New Delhi and Canberra, 1986, pp. 186–235.

The strength, resilience and viability of Brahmanical traditions seem to have been another factor creating conditions in which Sufis could estimate that the spirit of accommodation and assimilation, not claims of superiority and the show of spiritual power, would make them more acceptable as well as ensure the quick and sure success of their mission. Brahmanism had revived in medieval times in a quite spectacular fashion. In the 640s, when the Chinese pilgrim Hsuan Tsang visited India, he saw the Indo-Gangetic plains studded with Buddhist *chaityas* and *vihāras*. But early in the eleventh century, when al-Biruni was in India, he met only Brahmans who could help him in his pursuit of Indic sciences. By the middle of the fourteenth century, north Indians had completely forgotten the great Buddhist ruler Ashoka, who was to be rediscovered only by Europeans in the nineteenth and twentieth centuries. When Firuz Tughlaq found an Ashokan pillar and proposed to install it on the rooftop of his palace, he found no one in Delhi and in its vicinity who could read the edicts inscribed on it in the old Prakrit script.

The later Brahmanical revival showed, however, an enormous assimilative capacity. It absorbed Buddhism, integrated some of its rituals and beliefs, adopted tribal religious practices and deities, and admitted numerous non-Brahmanical customs and occupational groups into the Brahmanical *samskāra* and *varna* system. Migrations and resettlements of Brahmans, the new *dāna* rituals, and an emerging uniform culture buttressed by the increasing institutionalization of *tīrthas*, all provided new sources of power to the Brahmans.[65] The Brahmans seem to have used their newly acquired social authority to lend additional vitality to Brahmanism, which

[65] For a recent excellent analysis of the issue, see Kunal Chakrabarti, *Religious Process: The Puranas and the Making of a Regional Tradition*, Delhi, 2001; see also B.N.S. Yadava, *Society and Culture in Northern India in the Twelfth Century*, Allahabad, 1973, chapters 1 and 8; R.S. Sharma, *Social Change in Early Medieval India*, Delhi, 1969; B.P. Mazumdar, *Socio-Economic History of Northern India, 1130–1194*, Calcutta, 1960, chapters 3 and 14; B.P. Mazumdar, 'Epigraphic Records on Migrant Brahmans in North India (1030–1225)', *Indian Historical Review*, vol. 5, 1978–9, pp. 64–86; B.D. Chattopadhyaya, *The Making*

they did by developing it into a remarkably resilent 'Hinduism'. By the fourteenth century the term 'Hindu' had, significantly, begun to denote a religious culture encompassing all such cults and traditions as had originated and developed within the geographical limits that the term had hitherto stood for. Early medieval Persian accounts identified as 'Hindu' almost all indigenous religious traditions, including those which had an evidently anti-Brahmanical stance. In the sixteenth century, both the language and the contents of Tulsi Das's *Rāmcharitmānas*—the medieval Awadhi reworking of the ancient Sanskrit classic of Valmiki—showed how Brahmanism could extenuate, conciliate, and even appropriate dissent and protest.

## Towards a Reaffirmation

I have, in the foregoing section, outlined a counter-reaction of sorts, or a concurrent ethos and tendency which went against the grain of the flexibility and accommodation shown by the less stringent and orthodox practitioners of Indian Islam. Yet I do not intend to suggest that the message of the alternative of greater Islamic orthodoxy enshrined in the *akhlāq* texts, the liberal ethos of Persian literary culture, and Sufi attempts at assimilation were all simply lost in the din of this contestation. A non-sectarian and open-ended cultural politics, with the endeavour of balancing the conflicting claims of different communities, continued to assert its presence. Sufi legends that had earlier associated India with Islamic traditions remained strong. The noted eighteenth-century scholar Ghulam 'Ali Azad Bilgrami reiterates, in his Arabic history *Subḥat al-Marjān fī Ās̤ār-i Hindūstān*, that 'India was the site of the first revelation, the first mosque on Earth, and the place from which pilgrimage was first performed.' Using the Sufi concept of the Prophet Muhammad's

*of Early Medieval India*, Delhi, 1996; R.N. Nandi, 'Client, Ritual and Conflict in the Early Brahmanical Order', *Indian Historical Review*, vol. 6, nos 1–2, 1979–80, pp. 64–118.

primordial prophetic nature, Azad describes India as the place where the eternal light of Muhammad was first manifest in Adam, while Arabia was where it found final expression in the physical form of the Prophet: 'The black stone of Mecca descended with Adam, the staff of Moses grew from a myrtle that Adam planted on the peak, and all perfumes and craft tools derive from Adam's descent to India.'[66]

Thus, even among the *'ulamā'* who expressed reservations about the validity of the doctrine of *waḥdat al-wujūd*, there is to be found a plea for tolerance and dialogue in matters that are controversial. According to Shaikh 'Abd al-Haqq Muhaddis of Delhi—the noted traditionalist from Mughal India and the author of *A<u>kh</u>bār al-A<u>kh</u>yār*—the oft-cited biographical dictionary of Indian Sufis by Shaikh 'Abd al-Wahhab Muttaqi (whom we have noted above as an advocate for taking the juristic *sharī'a* as a set of teachings for the ideal moral life)—also made a plea for careful reflection upon alternative opinions on matters of faith. 'One should first listen and consider', Muttaqi is reported to have said, 'whether one has really grasped what has been said or not; then one should, if possible, reconcile it with [what one believes to be] the truth, otherwise one should reject it. If even that is not possible, one should just leave it aside and go one's way, without allowing one's faith to be shaken.'[67] Muhaddis of Delhi also quotes his father, Shaikh Saif al-Din (d.1582), a Sufi scholar, as saying that 'in a learned discussion you should not become prickly and hurt others. If you think the other person is right, agree with what he says; if he is not in the right, try once or twice to convince him. If he still refuses to change his view, tell him that you are saying what appears to be true according to your knowledge, but it is possible that what he says is correct, and there is no need for dispute.'[68]

[66] Cited in Carl W. Ernst, *Eternal Garden: Mysticism, History, and Politics at a South Asian Sufi Center,* Albany, 1992, p. 29.

[67] *A<u>kh</u>bār al-A<u>kh</u>yār*, p. 277.

[68] Cited in K.A. Nizami, *Ḥayāt-i Shai<u>kh</u> 'Abd al-Ḥaqq Muḥaddis Dihlawī*, Delhi, 1953, p. 78.

Whatever the nature of the connections of the Shaikh of the Naqshbandi Mujaddidi order with Shahjahan and Aurangzeb, it is difficult to suggest that they fundamentally influenced the course of Mughal politics. Again, Shahjahan had close relations with Shah Mir (d.1633), a Qadiri Sufi who believed in *waḥdat al-wujūd*. He also had faith in Shah Muhibb-Allah, whose response to a question in regard to the Hindus which he put through his son, Prince Dara Shukoh, is worth noting. Shah Muhibb-Allah advised thus:

> It is impertinent of me to give counsel, but justice requires that the welfare of the people be the concern of administrative officers, whether the people be believers or unbelievers, for they have been created by God, and the person who took the lead in being merciful to the righteous and the evil-doers, the believers and the unbelievers was the Prophet of God. This is recorded in [the history of] his victories and is stated in the Qur'an.[69]

Also relevant here is Shaikh 'Abd al-Rahman Chishti's evaluation of Mughal rule, which we noted earlier as unmistakeably arguing tolerance. Many *wujūdīs* felt strongly enough to defend the doctrine even in the face of a contrary imperial order. Aurangzeb took grave exception to the contents of Shah Muhibb-Allah's *Risāla-i Taswīyya*, seeing it as a restatement of Ibn al-'Arabi's *Fuṣūṣ al-Ḥikam*, and demanded an explanation. Shah Muhibb-Allah, who was close to Dara Shukoh, was dead by this time. The emperor therefore ordered one of the deceased saint's disciples, Shaikh Muhammadi, to explain the controversial passages in the *Risāla*, and in case he could not reconcile these with the *sharī'a*, all copies of the work were to be burnt. The shaikh replied that he was yet to reach the high and sublime mystic stage from which his master had spoken, and that when he acquired such status he would write the commentary, as desired. As for reducing the tract to ashes, the emperor himself could do this much better, he said, as there was much

[69] *Maktūbāt-i Shāh Muḥibb-Allāh Ilāhābādī*, MS. Subhanallah Collection, Maulana Azad Library, Aligarh Muslim University (AMU), Aligarh.

more fuel required by the royal kitchens than by ordinary households.[70]

Thus, the Naqshbandi Mujaddidi doctrine of *waḥdat al-shuhūd* could hardly shake the foundations of the doctrine of *waḥdat al-wujūd*, let alone dislodge it: there was still a widespread belief in its truth in the eighteenth century. Shah ʻAbd al-Rahim (d.1719), the father of the better-known Shah Wali-Allah (d.1763); Mirza ʻAbd al-Qadir Bedil (d.1720), the noted Persian poet; Mir ʻAli Muttaqi (d.1730), father of the famous Urdu poet Mir Taqi 'Mir' (d.1810)—all upheld and expressed their faith in this doctrine.[71] It is in the context of its wide acceptability that we must appreciate some Naqshbandi attempts—such as that by Shah Wali-Allah in his *Faiṣla-i waḥdat al-wujūd wa'l shuhūd*—at reconciliation between the two doctrines, suggesting that the difference between them was merely semantic.[72] This was part of Shah Wali-Allah's larger mission of *taṭbīq* (synthesis, reconciliation) of diverse views in religious matters. Indeed, his endeavour in *taṭbīq* of the different schools of jurisprudence, his concept of *dīn* as 'that nature on which the changes of age and time have no effect, and upon which all the prophets are agreed', shows that even in unexpected circles there was interest in maintaining the idiom of politics and power that the Mughals had chosen.[73]

[70] Rizvi, *History of Sufism*, vol. II, pp. 270–1.

[71] Cf. Shah Wali-Allah, *Anfās al-ʻĀrifīn*, p. 48; *Ruqʻāt-i Mirzā ʻAbd al-Qādir Bidil*, f. 26a; Mir Taqi Mir, *Zikr-i Mīr*, p. 18, English transl. C.M. Naim, Delhi, 1999, pp. 27–69.

[72] For a discussion of this text, see Burhan Ahmad Faruqi, *The Mujaddid's Conception of Tauhid*, Lahore, 1940, pp. 95–100; J.M.S. Baljon, *Religion and Thought of Shah Wali Allah Dihlawi, 1703–1762*, Leiden, 1986, pp. 56–63. See also Barbara D. Metcalf, *Islamic Revival in British India*, pp. 16–45, for a discussion on the eighteenth-century transition in the *ʻulama's* position and Shah Wali-Allah.

[73] Shah Wali-Allah, *Ḥujjat-Allāh al-Bāligha*, Arabic text with Urdu transl. by ʻAbdul Haq Haqqani, Lahore, n.d. p. 44. However, Shah Wali-Allah limited his references to the Jewish prophets alone. He wrote a commentary on the *Muʼaṭṭā*,

In general, Shah Wali-Allah is known for his revivalism, and also for having called a *jihād* for the final establishment of a pan-Islamic society. It is not my intention here to dispute this understanding. I wish only to point out that what Shah Wali-Allah took pride in was his extraordinary capacity to reconcile the injunctions of the Qur'an and *Ḥādīṣ* (*manqūlāt*) with the rational sciences (*ma'qūlāt*). He believed that differences between the different schools of jurisprudence, as well as between jurists and Sufis, could be eliminated with a judiciously balanced use of *burhān* (demonstrated proof), *wijdān* (intuition), and *manqūl* (traditional knowledge). He used and adapted materials from all directions simultaneously to produce his synthesized system.[74] In the context of Mughal India, the significance of this feature can be appreciated by the fact that, in Shah Wali-Allah's evaluation, Sirhindi occupied a special position in the history of Islamic thought because he too had attempted a reconciliation between *taṣawwuf* and *sharī'a*: he thus considered Sirhindi his predecessor. Shah Wali-Allah's position was, however, clearly a departure, and his principle of *taṭbīq* therein yet further evidence for the view that 'the door of *ijtihād*' was still open.

We also have echoes of the Nasirean *akhlāq* in Shah Wali-Allah's writings, in particular in his discussions of the idea of *irtifāqāt*. He writes that the *sharī'a*s of different prophets differed on account of different material circumstances:

> It is a known fact that the *sharī'a*s of the [various] prophets have differed due to certain causes and expediencies. The injunctions of the *sharī'at* had to pay due consideration to these. For example,

---

a collection of the *Ḥadīṣes* by Imam Malik ibn Anas, who founded the Maliki school of jurisprudence, one different from the Hanafi school which Shah Wali-Allah had inherited. He also wrote a treatise, *Al-Inṣāf fī bayān-i asbāb al-ikhtilāf*, to explain the reasons for difference and diversity in opinions. Again, part of his *Ḥujjat-Allāh* is a commentary on a famous *Ḥadīṣ* anthology, *Mishkāt al-Maṣābīh*, wherein he used all the schools of jurisprudence.

[74] Fazlur Rahman, *Revival and Reform in Islam*, pp. 171–203; Ahmad Dallal, 'The Origins and Objectives of Islamic Revivalist Thought, 1750–1850', *Journal of the American Oriental Society*, vol. 113, no. 3, 1993, pp. 341–59.

when the people of the Prophet Noah were physically strong and sturdy, fasting during the day was prescribed for them in order to suppress the fury of their animal power. But as the followers of the Prophet Muhammad were constitutionally weak, they were absolved of the observation of continuous fasts. In like manner, property acquired through booty was not made lawful for people in the past, but had been made so for those who came later because of their weakness. According to the Law of Moses, Jerusalem was the direction fixed for offering prayer, while the followers of the Prophet Muhammad were asked to turn their faces towards the Ka'aba. In the Mosaic Law, the penalty for intentional murder was retaliation, but in Islamic Law a fine is also allowed (provided the heirs of the murdered be content with that).[75]

More interesting is Shah Wali-Allah's discussion of political organization. In his understanding, the populace virtually constitutes one single being. If an individual feels pain somewhere, the whole society feels it—in the same way as the human body feels pain when one part of it is injured. As it is not possible for an individual to fulfill his needs alone, he has to live and co-operate with others. Each individual has a separate occupation, but mutual co-operation eventually results in the formation of a social and political order.[76]

In Shah Wali-Allah's line his son, Shah Rafi' al-Din (d.1833), as well as Isma'il Shahid (d.1831) in the early stage of his career, turned out to be *wujūdīs*. Mirza Mazhar Jan-i Janan (d.1784), another Mujaddidi Naqshbandi luminary of the period, remained a *shuhūdī*, whose efforts again were to reconcile differences. His position in relation to Hindu religion is noteworthy. In response to a query from one of his disciples, he wrote at length:

What we know from the ancient books of the people of India is that at the time when the human world was created, Divine Mercy

[75] These quotations are a paraphrase of Shah Wali-Allah's text in G.N. Jalbani, *Teachings of Shah Waliyullah*, Lahore, 1967, p. 101. For the original Arabic, see *Ḥujjat-Allāh al-Bāli<u>gh</u>a*, Cairo, 1936/1355 H, vol. I, pp. 86–7 and 90.

[76] Jalbani, *Teachings of Shah Waliyullah*, p. 133. For the original Arabic, see *Ḥujjat-Allāh al-Bāli<u>gh</u>a*, p. 43.

revealed the book called the *Veda* through Brahma, an angel, who is the root cause of the creation of the world. The book which is divided into four parts, comprising the commandments regarding obligatory and prohibited acts as well as stories of the past and forecasts about the future. The sages of ancient times derived from Book Six separate *dharmas*, which they called *Dharma Shāstra*, on the lines of our *'ilm-i kalām* (apologetics). Their religious leaders have similarly divided mankind into four groups; and fixed one of these for every group.

The branch of science, similar to our *'ilm-i fiqh* (jurisprudence) which delineates the details of these systems, is called *Karma Shāstra*. This defines the scope of human acts. There is no scope for the abrogation of commandments (*faskh-i aḥkām*), but there is space for modification in the law, to suit the changes that occur from time to time. Again, time in their *dharma* is divided into four ages (*yugas*), with a definite pattern of life for each *yuga*. The later leaders' interpretations are interpolations and are not reliable.

All these groups believe in the *Vedas* and in the oneness of God; they believe in the end of this world and reward and retribution for good and bad deeds on the day of Resurrection. Their religious leaders are masters of their own religions and rational sciences, methods of self-discipline and sublimation of the human soul. The practice of idol-worship among them is for different reasons; it is not polytheism (*shirk*). They have divided the span of human life into four parts; the first to acquire learning and etiquette, the second dedicated for children and earning a livelihood, the third for correction of the self and pious deeds, and the fourth for renunciation, which they regard as the zenith of human accomplishments. On this according to them depends the final deliverance (*najāt-i kubrā, mahā-mukt*). The rules and regulations of their religion were highly developed and are now abrogated. In our books there is little mention of the ancient abrogated religions other than Judaism and Christianity.

According to the Qur'an, each community had a prophet, God has not left India without Prophets. An account of them together with details of their piety is available in their books. One could estimate the level of their accomplishments from the cultural legacy of this land. Divine Mercy did not ignore the requirements of the people of this country. Obedience to the Prophets who came before our Prophet was obligatory for their communities, without any concern for the Prophets of other communities. In succession to our Prophet, no other Prophet will have to be followed till the end of this world, all over in the East and the West. Those who refused to obey our Prophet during the one thousand and eighty years that have elapsed since his advent were infidels, but not those who had lived earlier.

Since the Qur'an is silent about many Prophets, it is good that we adopt a liberal view of the Prophets and religions of India. The same should be our attitude with regard to the people of ancient Persia, and for that matter of all other countries. No one should be called a *kāfir* without a definite reason. The underlying idea behind the idolatry of the people of India is that some of the angels to whom God has given some kind of control over the world, or some of the past saints who still exert influence over this world after their deaths, or even some living sages who are immortal like Khizr [Elias], are represented in the idols towards whom they turn with reverence. Through meditation they establish an association with the original persons, and thus seek succour in the resolution of their needs, in this world and in the life hereafter.

[Now] this act of theirs resembles the Sufi practice of *z̤ikr-i rābiṯa* or *taṣawwur-i shai<u>kh</u>*, in which the disciple concentrates in meditation on the visage of his *pīr* (preceptor) and thus draws inspiration from him. The only difference between these two practices is that the Sufis do not make a physical image of the *pīr*. At any rate, idolatry in India has no connection whatsoever with the idolatry of pre-Islamic Arab infidels, who believed the idols were not mere agents of God; they had power in their own rights, were gods on earth while God (*<u>Kh</u>udā*) in heaven was the god of heaven alone. This was *shirk* (polytheism). The prostration of Indians before idols is a form of salutation (*tahniyat*), which they call *dandawat* and is performed in place of routine salutation (*salām*) in their tradition [*maz̤hab*] before father, mother, teacher and spiritual preceptor as well. This is not done by way of worship [and is not thus *shirk*]. As for belief in the transmigration of soul (*tanasu<u>kh</u>*), it does not imply infidelity.[77]

Mirza Mazhar's view was in sharp contrast to the one that Badauni expressed in his *Najāt al-Rashīd*. Mirza Mazhar reiterated his

[77] *Maqāmāt-i Maz̤harī*, ed. and transl. M. Iqbal Mujaddidi, Lahore, 1983, pp. 499–500; *Mirzā Maz̤har Jān-i Jānān ke <u>Kh</u>uṯūṯ*, transl. Khaliq Anjum, Delhi, 1962, pp. 93–5.

position in the presence of his spiritual preceptor, Haji Muhammad Afzal of Siyalkot. Once, a disciple of the Haji related to the latter a dream in the Mirza's presence. He saw in this dream a field full of fire, in the midst of which was seated Krishna, while Rama stood at the edge. When the dream was interpreted by someone present to mean that the two were punished by the fires of hell, Mirza Mazhar intervened: the fire that came in the dream he interpreted as the fire of love, and as Krishna sank into it, himself being in the middle of the fire, this indicated his involvement in ecstasy. On the other hand Ram, who followed the path of asceticism, was at the edge of the fire.[78] This dream and the views it entails have special significance, for we have no such episode in earlier Sufi texts. Even in the circle of the Chishtis, as we noticed above, Khwaja Mu'in al-Din was considered the only prophet-like figure of India.[79]

In the early 1740s the institution by Khwaja Muhammad Nasir 'Andalib (d.1759) of a Sufi order separate from the main Naqshbandi Mujaddidis, to which he had belonged, is also not without significance. Khwaja 'Andalib was a disciple of Shaikh Muhammad Zubair (d.1740), a direct descendant of Shaikh Ahmad Sirhindi. He was also closely associated with Shah Sa'd-Allah Gulshan, and the order, which was called *ṭarīqa-i Muḥammadiya*, was founded after the death of his *pīr*. He discussed and elaborated upon the principles of his new *ṭarīqa* not in an unalloyed treatise on Sufi doctrines or *malfūẓ*, but in a book of the *dāstān* genre (fables or tales), which he and others narrated while mourning the death of their preceptor, Shah Gulshan. Their *dāstān* revolves around the exploits of a prince, and reads like an imagined construction of the process of the making of Mughal political culture. Whether 'Andalib took that occasion, i.e. mourning the death of his master, to give vent through this narrative to his own feelings over the threats his vision of power

[78] *Bashārāt-i Maẓhariya*, Aligarh MS. For this reference, I am grateful to Dr F.A. Qadri of Northeastern Hill University. For Badauni's position, see Zilli, 'Badauni Revisited', pp. 143–68.

[79] See 'Abd al-Rahman Chishti, *Mir'āt al-Asrār*, f. 229b.

and political culture encountered—and whether the establishment of a new Sufi order distinct from the Naqshbandi Mujaddidis was intended to be a device to meet these threats—are questions which need to be addressed in some depth, and which I have tried to do elsewhere, in a limited way.[80] My purpose here is to draw attention to the fact that Khwaja 'Andalib's son and successor Mir Dard (d.1785), who further elaborated the rules of the new order in his major works, even as he defended the doctrine of *waḥdat al-shuhūd*, was virtually a *wujūdī* in his poetry. He also integrated *samā'* (music), considered so alien to the Naqshbandi Mujaddidis, into the Muhammadiya *ṭarīqa*.[81] In this connection, some verses of this poet may be in order here:

*Waḥdat ne har ṭaraf tere jalwe dikhā diye*
*parde ta'ayyunāt ke jo the uthā diye*

(The Oneness [of Being] has displayed Thy splendours all around,
the veils of distinctions have all been removed.)

*Shaikh ka'ba hoke pahunchā, ham kanisht-o-dair se*
*Dard manzil ek thī, tuk rāh hī kā pher thā.*

(The Shaikh reached here through the Ka'ba, we through the temples,
the destination was the same, O Dard, though we trod different roads.)

[80] Compare *Nāla-i 'Andalīb*, Bhopal, 1893/1310 H, Preface. For further elaboration of the rules of the order, also see his son Khwaja Mir Dard's *'Ilm al-Kitāb*, Delhi, 1891/1308 H. It has been suggested that the name 'Muhammadiya' was given to the Sufic order in order to emphasize its authenticity and purity, and that this was a kind of neo-Sufism in different parts of the Muslim world in the nineteenth century to meet the threat which Muslims encountered in the wake of but not necessarily in response to the Western domination of their world. Cf. Fazlur Rahman, *Islam*, London, 1966, pp. 166 and 205–11. It is, however, significant that in Delhi the *Ṭarīqa-i Muḥammadiya* was founded much before European domination of the city.

[81] Muhammad Umar, *Islam in Northern India, during the Eighteenth Century*, Delhi, 1993, pp. 127–9.

*Jin ke sabab se dair ko tū ne kiyā kẖarāb*
*ay Shaikẖ un buton ne mere dil mein ghar kiyā*[82]

(The idols that made you turn the temple desolate,
O Shaikh! They've chosen my heart for their home.)

Indeed, the reconfiguration of the message of non-sectarianism
carried from Persian poetry into Urdu poetry further illustrates the
fact that the forces in opposition to a fixed and narrowly religious
and political outlook had not abated. With this narrowed the gap between a high Persianized court and the culture of the people (of the
cities). This language, known in its early form as Hindi, Hindavi, or
Rekhta,[83] had long been in use outside the court. Mas'ud Sa'd Salman in the Ghaznavid period is reported to have had a *dīwān* in
Hindavi. Sufis used the language to reach the people and propagate
their ideas. Poems and verses in Hindavi mixed with Persian are
attributed to Amir Khusrau. We have seen that some of the Deccan
sultans also experimented with it as a medium of poetry. And,
despite the Mughal fascination for Persian, the language seems to
have entered the portals of their court sometime towards the last
decades of the seventeenth century.

The compilation of the *Tuḥfat al-Hind* by Mirza Khan in the later
years of Aurangzeb's reign possibly signified a serious and organized effort to persuade the Mughal elite to learn Hindavi, as also
the local Nagari script. The book, divided into seven chapters dealing with different popular branches of Indian sciences, begins with
an analysis of the Nagari alphabet, script, and essential Hindi grammar. At the end of the book (*kẖātima*) is a detailed glossary of the
words, phrases, idioms and similes used by the people of Hind.[84]
Mirza Khan wrote the book for the use of Mughal princes, with the

---

[82] For Mir Dard's verses, see Jamil Jalibi, *Tarikh-i Adab-i Urdu*, Delhi, 1993:
vol. 2, pt I, p. 493; pt II, p. 747; Ghulam Husain Zulfiqar, *Urdū Shā'irī kā Siyāsī
aur Samājī Pasmanẓar*, Lahore, 1966, p. 186.

[83] For a recent review of the history of the evolution of the language with its
different names, see Shamsur Rahman Faruqi, *Urdū kā ibtidā'ī zamāna: Adabī
tahẕīb-o-tārīkẖ ke pahlū*, Karachi, 1999.

[84] See, for instance, BN, MS., Blochet I, 235. Nurul Hasan Ansari has edited

intention of inspiring and equipping them to appreciate current indigenous sciences (*'ulūm-i mutadāwila-i Hindiya*). The noted late-seventeenth and early-eighteenth century Hindi poet Vrind was, reportedly, among the teachers of Prince Muhammad A'zam.[85] Again, the preparation of formal Hindi–Persian dictionaries, in particular *Gharā'ib al-Lughāt* by Mir 'Abd al-Wasi of Hansi, at this stage, was also perhaps an attempt in this direction, even though the principal objective of these dictionaries, as their compilers stated, was to provide Persian equivalents to Hindavi words in common use.[86]

There is also evidence of increasing interest on the part of the Mughals in Hindavi and Braj poetry in the early eighteenth century. Aurangzeb's grandson Prince Muhammad Rafi 'al-Shan wrote poetry in Hindi under the pen name 'Nyāy'ī'.[87] 'Abd al-Rahman 'Premi', a well-known *Rīti-kāl* poet, was patronized by Emperor Farrukh Siyar (r.1712–19).[88] One of his nobles patronized Nawaz, a Braj poet, who retold the *Shakuntalā*, adapted from the story in the

---

the Introduction and first five chapters and published the book from the Bunyad-i-Farhang-i-Iran, Tehran, 1975/1354*sh.* In this edition however, the first part and Introduction (*muqaddima*) are not printed in full, and the Hindi alphabet in Nagari characters has been omitted. Also see Mirza Khan, *A Grammar of the Braj Bhākhā: The Persian Text Critically Edited from Original MSS., with an Introd., Translation and Notes, Together with the Contents of the Tuḥfat ul-Hind*, ed. M. Ziauddin, Foreword by Suniti Kumar Chatterjee, Calcutta, 1935.

85 Compare Vrind, *Vrind Satsāi*, ed. Bhagwandeen, Allahabad, 1908, editor's Introduction; see also R.C. Shukl, *Hindi Sahitya ka Itihas*, Kashi, 1975/2032 VS.

86 Compare Mas'ud Husain Rizvi Adib, 'Urdū kī Qadīm Lughat', reprinted in the *Journal of the Khuda Bakhsh Oriental Public Library*, Patna, 1993, Special No. *Intikhāb az Risāla Hindūstanī*, Allahabad, 1931–48, p. 18, for the Preface of *'Ajā'ib al-Lughat*, which Ajmeri Palwali compiled, basing himself on 'Abd al-Wasi's *Gharā'ib*, some time in the early eighteenth century.

87 Muhammad Hadi Kamwar Khan, *Tazkirat-us-Salāṭīn Chaghtā*, ed. Muzaffar Alam, Bombay, 1980, p. 157.

88 'Abd al-Rahman Premi, *Nakh-shikh*, ed. Iqbal Ahmad, Bombay, 1959, editor's introduction. For an analysis of his poetry, see also Sandhya Sharma, 'Aspects of Society and Culture in *Reeti* Poetry', unpublished Ph.D. dissertation, Jawaharlal Nehru University, New Delhi, 2000.

*Mahābhārat*, the play by Kalidas, and the popular *kathā*. Nawaz then earned the coveted title of *kabīshwar*, or poet laureate, from the emperor.[89] The title, in contrast to the one of *Kab* [Kavī]-*rāi* awarded by Shahjahan, assumes special significance in view of the fact that, at Farrukh Siyar's court, there was no poet laureate in Persian. It was in the face of the reassertion of regional forces that the Mughals accorded a respectable position to Hindi at their court. There were few Iranians now seeking their fortune in Delhi, and the influence of those who came to Lucknow was limited largely to religion.[90] The Mughals' experience in the Deccan, where the sultans had encouraged the local language even for administration, may also have persuaded them to change to Hindi. It is significant that it was a Dakkani poet, Wali of the Deccan (d.1744), who is believed to have been the first major poet to have set the diction of Urdu in Delhi.[91]

In the eighteenth century, after Wali of the Deccan had shown how one could combine Persian and Indian aesthetics, the language began to grow as a rival to Persian in poetry, and fast became a favourite with kings and princes, and with major writers and poets of the period. A contemporary writer, 'Ashiqi' 'Azimabadi, recounts a telling anecdote in this context:

> On account of my training and temperament, I was inclined to write poetry in Persian. I used to go for corrections to Siraj al-Din 'Ali Khan Arzu. One day, Khan-i Arzu said to me: 'The stature of Persian

[89] Nawaz, *Shakuntalā*, Varanasi, 1924; see also an Urdu prose version of the same prepared by Kazim Ali Jawan, in 1801, reprinted with introduction and notes by Muhammad Aslam Quraishi, Lahore, 1963; Mas'ud Hasan Rizvi Adeeb, 'Nawāz aur Shakuntalā Nātak, *Nuqush*, Lahore, June 1963. See also Romila Thapar, *Sakuntala: Texts, Readings, Histories*. New Delhi, 1999.

[90] For Lucknow's links with Iran and Iraq during this period, see J.R.I. Cole, *Roots of North Indian Shi'ism in Iran and Iraq: Religion and State in Awadh, 1722–1859*, Delhi, 1989. See also Michael H. Fisher, *A Clash of Cultures: Awadh, the British, and the Mughals*, Delhi, 1987.

[91] Muhammad Husain Azad, *Āb-e Ḥayāt: Shaping the Canon of Urdu Poetry*, English transl. and edition by S.R. Faruqi and Frances Pritchett, New Delhi and New York, 2001, pp. 110–14; Jamil Jalibi, *Tārīkh-i Adab-i Urdū*, vol. I, Delhi, 1983, pp. 529–57.

poetry is very high indeed. [But] Our language is Hindi. Even if people from Hind have raised Persian to a great level, even so, before the Iranians and poets from the past whose language this was, our efforts are like showing a mere lamp to the sun. Until now there has not been any major master in *rekhtagū'ī*. Therefore, if we make efforts in terms of this [vernacular], we will also naturally become masters in this part of the world.' This advice seemed excellent to me. From that day on, I began to compose poetry in *rekhta*, and in a brief period, I became one of the master-poets of that language.

We can thus see the dilemma in which even an acknowledged defender of Indian Persian, such as Arzu, saw himself. The point can be developed further with respect to another major figure of eighteenth-century literary culture, Mirza Muhammad Rafi 'Sauda' (d.1781), who wrote verses in the form of a real or imagined dialogue with a Persian-speaking poet (*fārsī-dān*). The latter, asked by Sauda to correct his verse, tells the great poet that Indians will never be anything but the butt of ridicule and contempt by native speakers of the language. The following conclusion is thus reached:

*Ko'i zabān ho, lāzim hai khūbī-ye maẓmūn*
*Zabān-i furs par kuchh munḥaṣir sukhan to nahīn.*

(Whatever the tongue, what counts is an idea's excellence.
Poetry is not confined to the language of Fars alone.)

*Kahān tak unkī zabān tū durust bolegā*
*Zabān apnī mein tū bāndh ma'nī-ye rangīn.*

(How long will you strive to speak their tongue?
Compose colourful thoughts in your own language.)

These illustrative texts and anecdotes may help us understand how Urdu in northern India, within a relatively brief period of about a hundred years, achieved a status similar to that of Persian in poetry and other literary forms.[92] However, in the rise of Urdu there were also a number of other contributing factors. To begin with, there was the emergence of a new elite in Delhi, composed of newly successful trading communities, service gentry with their own high

[92] See Jamil Jalibi, *Tārīkh-i Adab-i Urdū*, vol. II, pt 2, Delhi, 1995, pp. 654–5.

cultural aspirations, and former regional elites, all of whom were for various reasons increasingly relocating into the centre. They were derided by writers who had previously enjoyed the patronage of the old nobility (i.e. *khanazads*) as, for instance, 'mean and ignoble' (*arāẕīl*), 'the jackals who had replaced the lions', and 'crows who cawed in place of the songs of the nightingale'. This new class began to be characterized in contemporary chronicles as *umarā'-i jadīd* (lit. 'new nobles', the *nouveau riche*), and their newfound successes were condemned as 'riches . . . bestowed on dogs and donkeys'. But it was during this period, while the glitter of the royal palace and the *ḥavelīs* of the erstwhile grand old nobles were on the wane, that many among these 'upstarts' took up the task of lavishing patronage on dancers, musicians, poets, and other such artistes. Many of them also themselves figured in contemporary *mushā'iras*, both as hosts and as participating literati.[93] However, this class was not so comfortable with Persian, and preferred to see the elegance of elite Persian integrated into the spoken language that they considered their own—namely, Hindavi. They responded to the abuse thrown at them by the erstwhile elites—to the effect that their culture was 'rustic' and their language 'ignorant'—with an attempt to show that, on the contrary, their literary idiom was equally capable of elegance and sophistication. They buttressed this position by encouraging active appropriations of Persian vocabulary, metaphors and allusions into an increasingly refined register of Hindavi.

It is against this background that we can appreciate another factor in the rise of Urdu. It is of no small importance that two of the greatest poets—Mir and Sauda—in the historical trajectory of Urdu

[93] For some evidence see Khush-Lal Chand, *Nādir al-Zamānī*, MS., British Museum, Or. 1654, ff. 111a–13a; Dargah Quli Khan, *Muraqqa'-i Dihlī*, edited with Urdu translation and notes by Nurul Hasan Ansari, Delhi, 1982, pp. 39 and 110; see also Chander Shekhar and Shama Mitra Chenoy's Introduction to their English translation of the *Muraqqa'* (Delhi, 1989) for a discussion of the state of art in Delhi in the eighteenth century; Naim Ahmad, ed., *Shahr-Āshūb*, Delhi, 1968, pp. 43–8 and 54–76; Ghulam Husain Zulfiqar, *Urdū Shā'irī ka Siyāsī aur Samājī Pasmanẓar*, Lahore, 1966, pp. 145–226; Frances Pritchett, 'A Long History of Urdu Literary Culture, Part 2: Histories, Performances, and Masters', in Sheldon Pollock, ed., *Literary Cultures in History*, pp. 864–911.

poetry flourished during this earliest period of Urdu literary culture, and through their talents gave the emerging literary idiom the stamp of credibility. In their poetry the new elite found its aspirations realized. Their poetry certified that Urdu could reach the heights that had hitherto been assumed to be the preserve of Persian alone.

This trend was so successful that we find, in the latter half of the eighteenth century, even the Mughal emperor Shah Alam, and certain Mughal princes, composing poetry in Hindi and Rekhta. And though Persian continued as the dominant vehicle for serious prose, it is notable, for instance, that the emperor's *'Ajā'ib al-Qiṣaṣ* was among the first major specimens of Urdu prose as well.[94]

The Mughal emperor Shah 'Alam II (r.1761–1818) and certain other Mughal princes, such as Mirza 'Azfari', composed poetry in Hindi and Rekhta, even as Persian continued for some time to dominate serious writings in prose. Europeans identified the language of the Nawab of Lucknow in the 1770s as Hindi. Evidently, all this must have affected the dominance of Persian, and led to the development of a common culture. In view of the fact that even the language of Persianized Mughal elites was now increasingly called Hindi, it is difficult to discern if the attempts at blending and enriching this with Persian metaphors and similes might have encouraged the conditions for its division into Urdu and Hindi in this period.[95] The understanding that this division was along religious

[94] Cf. Shah 'Alam II, *Nādirāt-i Shāhī*, ed. Imtiaz 'Ali Khan 'Arshi, Rampur, 1944; *idem*, *'Ajā'ib al-Qiṣaṣ*, ed. Sayyid 'Abdullah, Lahore, 1965; Mirza 'Ali Bakht Zahir al-Din 'Azfari', *Wāqi'āt-i Aẓfarī*, ed. T. Chandrasekharan and Saiyid Hamza Husain 'Umari, Madras, 1957.

It is interesting to note in this connection that Mirza Azfari also makes a plea for the revival of Turkish as a replacement for Persian as the official language of the royal household, which one can speculate may also have tilted the balance against Persian, and widened the niche for Hindavi. Cf. Sayyid Abdullah, *Fārsī Zubān o Adab*, Lahore, 1977, pp. 290–2.

[95] For a discussion on the Persianization of Hindavi, see Amrit Rai, *A House Divided: The Origin and Development of Hindi/Hindavi*, Delhi, 1984, pp. 226–84. In Amrit Rai's opinion the seeds of the Urdu–Hindi divide of the later period along religious lines were already sown in terms of the eighteenth-century Persianization of the language. See also Faruqi, *Urdū kā ibtida'ī zamāna*, pp. 141–78.

lines needs reconsideration. Hindi/Urdu signified the region's rise against the Persianized Mughal centre. The process of Hindi-ization of Mughal Delhi, as we saw above, is to be seen in the context of the emergence of the new local elites, who also included people from the regions that had settled in Delhi. This Delhi elite echoed and implemented the growing aspirations of the other regions to dislodge Persian and replace it with local dialects. But in Delhi itself the attachment to the symbols of Mughal refinement and cultural prestige remained strong, and what really emerges now is a composite mix: Persian is indeed replaced by Hindavi, but a Hindavi selfconsciously ornamented and embellished by Persian cultural idiom.

In a sense, one might say that Delhi was simply one region among many, all of which were trying to assert the power of their local idiom. But its inextricable association with the Mughal court gave Delhi's Hindavi a distinct prestige and advantage as cultural capital unavailable in, say, the Deccan. The Delhi register of Hindavi was—perhaps uniquely—capable of incorporating Persian vocabulary without changing accent or intonation. This also perhaps explains how, in this process, Hindavi dislodges the erstwhile Dakkani, and, more than that, the Braj Bhasha of the geographically larger surrounding area which had earlier appealed to the Mughal elites. It is this idiom that came to be known as the language of Delhi (*zabān-i urdū-i mu'allā-i Shāhjahānābād*), and which also saw in course of time the idioms of other regional centres—whether Hindu or Muslim—as potent, but lesser, rivals. The so-called Delhi–Lucknow rivalry provides the best-known example of this phenomenon. It is much later that the Delhi and Lucknow Hindi idiom began to be identified as 'Muslim', as opposed to the one associated with 'Hindu' Benares.[96] Like Persian in the heyday of the Mughals, the

[96] For a discussion on the evolution of Hindavi-Hindi as *zubān-i Urdū*, see Shamsur Rahman Faruqi, *Urdū kā Ibitidā'ī Zamāna*; for the Delhi-Lucknow rivalry, see Carla Petievich, *Assembly of Rivals: Delhi, Lucknow, and the Urdu Ghazal*, Delhi, 1992; for discussion on the Hindi–Urdu divide, see for example, Christopher R. King, *One Language, Two Scripts: The Hindi Movement in Nineteenth Century North India*, Delhi, 1994; Vasudha Dalmia, *The Nationalization*

new Hindi, Hindavi, or Urdu was enriched by Hindus and Muslims alike. It carried the message of a liberal and catholic approach to life, finding echoes among most poets of the period. Note, for instance the following verses by Sauda.[97]

*Maqṣūd dard-i dil hai, Islām hai na kufr*
*phir har gale mein subḥa-o-zunnār kyon na ho.*

(The destination is a heart in pain [for others' sake],
not Islam or infidelity.
Why should there not then be a rosary and a sacred thread,
around each neck?)

*Ka'ba sau bār woh gayā to kyā*
*jis ne yān ek dil mein rāh na kī*

(What if he visited Ka'ba a hundred times,
when he failed to win a single heart over here.)

*Ka'be kī ziyārat ko ay Shai<u>kh</u> main pahunchūngā*
*mastī se mujhe bhūle jis din rah-i mai<u>kh</u>āna.*

(O Shaikh, I'll arrive at the Ka'ba for pilgrimage on that day,
When I forget the way to the tavern in my inebriation.)

*Āyā hūn tāza-dīn ba ḥaram Shai<u>kh</u>onā mujhe*
*pūjā namāz se bhī muqaddam bahut hai yān.*

(I have come to the Haram, I am fresh in faith,
I prefer *pūjā* even over *namāz* here, O Shaikh!)

*Ka'ba agarche ṭūṭā to kyā jā'e<u>gh</u>am hai Shai<u>kh</u>*
*kuchh qaṣr-i dil nahīn ke banāya na jā'egā.*

(If the Ka'ba has been demolished, worry not, O Shaikh!
Was it an abode of the heart, that it cannot be rebuilt?)

---

*of Hindu Traditions: Bharatendu Harishchandra and Nineteenth-century Banaras*, Delhi, 1997; Alok Rai, *Hindi Nationalism*, Hyderabad, 2001.

[97] For these verses and also for the subsequent ones from Sauda and Qa'im Chandpuri, see Jalibi, *Tārī<u>kh</u>-i Adab-i Urdū*, vol. 2, pt II, pp. 493, 680 and Zulfiqar, *Urdū Shā'irī kā Siyāsī aur Samājī Pasmanẓar*, pp. 183 and 186.

Or the following verse from Qa'im Chandpuri (d.1793):

> *Jis muṣallā pa chhiṛakye na sharāb*
> *apne ā'īn mein woh pāk nahīn.*
>
> (That prayer-mat on which you do not sprinkle wine,
> is not pure in the religion I hold.)

Also of significance in this respect were some eighteenth-century social practices. Holi was one important festival that the Mughals had encouraged and celebrated, and the practice continued at the local and regional courts, sometimes with even greater enthusiasm. The nawabs and nobles in eighteenth-century Bengal, for instance, actively participated in Holi. On one occasion Nawab-Shahamat Jang and Saulat Jang, nephews of Ali 'Vardi Khan, the Nawab of Bengal (r.1741–56), played Holi for several days together in Motijhil at Murshidabad, as we see from the following description:

> On this occasion about 200 reservoirs were filled with coloured water, heaps of *abīr* (red powder) and saffron were collected and more than five hundred dancing-girls, dressed in costly robes and jewels, appeared in a body every morning and evening, mustering from different parts of the garden.

In the same way, Nawab Shuja' al-Din Muhammad Khan also celebrated Holi.[98] Writing about the situation from the perspective of the late eighteenth century, Ghulam Husain Tabataba'i says:

> As for the Holi itself, it is again a festival of Hindoo institution, but held so sacred amongst our delicate grandees, and so very obligatory, that they never fail to spend a great deal of money on dancers, and such kind of spectacles, and especially, in making presents to low people, who, at such a particular time, are in a position of acknowledging those favours by the liberty of giving to the donors, as well as to each other, a great deal of abusive and shameful language, and that too not in obscure terms, but in the broadest and coarsest

[98] Munshi Salimullah, *Tārīkh-i Bangāla*, reprint, Dacca, 1981, p. 105; *Muẓaffar-Nāma*, Khuda Bakhsh Library, Patna, MS., pp. 866–87a.

language, and by naming every thing by its proper term, without any regard to rank, station, or decency.[99]

Holi thus turned out to be a festival observed by Hindus and Muslims alike. An early-nineteenth-century account of the festival, as celebrated somewhere near Delhi, is noteworthy:

> Today is the festival of Hoolee, and our camp is a scene of unbounded rejoicing. The servants and other followers, both Hindoos and Mahommadans, are strolling about in groups accompanied with the clashing of rude music, to which they add yells of merriment, and songs, specially chanted upon this holiday. They are provided with quantities of a red powder, which they throw at each other, and besides, mix it with water, and squirt the concoctions, with extreme ingenuity, by means of monster syringes at all comers. Here we see crowds of young urchins, their eyes on fire with innocent subtlety, splashing a venerable Mahommadan whose long beard soon reeks with the crimson stream of Hoolee water, while, he in turn, shaking with laughter, envelops them suddenly in the cloud of rosy powder.
>
> 'Hoolee, Hoolee!' is the cry. There you see a neat and staid khidmutgar, his wide dress dyed with a hue like the rich red beams of daybreak, leaping with frenzied mirth to the eloquent melody of tom-toms, regardless of tent ropes and tent pins, in the midst of a throng of coolies, smiling at all, and enchanted with himself; now he disappears in whirlwinds of ruby dust, now he rises beneath rainbows of blushing waterdrops, which career arching over his head. Sometimes he pursues, sometimes he runs away. While shrieks of ecstasy are heard, 'Hoolee! Hoolee! Hoolee! Hoolee!' Here we have a muscular sepoy, vociferating, and twirling like a dancing Durwesh, an excited statue of red-granite; and look, you, at that laughing Hindoostanee girl, whose supple figure moves as gracefully as a Lotus stem, in an imperceptible eddy whose large black eyes are liquid with excess of delight, her thin white garment spotted and streaked with carmine water, bending her neck, and putting her little hand into a large bag, and taking out as much of the glowing powder, as it will

[99] Ghulam Husain Tabataba'i, *Siyar al-Muta'akhkhirīn*, English trans. by M. Raymond, *alias* Haji Mustafa, Calcutta, 1902, reprinted 1991, pp. 144–5.

> hold—'Hoolee! Hoolee! Hoolee! Hoolee!' All is uproar, all is confusion, all is pleasure![100]

There were also fairs in which the different communities participated.[101] Then there were religious organizations with members from both religious communities. There were Hindus who observed Muslim rituals and ceremonies such as Muharram, *Yāzdahum* (celebration of the birth anniversary of the founding father of the Qadiri Sufi *silsila*), and *Bārah Wafāt* (the birthday of the Prophet Muhammad).[102]

All this, in large measure, received nourishment from the extension of the boundaries of the *sharī'a* in *akhlāq* texts within the Nasirean tradition. Nasirean ethical norms continued to be pronounced in Persian, and then for some time also in Urdu. If an orthodox mulla, on the one hand, made a plea for the entire resources of the state to be earmarked only for the maintenance of the clergy,[103] on the other the compilers of *akhlāqī* digests kept reiterating that:

> The finest pleasure in life and the most gracious divine benevolence in both the worlds [for a man] is to acquire the joys [of living] in the ever green garden of good name and to endear himself as a cherished and rare precious object to the followers of each and every religion. He will earn this fortune when he cleans his heart of all the dregs of bigotry, and hurts none with his baseless ideas and inappropriate criticisms. He should however be loyal to the injunctions of the religion he is born in, the one that God considered for him good. He

[100] Cf. William Lloyd and Alexander Gerard, *Narrative of a journey from Caunpoor to the Boorendo pass, in the Himalaya Mountains via Gwalior, Agra, Delhi, and Sirhind; by Major Sir William Lloyd. And Captain Alexander Gerard's account of an attempt to penetrate by Bekhur to Garoo, and the Lake Manasarowara: with a letter from the late J.G. Gerard, Esq. detailing a visit to the School and Boorendo passes, for the purpose of determining the line of perpetual snow on the southern face of the Himalaya*, vol. I, London, 1841, pp. 41–5.

[101] Of interest in this connection is the Urdu poet Nazir Akbarabadi's description of 'Baldevji ka Mela' at Agra. Nazir also writes on Holi. See *Kulliyāt-i Naẓīr Akbarābādī*, Lucknow, 1951, pp. 432 and 451–8.

[102] Muhammad Umar, *Islam in Northern India*, p. 387.

[103] Zafarul Islam, 'Nature of Landed Property in Mughal India'.

should not step out of the limits of his own religion. For, if he acts otherwise, people will regard him as faithless and untrustworthy. Still, he should ever keep in mind that it is the same one God who has created the [different] religions and is the Keeper of all the classes of peoples. And this too is [a sign of] His manifest benevolence and perfect prudence that there is a separate path for each religion, suitable to its own milieu, and that everyone is endowed with an special direction. As He adorned the garden of this world with a variety of trees and colourful flowers, likewise He created various religions and made the heart burn with a desire to recognize Him [through the diverse ways]. If there is a mosque, there is a call for prayer in His name, if a temple, the bells are sounding for the same aim.

I am amazed at the hostility between Islam and unbelief.
For, both the Ka'ba and the idolhouse are illumined with the same lamp.

Thus, it is necessary that everyone scours his heart free of dirt, treats the people of other faiths as his brothers, and keeping himself away from the thorns of dispute takes his residence in the heaven-like garden of unity and accord.

The peace in both the worlds is embodied in these two words:
'kindness' to friends and 'courtesy' to foes.

Whichever the place of worship he comes across, he should show respect to it, and whoever the religious leader he meets, he [must] be reverent to him. He should not defile the fresh spring of unity by indulging in religious disputations. For ages the people have quarrelled over religious matters, but still they are left unresolved and unfinished.[104]

[104] Durga Prashad, *Makhzan al-Akhlāq*. Sandila, 1899/1317 H, pp. 59–60.

CHAPTER 6

# Concluding Remarks

The main conclusions to be emphasized from the foregoing discussion are that despite the complexities that emerge from our survey of several centuries of Indo-Islamic interaction, it seems of importance to examine this history within the framework of an even larger history, namely that of Islam from its very beginning. In this connection, it is clear that a creative tension existed from the very start of Islamic history, concerning those views and practices that could or could not be accommodated within the framework of that which was considered properly 'Islamic'. The traditions of the Prophet (*ḥadīs̤*), to the effect that 'disagreements in my community (*ikhtilāf-u ummatī*) are a blessing', may have initially lent legitimacy to the view that a certain plurality of opinions was natural and even desirable in this context. However, it became clear soon enough that this notion of 'pluralism' was largely confined to the legal sphere, while dogmatics were to be excluded from this flexible definition. Hence, 'heresiographies' came to be written in order to define what was beyond the pale, of which a particularly comprehensive example comes from the mid-eleventh century, in the form of Shahristani's noted *Kitāb al-milal wa'l niḥal* (Book of Religions and Sects). In the world where works such as this were read and written, it was evident that a sphere existed of 'heretics and renegades' (*zindīq* and *mulḥid*), who would never be integrated into the mainstream of Islamic thought.

This obviously targeted a number of early Muslim thinkers and philosophers who were influenced by Hellenic traditions, and whose radical questioning posed problems for such foundational issues as the very nature of prophethood.[1] Indeed, some of the major works of heresiography even refuse these 'deviant' philosophers a place in their discussion of Islam, preferring to locate them elsewhere, even while speaking of groups of unbelievers and pagans. Since the risk was that those who 'deviated' too far from normative practice would be expelled from the community of believers (even in its expanded notion of the so-called seventy-three sects), this realization conditioned the strategies adopted by those who held views that might be considered heterodox. Thus, rather than unnecessarily provoking conflict, it is clear that means were sought from the twelfth century onwards to accommodate a certain measure of difference within the circle of what was considered to be acceptable Islamic practice by taking a rather different tack than that of the overt challenge posed by the philosophers of the early centuries of Islamic history.

In this second phase—which produces a new form of reflection of which the works of Nasirean *akhlāq* in Persian are a characteristic part—the strategy is of a far more delicate and nuanced challenge, one that relies on semantic displacement rather than calling into question the very large structures of prophethood and revelation, or the accepted canon of early Islamic texts. The texts that follow the model of Nasir al-Din Tusi thus inevitably begin with a proper sequence of references to the Creator and the Prophet, and seek initial legitimacy by inserting their authors into a system of erudite references that makes their texts immediately recognizable to fellow Muslims. Thus, even though these works derive from Aristotle's *Nicomachea*, they nevertheless came to be accepted as a proper part of Islamic writings. The formal similarities between these treatises of political ethics and other treatises of a purely religious nature (which were, paradoxically intended, among other things, to be refutations of the Hellenic tradition), may also have lent them some weight of legitimacy. The acceptability of Tusi's

[1] For a recent discussion around this question, see Sarah Stroumsa, *Freethinkers of Medieval Islam: Ibn al-Rāwandī, Abū Bakr al-Rāzī and Their Impact on Islamic Thought*, Leiden and Boston, 1999.

text, it has been noted, was partly a function of the particular conjuncture in which the Islamic lands found themselves in the wake of the great Mongol expansion under Chengiz Khan and his immediate successors. However, these immediate causes cannot provide us a real reason for the persistence of such thinking after the critical moment of the thirteenth century had passed: the reasons for this must be sought elsewhere.

In the same phase, *taṣawwuf* emerged as an institution, not always restricted by the bonds of the codified law, that is the *sharī'a* of the jurists, in its search for religious truth and the rules for regulating civil society. Time and again, theologians and other purists expressed doubts regarding the validity, for instance, of Ibn al-'Arabi's doctrine and many of the other esoteric features of Sufi life and practice. Indeed, there was even a plea for declaring it against the Qur'an and the Sunnat (Traditions) of the Prophet altogether. *Taṣawwuf*, however, continued to be an integral part of Islam, and interestingly even those who opposed it sometimes sought to pose their opposition in Sufi terms in order to make their arguments more effective.

In general, it is my view that the interaction of Islam with other traditions generated tensions that might not have emerged in terms of the internal dialectics of the Islamic tradition itself. These tensions were thus prerequisites for the creation of both a conceptual and an institutional space where accretions and innovations (*bid'a*) could take place, leaving open the possibility of their eventual integration into the mainstream understanding of what was Islam. A figure such as Akbar, criticized in harsh terms by the Naqshbandi–Mujaddidi order, even to the point of implying that he had ceased to be a Muslim, could thus be seen as perfectly acceptable to members of another no-less-respectable Sufi order such as the Chishtis, to whom 'Abd al-Rahman Chishti belonged. Chishti writes in the context of his account of Khwaja Mu'in al-Din:

> Reinforced with Divine help, Akbar ascended the throne of Delhi like the dazzling sun at an auspicious hour, at the age of fourteen after the death of his high-statured father, Humayun. The local power-

> mongers then disappeared everywhere, as stars are outshone [by the rise of the sun], with no trace of their power visible anywhere today. God made him and his descendants the sole rulers of all the regions of Hindustan. Akbar was unusually devoted to the great Khwaja, paid visits to the holy city of Ajmer several times on foot, built a majestic mosque, several mansions and a wall around the city for the protection and comfort of its residents, conferred cash and land grants on the Khwaja's descendants and the attendants of the shrine, earmarked [the revenues of] some villages for the expenses of the *langar* (free public kitchen) and appointed an official (*mutawallī*) to take care of the needs of the visitors and dervishes who live there. These grants continue till date. As a matter of fact, for the fifty years of his reign, the emperor remained fully devoted to the Khwaja. May God bless him (*raḥima-hu Allāh*).[2]

In 'Abd al-Rahman Chishti's memory, then, Akbar was not simply a Muslim, but a true and pious Muslim until his death. Similarly, there seems to be an interesting explanation from the Sufi tradition for the troubles afflicting the Mughal state in the late seventeenth century, as we see from a Chishti *tazkira*, *Sawāṭi' al-Anwār*. The author of this *tazkira* describes the annual visit to Delhi of one Sayyid Gharib-Allah ibn Sayyid 'Abd al-Rasul, *khalīfa* of the Chishti master Shaikh Da'ud, a great grandson of Shaikh 'Abd al-Quddus Gangohi, on the occasion of the *'urs* festivities of Shaikh Qutb al-Din Bakhtiyar Kaki. He would preside over a special *samā'*, or musical séance, for his disciples and followers at the shrine. These were the days when the Mughal state had come to be associated with Sunni orthodoxy, and Aurangzeb had deputed *muḥtasibs* (censors) with the authority to enforce *sharī'a* in the everyday life of Muslims. Since the convening of a *samā'* violated the *sharī'a* norm, it is reported that a Naqshbandi shaikh (*pīrzāda*) who was close to Aurangzeb complained about the matter, and actually brought the *muḥtasib* to the shrine to call it to a halt. When Sayyid Gharib-Allah heard about the impending visit, he sought guidance from the soul (*rūḥāniyat*) of Shaikh Qutb al-Din as to how he should

[2] *Mir'āt al-Asrār*, fol. 236a.

react. In a vision, Sayyid Gharib-Allah then saw Shaikh Qutb al-Din emerge from his grave wearing flaming red robes with an enraged expression, reciting the following verse:

*Gulgūn libās kard sawār-i samand shud*
*Yārān hazar kunīd ki ātish buland shud*

(He put on red robes, rode on his steed
Beware, friends! A fire is raging.)

Gharib-Allah for his part understood the message and the musical gathering grew even more passionate. But the *muḥtasib* and the Naqshbandi shaikh eventually managed to shut down the *samā'*. What happened subsequently is a matter of significance for our purposes. The Naqshbandi shaikh who had escorted the *muḥtasib* died mysteriously within a few days. Aurangzeb was then compelled, according to the author of this *tazkira*, to leave Delhi, and was destined never to return. The emperor's absence from north India then led to chaos and the eventual end of Mughal authority.[3] All this was presented as the result of Qutb ul-Din Bakhtiyar Kaki's anger over the official interruption of a *samā'* at his shrine at the behest of a Naqshbandi shaikh. Thus the entire Mughal state unravelled, as a result of its refusal to tolerate a Chishti Sufi practice. The significant point here is that, according to the Naqshbandi Sufi tradition, what the *muḥtasib* tried to do was in complete accord with Islamic tenets. But, according to the Chishti tradition, the very act of the *muḥtasib* caused the downfall of an 'Islamic' power. Thus we can see that there was no single dominant Islamic tradition or any single reading of the *sharī'a* which shaped and determined the course of Muslim polity in pre-colonial India. In fact, different

[3] Muhammad Akram ibn Shaikh Muhammad 'Ali ibn Shaikh Ilah Bakhsh, *Sawāṭi' al-Anwār*, British Library, London, OIOC, MS. 654, ff. 444a–444b. There are a number of other explanations in Sufic texts that similarly locate the loss of Muslim political power and sufferings of Muslim society in terms of an insult to a Sufi saint. See, for one such instance, with reference to the thirteenth-century Mongol disaster: Ashraf Jahangir Simnani, *Maktūbāt-i Ashraf*, 1, Urdu transl. Mahmud 'Abd al-Sattar, Tanda, District Ambedkarnagar, 1998, pp. 164–75.

Islamic traditions were often at loggerheads with one another. The *umma* was rarely united in historical Islam.

This takes us to a further point, for it has not been the intention here to reduce the entire process of the creation of a new normative vocabulary to purely 'objective' and institutional interactions. The pivotal role played by some thinkers and political actors in these processes cannot be denied either, and we must at least give due weight to the fact that our sources themselves insist on the importance of certain emblematic or charismatic figures in the processes that we have set out above. The idioms of power that existed in the Indo-Islamic polities that we have analysed thus emerged from a complex of processes, some purely political, others involving the interaction of the political and the religious, and still others drawing sustenance from issues concerning language and identity. It has not been my intention here to idealize the polity that produced these diverse reflections, nor to suggest that a generalized tolerance or liberalism was the norm either at the time of the Sultanate of Delhi or the Mughals who succeeded thereafter. For it should not surprise us either that a complex, diverse and evolving polity threw up solutions for social management that were themselves contested, or that the lines were periodically redrawn in such a contest. After all, the problems with which these diverse actors—Sufis, poets, rulers, counsellors and divines—grappled over the centuries are still with us in some measure.

This book has primarily been concerned with the realm of ideas and conceptions, less so with details of the actual administrative arrangements or institutions that emerged in the centuries that have been considered here. The historian of political and social questions will be aware that the idioms of power that we have discussed were neither a perfect reflection of realities, nor a matrix that wholly determined the functioning of institutions. The interaction was a complex one, yet a comparative reflection with other polities and societies of that period shows that the idioms in which political ideas and ideals were expressed in Indo-Islamic polities had much that was original about them.

# Bibliography

## A. Primary References (Manuscripts, Editions, and Translations)

Abu'l Faẓl, *Ā'in-i Akbarī, I*, edited by H. Blochmann, Calcutta: Bibliotheca Indica, 1872.

———, *Akbar-nāma*, edited by Agha Ahmad Ali and Abdur Rahim, vols 1 and 3, Calcutta: Bibliotheca Indica, 1873 and 1886.

———, *Inshā'-i Abu'l Faẓl*, Lucknow: Nawalkishor Press, 1863/1280 H.

'Afīf, Shams Sirāj, *Tārīkh-i Fīrūz Shāhī*, edited by Maulavi Wilayat Husain, Calcutta: Bibliotheca Indica, 1890.

'Alī Asghar bin Shaikh Maudūd, *Jawāhir-i Farīdī*, Lahore, 1884/1301 H.

'Andalīb, Khwāja Muḥammad Nāṣir, *Nāla-i 'Andalīb*, Bhopal: Maṭba' Shāhjahānī, 1894.

Anonymous, *Tāīkh-i Jā'is*, MS. Dr Abdul Ali Collection, Nadwat al-'Ulāma', Lucknow.

Aẓfarī, Mirzā Ẓahīr al-Dīn 'Alī Bakht, *Wāqi'āt-i Aẓfarī*, edited by T. Chandrasekharan and Saiyid Hamza Husain Umari, Madras: Government Oriental Manuscripts Library, 1957.

Ārzū, Sirāj al-Dīn 'Alī Khān, *Sirāj-i Munīr*, edited by S.M.A. Ikram, Islamabad: Iran Pakistan Institute of Persian Studies, 1988.

———, *Tanbīh al-Ghāfilīn*, edited by S.M.A. Ikram, Lahore: Punjab University, 1981.

———, *Muthmir*, edited by Rehana Khatoon, Karachi: Institute of Central and West Asian Studies, 1991.

———, *Majma' al-Nafā'is*, India Office Library, London, MS.I.O. 4015.

'Aufī, Sadīd al-Dīn Muḥammad, *Lubāb al-Albāb*, edited by Muhammad Abdul Wahhab Qazwini, E.G. Browne, and Muhammad Abbasi, Tehran: Kitāb Furūshī-y Fakhr-i Rāzī, 1982/1361 *sh.*

Ashūb, Mirzā Muḥammad Bakhsh, *Tārīkh-i Shahādat-i Farrukh Siyar wa Julūs-i Muḥammad Shāh*, British Museum, London, MS. Or. 1832.

Badā'ūnī, Mullā 'Abd al-Qādir, *Muntakhab al-tawārīkh*, edited by Kabiruddin Ahmad, Ahmad Ali & W.N. Lees, 3 vols, Calcutta: Bibliotheca Indica, 1865 and 1869; English transl. by W.H. Lowe, reprint, Delhi: Oriental Reprints, 1973.

Bābur Ẓahīr al-Dīn Muḥammad, *Dīwān*, edited by Denison Ross, *Journal of the Royal Asiatic Society of Bengal*, vol. 6, New Series, pp. 1–43, 1910.

———, *Bābur-nāma*, English transl. by A.S. Beveridge, Delhi: Oriental Reprints, 1970; also John Layden and William Erskine, Oxford: Oxford University Press, 1921, and W.M. Thackston, Washington D.C.: Smithsonian Institute and New York: Oxford University Press, 1996.

Bairam Khān, *Dīwān*, edited by S. Husamuddin Rashidi and Muhammad Sabir, Karachi: Institute of Central and West Asian Studies, University of Karachi, 1971.

Balkhī, Muẓaffar Shams, *Maktūbāt*, MS. Khudā Bakhsh Oriental Public Library, Patna; English transl. by S.H. Askari, *Patna University Journal*, vol. 12, 1958.

Banī Isrā'īl, Muḥammad Amīn, *Majma' al-Inshā'*, Bibliothéque Nationale de France, Paris, MS. Supplement Persan, 461.

Baranī, Ẓiyā al-Dīn, *Tārīkh-i Fīrūz Shāhī*, edited by Saiyid Hasan Khan, Calcutta: Bibliotheca Indica, 1862.

———, *Fatāwā-i Jahāndārī*, edited by Afsar Salim Khan, Lahore: Research Society of Pakistan, Punjab University, 1972. English transl. by Afsar Salim Khan, *The Political Theory of the Delhi Sultanate*, Allahabad: Kitāb Maḥal, n.d.

Bazmī, 'Abd al-Shukūr, *Dāstān-i Padmāwat*, edited by Amir Hasan Abidi, Tehran: Bunyād Farhang-i Iran, 1971/1350 *sh*.

Bīdil, Mirzā 'Abd al-Qādir, *Kulliyāt*, Kabul: Dapohni Maṭba'h. Also 1875, in 2 vols, Lucknow: Nawalkishor, 1922/1341 H.

Bilgrāmī, Ghulām 'Alī Āzād, *Khizāna-i 'Āmira*, Kanpur: Nawalkishor 1871; also Bibliothéque Nationale de France, Paris, MS Polier 2-Supplement Persan 946.

———, *Ma'āṣir al-Kirām*, vol. II, edited by Maulavi Abdul Haq, Hyderabad: 1913.

Bilgrāmī, Mīr 'Abd al-Wāḥid, *Haqā'iq-i Hindī*, translated by S.A.A. Rizvi, Kashi: Nāgrī Prachārinī Sabhā, 1957/2014 VS.

Bernier, François, *Travels in the Mogul Empire, 1656–1668*, English transl. by A. Constable, reprint, Delhi: S. Chand & Co., 1972.

Bisṭāmī. 'Alī bin Ṭaifūr, *Tuḥfa-i Quṭb Shāhī, Akhlāq-i Bādshāhī*, Bodleian Library, Oxford, MS. Ouseley 226.

Chishtī, 'Abd al-Raḥmān, *Mir'āt al-Asrār*, British Museum, London, MS. Or. 216.

———, *Mir'āt al Makhlūqāt*, India Office Library, London, MS. Or. 1883.

*Dabistān-i Mazāhib*, edited by Nazr Ashraf, Calcutta, 1809, also Kanpur: Nawalkishor, 1903/1321 H; also edited by Rahim Rizazadeh Malik, 2 vols, Tehran: Kitābkhāna-i Ṭahūrī, 1983/1362 *sh.*, English transl. David Shea and Anthony Troyer, 3 vols, London: Oriental Translation Fund of Great Britain and Ireland, 1843.

Dawwānī, Jalāl al-Dīn, *Lawāmi 'al-Ishrāq* or *Akhlāq Jalālī*, Lucknow: Nawalkishor, 1914; reprint Lucknow: Tej Kumar, 1957. English transl. W.F. Thompson as *Practical Philosophy of the Mohammadan People*, reprint Karachi: Karimsons, 1977.

Dihlawī, 'Abd al-Ḥaqq Muḥaddiṣ, *Akhbār al-Akhyār*, Deoband: Kutub-khāna Raḥīmiyā, n.d.

Faiẓī, Abu'l Faiẓ, Faiyāẓī, *Dīwān*, edited by A.D. Arshad, Lahore: Punjab University/Tehran: Furūghī, 1983/1362 *sh.*

———, *Inshā'-i Faiẓī*, edited by A.D. Arshad, Lahore: Majlis-e Taraqqī-ye Adab, 1973.

Fakhr al-Dīn Muḥammad bin Mubārak Shāh (Fakhr-i Mudabbir), *Ādāb al-Ḥarb wa'l-Shujā'a*, edited by Ahmad Suhaili Khwansari, Tehran: Iqbāl, 1967/1346 *sh.*

———, *Ā'īn-i Kishwardārī*, edited by Mohammad Sarwar Maulai, Tehran: Ḥaidarī, 1975/1354 *sh.*

Farangī Maḥallī, Mullā Niẓam al-Dīn, *Manāqib-i Razzāqiya*, Lucknow: Maṭba' Mujtabā'ī, 1896/1313 H.

Firdausī, Abu'l Qāsim, *Shāh-nāma*. 4 vols, Lucknow: Nawalkishor, 1870.

Firishta, Muḥammad Ibrāhīm, *Gulshan-i Ibrāhīmī*, better known as *Tārīkh-i Firishta*, vol. 1, Lucknow: Nawalkishor, 1864/1281 H. English transl., J. Briggs, in 4 vols, London, 1829.

Gangohī, Shaikh 'Abd al-Quddūs, *Rushd-nāma*, MS. Staatbibliothek, Berlin, Sprenger 827.

———, *Maktūbāt-i Quddūsiya*, Delhi: Matba' Aḥmadī, 1870/1287 H.

Ghaẓalī, Muḥammad bin Ḥāmid, *Naṣīḥat al-Mulūk*, edited by Jalal Homai, Tehran. English transl., F.R.C. Bagley, *Counsel for Kings*, London: Oxford University Press, 1964.

Ghulām 'Alī Shāh, *Maqāmāt-i Maẓharī*, Delhi, 1892, Urdu transl., Iqbal Mujaddidi, Lahore: Urdu Science Board, 1983.

Ghulām Sarwar, *Khazīnat al-Aṣfiyā'*, Lucknow: Maṭba' Ṣamar-i Hind, 1873.

Gīlānī, Abu'l Fatḥ, 1968, *Ruq'āt-i Abu'l Fatḥ Gīlānī*, edited by M. Bashir Husain, Lahore: Punjab University, 1967.

Gopal bin Govind, Persian translation of *Rāmāyana*. MS., Bibliothèque Nationale de France, Paris.

Gulbadan Begum, *Humāyūn-nāma*, Persian text edited and English transl. by A.S. Beveridge, reprint, Delhi: Idārah-i Adabiyāt-i Dellī, 1972.

Ḥāfiẓ Shīrāzī, *Dīwān*, edited by Muhammad Riza Naini Jalali & Nazir Ahmad, Tehran: Sāzmān-i Umūr-i Farhangī, 1971/1350 *sh.*; also edited and transl. into Urdu by Qazi Sajjad Husain, Delhi: Sabrang Kitābghar, 1967; also in English transl., Tehran: Wizārat-i Farhang-o-Irshād-i Islāmī, 1997/1376 *sh.*

Ḥajjī Shms al-Dīn Muḥammad Ḥusain Ḥakīm, *Intikhāb-i Shā'istaKhānī*, India Office Library, London, MS. 2210.

Hamadānī, Saiyid 'Alī, *Zakhīrat al-Mulūk*, Bibliothèque Nationale de France, Paris, MS. 760.

*Ḥujjat al-Hind*, British Museum, London, MS. Add.5602.

Ḥusainī, Ashraf Khān, *Raqā'im-i Karā'im*, edited by S. Azizuddin Husain. Delhi: Idārah-i Adabiyāt-i Dellī, 1990.

Ḥusainī, Qāẓī Ikhtiyār al-Dīn, *Akhlāq-i Humāyūnī*, Bibliothèque Nationale de France, Paris, MS. 767.

———, *Dastūr al-Wizārat*, Bibliothèque Nationale de France, Paris, MS. 768.

Ibn Miskawaih, Aḥmad ibn Muḥammad, *Tahẕīb al-Akhlāq*, edited by Qusṭanṭin Zurayq, Beyrut: American University Press, 1966.

Ibn Miskawaih, *al-Ḥikmat al-Khālida*, edited by Abd al-Rahman Badawi, Beyrut: Dār al-Andalus, 1986.

Injū, Mīr Jamāl al-Dīn Shīrazī, *Farhang-i Jahangīrī*, edited by Rahim Afifi, 3 vols, vol. I, Mashhad: University Press, 1972/1351 *sh.*

'Iṣāmī, Abd al-Malik, *Futūḥ al-Salāṭīn*, edited by S.A. Usha, Madras: Madras University, 1948.

Islam, Riazul, edited and transl., *A Calender of Documents on Indo-Persian Relations, 1500–1750*, 2 vols, vol. I, Karachi: Institute of Central and West Asian Studies, University of Karachi, 1979.

Jahāngīr, Nūr al-Dī Muḥammad, *Tūzak-i Jahāngīrī*, edited by Saiyid Ahmad Khan, Aligarh, 1864; English translation Alexander Rogers and Henry Beveridge, reprint, Delhi: Mushiram Manoharlal, 1968; also English transl. W.M. Thackston, Washington, DC: Smithsonian Institute and New York: Oxford University Press, 1999.

Jamālī, Ḥāmid bin Faẓl-Allāh, Kamboh, *Siyar al-'Ārifīn*, Delhi: Maṭba' Riẓvī, 1893/1311 H; Urdu transl., Muhammad Aiyub Qadiri, Lahore: Urdu Science Board, 1976.

Jān-i Jānān, Mirzā Maẓhar, *Khuṭūṭ*, Urdu transl. Kahliq Anjum, Delhi: Maktaba Burhān, 1962.

Jawān, Kāẓim 'Alī, *Shakuntalā*, edited by Muhammad Aslam Quraishi, Lahore: Majlis-e Taraqqī-ye Adab, 1963.

Kaikā'ūs, *Qābūs-nāma*, edited by Ghulam Husain Yusufi, Tehran: Bangāh-i Tarjuma wa Nashr-i Kitāb, 1966/1345 *sh.*

Kākī, Quṭb al-Dīn Bakhtyār, *Fawā'id al-Sālikīn* (Urdu), in *Hasht Bihisht*, Delhi: Maktaba Jām-i Nūr, n.d.

Kāmwar Khān, Muḥammad Hādī, *Taẕkirat-us-Salaṭīn Chaghtā* (Account of Post-Aurangzeb Period) edited by Muzaffar Alam, Bombay: Asia Publishing House, 1980.

Kāshifī, Ḥusain Wā'iẓ, *Akhlaq-i Muḥsinī*, Bombay, 1890/1308 H.

———, *Anwār-i Suhailī*, edited by Hakim Sayyid Shah Ahmad Ashraf Ashrafi, Allahabad: Ram Narain Lal Arun Kumar, n.d. English transl. Arthur A. Wollaston, London: John Murray, 1904. Description of the illustrations preserved in the British Library, London, J.V.S. Wilkinson, New York: William Edwin Rudge, *c.* 1929.

Kashmīrī, Bābā Naṣīb, *Nūr-nāma*, MS. Research and Publication Department, Srinagar, ACC No. 795.

Kashmīrī, 'Ināyatullāh Khān, *Kalimāt-i Ṭayyibāt*, edited by S. Azizuddin Husain, Delhi: Idārah-i Adabiyāt-i Dellī, 1982.

Khāfī Khān, Muḥammad Hāshim, *Muntakhab al-Lubāb*, vols II & III, edited by K.D. Ahmad and Wolseley Haig, Calcutta: Bibliotheca Indica, 1869 & 1925, English transl., portion dealing with Aurangzeb's reign, S. Moinul Haq, Karachi: Pakistan Historical Society, 1977; A.J. Syed, Bombay: Popular Prakashan, 1977.

Keshavdāsa, *Keshav-Granthāvalī*, edited by V.P. Mishra, Varanasi: N.P.S., 1969.

Khalīl, 'Alī Ibrāhīm Khān, *Ṣuḥuf-i Ibrāhīm*, edited by A.R. Bedar, Patna: Khudā Bakhsh Oriental Public Library, 1981.

Khāqānī, Ḥasan 'Alī bin Ashraf al-Munshī, *Akhlāq-i Ḥakīmī*, India Office Library, London, MS. 2203.

Khāqānī, Nūr al-Dīn Qāẓī, *Akhlāq-i Jahāngīrī*, India Office Library, London, MS. 2207.

Khusrau, Amī *I'jāz-i Khusrawī*, vol. I, Lucknow: Nawalkishor, 1875.

———, *Nuh Siphr*, edited by Wahid Mirza, Oxford: Oxford University Press, 1950.

———, *Dībācha-i Ghurrat al-Kamāl*, edited by S.H. Qasemi, in *Khusrau Nāma*, Special Number of *Majalla-i Taḥqīqāt-i Fārsī*, Delhi: Department of Persian, Delhi University, 1988, pp. 128–237.

Khwāndmīr, *Ḥabīb al-Siyar*, vol. IV, Tehran: Khayyām, 1973/1352 *sh.*

Lāldās, *Lāldās kā Bītak*, edited by M.B. Jaiswal and D.K. Sharma, Allahabad: Pranāmī Sāhitya Sansthān, 1966.

Magray, Saiyid 'Alī, *Tārīkh-i Kashmīr*, MS. Research and Publication Deptt. Srinagar, ACC No. 739.

*Mahābhārat*, Persian translation by Mīr Ghiyāṣ al-Dīn Qazwīnī, *alias* Naqib Khān, edited by S.M. Riza and N.S. Shukla, vol. I, Tehran: Kitābkhāna-i Ṭahūrī, 1979/1358 *sh.*

Maqrīzī, Taqī al-Dīn, *al-Mawā'iẓ wa'l I'tibār fi Zikr al-Khiṭaṭ-i wa'l Āmṣār*, Cairo: Būlāq, Ṣafar, 1853/1270 H.

Mas'ūd Sa'd Salmān, *Dīwān*, edited by Nasir Hayyiri. Tehran: Gulshā'ī, 1984/1363 *sh.*

Māwardī, Abul Ḥasan 'Alī bin Muḥammad, *al-Aḥkām al-Sulṭāniya*, edited by Muhammad Badr al-Din al-Nasani, Cairo: Ṣubaiḥ, 1909.

Minhāj-i Sirāj, *Ṭabaqāt-i Nāṣirī*, edited by W. Nassau Less, Khadim Husain and Abdul Hai, Calcutta: Bibliotheca India, 1863–64, English transl. H.G. Raverty, 2 vols, Repr., New Delhi: Oriental Reprints, 1970.

Mīr Aḥmad 'Alī Khān, *Akhlāq-i Muḥammad Shāhī*, Bodelian Library, Oxford, MS. Elliot 6.

Mīr Dard Khwāja, *'Ilm al-Kitāb*, Delhi: Maṭba' Ansārī, 1891/1308 H.

Mīr Taqī, *Zikh-i Mīr*, edited by Maulavi Abdul Haq, Aurangabad: Anjuman-i Taraqqī-ye Urdu, 1928, English transl., C.M. Naim, Delhi: Oxford University Press, 1999.

Mirzā Khān bin Fakhr al-Din Muḥammad, *Tuḥfat al-Hind*, edited by Nurul Hasan Ansari, Tehran: Bunyād Farhang-i Iran, 1977/1356 *sh.*; also M. Ziaduddin's *A Grammar of the Braj Bhakha: The Persian Text critically edited from the original Mss, with an introduction, translation and notes, together with contents of the Tuḥfat-ul-Hind*, Calcutta: Visva Bharati Book Shop, 1935.

Mirzā Muḥammad Mu'tamad Khān, *Iqbāl-nāma-i Jahangīrī*, edited by Abdul Hai, Ahmad Ali, and W. Nassau Lees, Calcutta: Bibliotheca Indica, 1865.

Mīr Khwurd, *Siyar al-Auliyā'*, edited by Chiranjilal, Delhi, Maṭba'-i Muḥibb-i Hind, 1885/1302 H.

Muḥammad Akram, *Sawāṭi' al-Anwār*, India Office Library MS. 654.

Muḥammad Kāẓim, *'Ālamgīr-nāma*, edited by Khadim Husain and Abdul Hai, Calcutta, Bibliotheca India, 1868.

Mullā Dā'ūd, *Chāndāyana*, edited by Mataprasad Gupta, Agra: Pramānik Prakāshan, 1967.

Munīr, Abu'l Barakāt Lāhorī, *Kārnāma-i Munīr*, edited by S.M.A. Ikram, Islamabad: Iran Pakistan Institute of Persian Studies, 1977.

Muṭribī Samarqandī, *Tazkirat al-Shu'arā'*, edited by A.G. Mirzoyef, Karachi: Institute of Central and West Asian Studies, University of Karachi, 1976.

———, *Khaṭirāt-i Muṭribī*, edited by A.G. Mirzoyef, Karachi: Institute of Central and West Asian Studies, University of Karachi, 1977; English transl. by Richard C. Foltz, *Conversations with Jahangir*, Costa Mesa, CA: Mazda Publishers, 1998.

Nāgorī, Ḥamīd al-Dīn, *Surūr al-Ṣudūr*, MS. Habibganj Collection: Maulana Azad Library, Aligarh Muslim University, Aligarh.

Najm-i Ṣānī, Muḥammad Bāqir, *Mau'iẓah-i Jahāngīrī: An Indo-Islamic Mirror for Princes*, edited and transl. by Sajida Sultana Alvi, New York: SUNY, 1989.

Naṣrullāh, Abu'l Ma'ālī Mīr. *Kalīla wa Dimna*, edited by Manuchihr Dānishpazhūh, Tehran: 1964/1343 *sh.*

Naẓīr Akbarābādī, *Kulliyāt-i Naẓīr Akbarābādī*, Lucknow, Nawalkishor, 1951.

Naẓīrī, Muḥammad Ḥusain Nishāpūrī, *Dīwān*, edited by Mazahir Musaffa, Tehran: Amīr Kabīr, 1961/1340 *sh*.

Niẓām al-Dīn Aḥmad, Khwāja, *Ṭabaqāt-i Akbarī*, 3 vols, vol. II, edited by B.De, Calcutta: Bibliotheca Indica, 1927.

Nihāwandī, ʻAbd al-Bāqī, *Ma'āṣir-i Raḥīmī*, vol. 3, edited by Hedayat Hosain, Calcutta: Bibliotheca Indica, 1931.

Niʻmat-Allāh, Maulānā, *Ganj-i Lāyakhfā*, MS. Khuda Bakhsh Oriental Public Library, Patna.

Qābil Khān, Shaikh Abu'l Fatḥ, *Ādāb-i ʻĀlamgīrī*, 2 vols, edited by A.G. Chaudhari, Lahore: Punjab University, 1971.

Qazwīnī, ʻAbd al-Nabī, *Tazkira-i Maikhāna* edited by Ahmad Golchin Maʻani, Tehran: Iqbāl, 1961/1340 *sh*.

Qalandar, Ḥamīd, *Khair al-Majālis*, edited by K.A. Nizami, Aligarh: Muslim University, 1959.

Polier, Antoine Louis-Henri, *Iʻjāz-i Arsalānī*, Bibliothèque Nationale, Paris, vol. 1, MS. English transl. Muzaffar Alam and Seema Alavi, *A European Experience of the Mughal Orient*, Delhi: Oxford University Press, 2001.

Premī, ʻAbd al-Raḥmān, *Nakh-Shikh*, edited by Iqbal Ahmad, Bombay: Hindi Sabhā, 1959.

Reis, Sidī ʻAlī, *The Travels and Adventures of Turkish Sidi Ali Reis*, transl. A. Vambery, London: Luzac & Co., 1899; reprint, Lahore: Al-Biruni, 1975.

Rūmī, Jalāl al-Dīn, *Maṣnawī-ye Maulānā Rūm*, 5 vols, vol. II, edited by Qazi Sajjad Husain, Delhi: Sabrang Kitābghar, 1976.

Rūzbihānī, Iṣfahānī, Faẓl-Allāh, *Sulūk al-Mulūk*, British Museum, London, MS. Or. 253. English translation, Muhammad Aslam, *Muslim Conduct of State*, Islamabad: University of Islamabad Press, 1974.

Sabzawārī, Ṭāhir Muḥammad ʻImād al-Dīn, *Rauẓat al-Ṭāhirīn*, Bodleian Library, Oxford, MS. Arch Swinton, Elliot 314.

Salīmullāh Munshī, *Tārīkh-i Bangāla*, reprint, Dacca: Bangladesh Historical Society, 1981.

Shāh ʻAlam II, *Nādirāt-i Shāhī*, edited by Imtiyaz Ali Khan ʻArshi', Rampur: Hindustānī Press, 1944.

———, edited by Sayyid Abdullah, Lahore: Taraqqī-ye Adab, 1965.

Shāh Muḥibb-Allāh Ilāhābādī, *Maktūb banām Mullā Jaunpurī*, Aligarh:

Maulana Azad Library MS. Zakhīra-i Aḥsan, no. 297.7/37, *Fārsī Taṣawwuf.*

Shāhjahānābādī, Kalīm-Allāh Shāh, *Kashkūl-i Kalīmī*, with Urdu transl., Delhi: Āstāna Book Depot, n.d.

Shāhjahānpūrī, Nawāb Muḥammed Khān, *Karāmāt-i Razzāqiya*, Hardoi: Maṭba' Muraqqa'-i 'Ālam, 1902/1319 H.

———, *Malfūẓ-i Razzāqī*, Lucknow: Maṭba' Mujtabā'ī, 1896/1313 H.

Shāh Walī-Allāh, *Ḥujjat Allāh al-Bāligha*, 2 vols, vol. 1, Cairo: Maṭba' Khairiya, 1904/1322 H.

———, *al-Inṣāf fī bayān-i Sabab al-Ikhtilāf fi al-Aḥkām al-fiqhiya* Cairo: Maktaba al-Salafiya, 1965/1385 H.

———, *Faiṣla-i Waḥdat al-Wujūd wa Waḥdat al-Shuhūd*, n.d.

———, *'Iqd al-Jīd fi al-Ijtihād wa'l Taqlīd*, Cairo: Maktab al-Salafiya, 1978/1398 H.

———, *Anfās al-'Ārifīn*. Urdu transl., Sayyid Muhammad Faruq al-Qadiri, Delhi: Maktaba al-Falāḥ, 1973/1393 H.

Shaikh Rukn al-Dīn, *Laṭā'if-i Quddūsiya*, Delhi: Maṭba' Mujtabā'ī, 1893/1311 H.

Shīrāzī, Mirzā Niẓām al-Dīn Aḥmad al-Ṣā'idī, *Ḥadīqat al-Salāṭīn*, edited by S. Asghar Ali Bilgrami, Hyderabad, 1931.

Sijzī Dihlawī, Amīr Ḥasan, *Fawā'id al-Fu'ād*, Lucknow: Nawalkishor, 1885/1302 H; also ed., Muhammad Latif Malik, Lahore: Mailk Sirājuddīn & Sons, 1966, English transl., Bruce Lawrence, New York: Paulist Press, 1992; also transl., Ziaul Hasan Faruqi, New Delhi, D.K. Printworld, 1996.

———, *Dīwān*, edited by Mas'ud Ali Mahvi, Hyderabad: Maktaba Ibrāhīm, 1934/1352 H.

Simnānī, Jahāngīr Ahsraf, *Maktūbāt-i Ashraf*, vol. 1, Urdu translation Mahmud Abd al-Sattar, Tanda, Distt. Ambedkarnagar: Dānish Book Depot, 1998.

Sirhindī, Shaikh Aḥmad, *Maktūbāt-i Imām Rabbānī*, vol. II, Lucknow: Nawalkishor, 1877/1294 H; reprint Istanbul, 1977.

Ṭabāṭabā'ī, Ghulam Ḥusain, *Siyar al-Muta'akhkhirīn*, vol. I, Lucknow: Nawalkishor, 1876.

Ṭālib Āmulī, *Kulliyāt-i Ash'ār-i Malik al-Shu'arā Ṭālib Āmulī*, edited by Tahiri Shihab, Tehran: Sanā'ī, 1967/1346 *sh*.

Tushtarī, Taqī al-Dīn Muḥammad al-Arjānī, *Jāwidān Khirad*, British Museum, London, MS. Or. 457; edited by Bihruz Sarvatiyan, Tehran: Musassasa-i-Muṭāla'-i-Dānishgāh-i McGill, 1976/1355 *sh*.

Ṭūsī, Naṣir al-Dīn, *Akhlāq-i Nāṣirī*, edited by Mojtaba Minavi and Ali Riza Haidari, Tehran: Shirkat Sahāmī Intishārāt-i Khwārizmī, 1976/1356 *sh*. English transl. G.M. Wickens, *The Nasirean Ethics*, London: George Allen & Unwin, 1964.

Ṭūsī, Niẓām al-Mulk, *Siyāsat Nāma/Siyar al-Mulūk*, edited by Hubert Darke, Tehran, 1962.

'Urfī, Muḥammad Jamāl al-Dīn Shīrāzī, *Dīwān*, Kanpur: Nawalkishor, 1915.

———, *Kulliyāt*, edited by Jawahar Vajdi, Tehran: Sanā'ī, 1990/1369 *sh*.

Vrind, *Vrind-Satsāi*, edited by Bhagwandeen, Prayag: Hindi Mandir, 1897.

Wālih Dāghistānī, 'Alī Qulī Khān, *Riyāẓ al-Shu'arā'*, Aligarh: Maulana Azad Library, Ms. Habibganj Fārsī 51-3-4; edited by Sharif Husain Qasemi, vol. I, Rampur: Raza Library, 2002.

Waṭwāṭ, Rashīd al-Dīn Balkhī, *Ḥadā'iq al-Siḥr Fī Daqā'iq al-shi'r*, edited by Abbas Iqbal, Tehran: Majlis, 1929/1308 *sh*.

## B. Secondary Sources

Abdul Haq, *Malik al-Shu'arā' Nuṣratī Bījāpūrī ke Ḥālāt aur Kalām*, Delhi: Anjuman-i-Taraqqī-ye Urdu, 1988.

Abdullah, S.M., *Adabiyāt-i Fārsī Meiñ Hindūwoñ Kā 'Hiṣṣa*, Lahore: Majlis-i Taraqqi-ye Adab, 1967.

———, *Mabāḥiṣ*, Delhi: Kutubkhāna Naẓīria, 1968.

———, *Fārsī Zubān-o-Adab: Majmūa'-i Maqālāt*, Lahore: Majlis-i Taraqqī-ye Adab, 1977.

Abidi, S. Amir Hasan, *Hindustānī Fārsī Adab*, edited by S.H. Qasemi, Delhi: Indo-Persian Society, 1984.

Acharya, Promesh, 'Pedagogy and Social Learning: *Tol* and *Pathshala* in Bengal', *Studies in History* (New Series), 10, 2 July-December, 1994, pp. 255–72.

Adeeb, Masud Husain Rizvi, *Lakhnau kā Shāhī Stage*, Lucknow: Adabistān, 1957.

———, 'Nawāz aur Shakuntalā Nātak', *Nuqoosh*, Lahore, June 1963.

———, 'Urdu kī Qadīm Lughat', reprinted in the journal of the Khudā Bakhsh Oriental Public Library, Patna, 1993, Special Number with Selections from *Hindustānī* Allahabad, 1931–48.

Ahmad, Aziz, *Islamic Modernism in India and Pakistan, 1857–1964*, London: Oxford University Press, 1967.

———, *An Intellectual History of Islam in India*, Edinburgh: Edinburgh University Press, 1969.

———, 'Safawid Poets and India', *Iran, Journal of the British Institute of Persian Studies*, 14, 1976, pp. 117–32.

———, 'Conversion to Islam in the Valley of Kashmir', *Central Asiatique Journal*, vol. 23, nos 1–2, 1979.

———, *Studies in Islamic Culture in the Indian Environment*, London: Oxford University Press, 1966, repr. Delhi: Oxford Unversity Press, 1998.

Ahmad, Dallal, 'The Origins and Objectives of Islamic Revivalist Thought, 1750–1850', *Journal of American Oriental Society*, vol. 113, no. 3, 1993, pp. 341–59.

Ahmad, Zahuruddin, *Pākistān meiñ Fārṣī Adab kī Tārīkh*, Lahore: Majlis-e Taraqqī-ye Adab, 1974.

Akhtar, Muhammad, *Mawdudi Ṣāḥib Akābir-i Ummat kī Naẓr meiñ*, Karachi: Kutubkhāna Maẓharī, 1976.

Algar, Hamid, transl., *Islam and Revolution: Writings and Declarations of Imam Khomeini*, Berkeley: Mizan Press, 1980.

Ali, M. Athar. *The Mughal Nobility Under Aurangzeb*, revised edn., Delhi: Oxford University Press, 1997.

al-Rasheed, Madavi, *A History of Saudi Arabia*, Cambridge: Cambridge University Press, 2002.

Amin, Shahid. 'On Retelling the Muslim Conquest of India', in Partha Chatterjee and Anjan Ghosh, eds, *History and the Present*, Delhi: Permanent Black, 2002.

Ansari, Muhammad Reza, *Bānī-ye Dars-i Niẓāmī: Mullā Niẓāmuddīn Muḥammad Farangī Maḥallī*, Lucknow: Farangī Maḥall Kitābghar, 1973.

———, *Taẕkira-i 'Ḥaẓrat Saiyid Sāḥib Bānsawī* (Urdu), Lucknow: Farangi Mahall, 1986.

Appleby, R. Scott, ed., *Spokesmen for the Despised: Fundamentalist*

*Leaders of the Middle East*, Chicago: University of Chicago Press, 1997.

Aquil Raziuddin, 'Sufi Cults, Politics and Conversion: The Chishtis of the Sultanate Period', in *Indian Historical Review*, vol. 22, nos 1–2, July 1995 and January 1996, pp. 190–7.

———, 'Miracles, Authority and Benevolence: Stories of *Karamat* in Sufi Literature of the Delhi Sultanate', Anup Taneja, ed., *Sufi Cults and the Evolution of Medieval Indian Culture*, Delhi: Indian Council of Historical Research, 2003.

Askari, S.H. and Ahmad, Q., *A Comprehensive History of Bihar*, vol. 2, Patna: K.P. Jaiswal Research Institute, 1984.

Ayalon, David, *Outsiders in the Lands of Islam: Mamluks, Mongols, and Eunuchs*, London: Variorum Reprints, 1988.

Azad, Muhammad Husain, *'Āb-e Ḥayāt: Shaping the Canon of Urdu Poetry*, English transl. and edition S.R. Faruqi and Frances Pritchett, Delhi: Oxford University Press, 2001.

Baig, M. Safdar Ali. 'Amir Khusrau: His Beliefs and the Sufi Tradition', in *Life, Times and works of Amir Khusrau: Commemoration Volume*, Delhi: Seventh Centenary National Amir Khusrau Society, 1975.

Baljon, J.M.S., *Religion and Thought of Shah Wali Allah Dihlawi, 1703–1762*, Leiden: E.J. Brill, 1986.

Bayly, Susan, *Saints, Goddesses and Kings: Muslims and Christians in South Indian Society*, Cambridge: Cambridge University Press, 1984.

———, 'Islam and State Power in Pre-colonial South India', *Itinerario*, vol. 12, no. 1, 1989, pp. 143–64.

Behl, Aditya and Simon Wieghtman, with Shyam M. Pandey, Introduction to their edition of *Madhūmālatī of Mīr Sayyid Manjhan Shattārī Rājgīrī*, Delhi: Oxford University Press, 2000.

Behl, Aditya, 'Rasa and Romance: The *Madhumālatī* of Shaikh Mañjhan Shattārī', Ph.D. dissertation, University of Chicago, 1995.

Binder, Leonard, 'Al-Ghazali's Theory of Islamic Government', *The Muslim World*, vol. XLV, no. 3, July, 1995.

Blochet, Edgar, *Catalogue des Manuscripts Persans*, vol. II, Paris: Leroux, 1912.

Blochmann, H., 'Preface to the English transl. of the *'A'īn-i Akbarī'*. reprint, Delhi: Oriental Reprints, 1965.

———, 'Contributions to Persian Lexicography', *Journal of the Royal Asiatic Society of Bengal*, vol. 37, part 1, 1868–9, pp. 1–72.

Bosworth, C.E., *The Ghaznavids*, Edinburgh: Edinburgh University Press, 1963.

———, 'The Development of Persian Culture under the Early Ghaznavids', in *Iran: Journal of the British Institute of Persian Studies*, vol. 6, 1968, pp. 33–44.

Brown, Anthony, *Oil, God, and Gold: The Story of Aramco and the Saudi Kings*, Boston: Houghton Mifflin, 1999.

Brown, Daniel W., *Rethinking Tradition in Modern Islamic Thought*, Cambridge: Cambridge University Press, 1996.

Browne, Edward G., *A Literary History of Persia*, vol. II, reprint, Cambridge: Cambridge University Press, 1969.

Calmard, Jean, 'Les Rituels shiites et le Pouvoir, L'imposition de shiisme safavide: eulogies et malediction canoniques' in Jean Calmard, ed., *Etudes Safavides*, Paris-Tehran: Institut Francais de Recherche en Iran, 1993.

Canfield, Robert L., ed., *Turko-Persian in Historic Perspective*, Cambridge: Cambridge University Press, 1991.

Chakrabarti, Kunal, *Religious Process: The Puranas and the Making of a Regional Tradition*, Delhi: Oxford University Press, 2001.

Chandra, Satish, *Parties and Politics at the Mughal Court, 1707–1740*, repr. Delhi: Peoples Publishing House, 1972.

Chandra, Savitri, *Social Life and Concepts in Medieval Hindi Bhakti Poetry: A Socio-Cultural Study*, Delhi: Chandayan, 1983.

Chattopadhyaya, B.D., *The Making of Early Medieval India*, Delhi: Oxford University Press, 1996.

Cohn, Bernhard, 'The Command of Language and the Language of Command' in Ranajit Guha, ed., *Subaltern Studies IV: Writings on South Asian History and Society*, Delhi: Oxford University Press, 1984, pp. 284–95.

Cole, J.R.I., *Roots of North Indian Shi'ism in Iran and Iraq: Religion and State in Awadh, 1722–1859*, Delhi: Oxford University Press, 1989.

Coulson, N.J., *History of Islamic Law*, Edinburgh: Edinburgh University Press, 1964.

Dalmia, Vasudha, *The Nationalization of Hindu Traditions: Bharatendu Harischandra and Nineteenth-century Banaras*, Delhi: Oxford University Press, 1997.

Damrel, David W., 'The "Naqshbandi Reaction Reconsidered', in *Beyond Turk and Hindu: Rethinking Religious Identities in Islamicate South Asia*, Gainesville, Fl: University Press of Florida, 2000, pp. 176–98.

de Boer, T.J., *The History of the Philosophy of Islam*, English translation, Edward R. Jones, London: Luzac & Company, 1933, reprint, New York, 1967.

De Corancez, L.A.O., *The History of Wahhabis, from their Origin until the End of 1809*, Reading, UK: Garnet Publishing, 1995.

Dehlavi, Nazir Ahmad, *Ibn ul-Waqt*, English translation by Muhammad Zakir as *Man of the Moment*, Delhi: Orient Longman, 2001.

Derrett, J. Duncan, *Religion, Law and the State in India*, London: Faber and Faber, 1968.

Digby, Simon, 'Hawk and Dove in Sufi Combat', *Pembroke Papers*, I, 1990.

———, 'Shaykh 'Abd al-Quddūs Gangohī', *Medieval India: A Miscellany*, vol. III, Bombay: Asia Publishing House, 1979, pp. 1–60.

———, '*Qalandars* and Related Groups: Elements of Social Deviance in the Religious Life of the Delhi Sultanate of the 13th and 14th Centuries', *Islam in Asia*, vol. 1, edited by Yohanan Friedmann, Boulder, Colo.: Westview Press, 1984.

———, 'Sufi Shaykh and the Sultan: A Conflict of Claims to Authority' *Iran*, XXVII, 1990, pp. 71–81.

Eaton, Richard M., *The Sufis of Bijapur: Social Roles of the Sufis in Medieval India, 1300–1700*, Princeton: Princeton University Press, 1978.

———, *The Rise of Islam and the Bengal Frontier, 1204–1760*, Berkeley: University of California Press, 1993.

———, *Essays on Islam and Indian History*, Delhi: Oxford University Press, 2001.

———, ed., *India's Islamic Traditions*, Delhi: Oxford University Press, 2003.

Eickelman, Dale F., and James Piscatori, *Muslim Politics*, Princeton: Princeton University Press, 1996.

Ernst, Carl W., *Eternal Garden: Mysticism, History and Politics at a South Asian Sufi Center*, Albany: SUNY Press, 1992.

Esposito, John L., *Islam and Politics*, 3rd edition, Syracuse, NY: Syracuse University Press, 1991.

———, *Islam: The Straight Path*, New York: Oxford University Press, 1991.

———, *The Islamic Threat: Myth or Reality?* New York: Oxford University Press, 1999.

Ethé, H., *Catalogue of the Persian Manuscripts in the Library of the India Office*, vol. 1, Oxford: Horace Hart, Printer to the University, 1903.

Euben, Roxanne L., *Enemy in the Mirror: Islamic Fundamentalism and the Limits of Modern Rationalism*, Princeton: Princeton University Press, 1999.

Ewing, Kaherine P., '*Malangs* of the Punjab: Intoxication or *Adab* as the Path of God', *Moral Conduct and Authority: The Place of Adab in South Asian Islam*, edited by Barbara D. Metcalf, Berkeley: University of California Press, 1984, pp. 357–71.

———, *Shari'at and Ambiguity in South Asian Islam*, Delhi: Oxford University Press, 1988.

Fakhry, Majid, *A History of Islamic Philosophy*, New York: Columbia University Press, 1970.

———, *Ethical Theories in Islam*, Leiden: E.J. Brill, 1994.

Farangi Mahalli, Muhammad Abdul Bari, *Fuyūẓ-i Haẓrat Bānsa* (Urdu), Lucknow: Isha'at-ul-Ulum Press, Farangi Mahall.

Farooqi, Naimur Rahman, *Mughal–Ottoman Relations: A Study of Political and Diplomatic Relations between Mughal India and the Ottoman Empire, 1556–1748*, Delhi: Idārah-i Adabiyāt-i Dellī, 1989.

Faruqi, Burhan A., *The Mujaddid's Conception of Tawhid*, Lahore: Muhammad Ashraf, 1940.

Faruqi, S.R., *Urdu kā Ibtadā'i Zamāna: Adabī Tahẕīb-o-Tārīkh ke Pehlū*, Karachi: Aaj Publications, 1999.

Faruqi, Ziyaul Hasan, *The Deoband School and the Demand for Pakistan*, New York: Asia Publishing House, 1963.

Faruqui, Abdul Hamid, *Chandra Bhan Brahman: Life and Works with a Critical Edition of His Diwan*, Ahmedabad: Khalid Shahin Faruqui, 1966.

Fischell, Walter J., 'Jews and Judaism at the Court of the Mughal Emperors in Medieval India', *Proceedings of the American Academy for Jewish Research*, vol. 18, 1948–49, pp. 133–77.

Fisher, Michael H., *A Clash of Cultures: Awadh, the British, and the Mughals*, Delhi: Manohar Publications, 1987.

Foltz, R., 'Two Seventeenth Century Central Asian Travellers to Mughal India', *Journal of the Royal Asiatic Society*, third series, vol. 6, part 3, October 1996, pp. 367–77.

Fouchecour, Charles Henry, *Moralia: Les notions morales dans la litterature persane du 3/9 au 7/13 siecle*, Paris: Institut Français de Recherche en Iran, 1986.

Fraser, Cary, 'In Defense of Allah's Realm: Religion and Statecraft in Saudi Foreign Policy Strategy', *Transnational Religion and Fading States*, edited by Susanne H. Rudolph and James Piscatori, Boulder, Colo.: Westview Press, 1997, pp. 212–40.

Friedmann, Yohanan, *Shyakh Ahmad Sirhindi, An Outline of His Thought and a Study of His Image in the Eyes of Posterity*, Montreal: McGill University, Institute of Islamic Studies, 1971.

———, 'Medieval Muslim Views of Indian Religions' ,*Journal of American Oriental Society*, vol. 95, 1975.

———, *Tolerance and Coercion in Islam: Interfaith Relations in the Muslim Tradition*, Cambridge: Cambridge University Press, 2003.

Ghani, Abdul, 'Tanqīdī Shu'ūr kā Irtiqā', S.F. Mahmud (general editor), *Tārīkh-i Adabiyāt-i Musalmānān-i Pākistān-o-Hind, vol. 4, Fārsī 'Adab II*, edited by Maqbul Badakhashani, Lahore: Punjab University, 1971, pp. 455–71.

Ghani, M.A., *A History of Persian Language and Literature at the Mughal Court (Babur to Akbar)*, in three parts, Allahabad: Indian Press, 1929–30.

———, *Pre-Mughal Persian Poetry in Hindustan*, Allahabad: Allahabad Law Journal Press, 1941.

Ghosh, J.C. *Bengali Literature*, London: Oxford University Press, 1948.

Gibb, H.A.R., *Studies on the Civilization of Islam*, edited by Stanford Shaw and William Polk, London: Routledge & Kegan Paul, 1962.

Gilmartin, David, 'Customary Law and *Sharī'at* in British Punjab', in *Sharī'at and Ambiguity in South Asian Islam*, edited by Katherine P. Ewing, Delhi: Oxford University Press, 1988, pp. 43–62.

———, and Bruce Lawrence, eds, *Beyond Turk and Hindu: Rethinking Religious Identities in Islamicate South Asia*, Gainesville, University of Florida Press, 2000.

Golchin Ma'ani, Ahmad, *Kārvān-i Hind*, 2 vols, Mashhad: Āstan-i Quds Riẓavī, 1990.

Gopal, S. and R. Champakalakshmi, eds, *Tradition, Dissent and Ideology: Essays in Honour of Romila Thapar*, Delhi: Oxford University Press, 1996.

Habbi Joseph & Hikmat Najib, Introduction to their edition of Hunayn bin Ishaq's *Aristotle's Meteorology*, Baghdad: Majma' al-Lughat al-Suryāniyah, 1976.

Habib, Irfan, 'For a Political Theory of the Mughal Empire: A Study of the Ideas of Abu'l Fazl', *Proceedings of the Indian History Congress*, 59th Session, Patiala, 1998, pp. 332–53.

Habib, M., 'Chishti Mystic Records of the Sultanate Period', K.A. Nizami, ed., *Politics and Society During the Early Medieval Period*, vol. I, Delhi: Peoples Publishing House, 1974.

———, 'Life and Thought of Ziauddin Barani', *Politics and Society during the Early Medieval India*, edited by K.A. Nizami, Delhi: Peoples Publishing House, 1974.

Habibullah, A.B.M., *The Foundation of Muslim Rule in India*, reprint, Allahabad: Central Book Depot, 1976.

Hadi, Nabi, *Mughaloñ ke Malik al-Shu'arā'*, Allahabad: Asrār Karīmī Press, 1978.

Hali, Khwaja Altaf Husain, *Ḥayāt-i Jāved*, Lahore: Ishrat Publishing House, 1965.

Hallaq, Wael B., 'Was the Gate of *Ijtihad* Closed'? *International Journal of Middle Eastern Studies*, vol. 16, no. 4, 1984, pp. 3–41.

———, *Law and Legal Theory in Classical and Medieval Islam*, Aldershot, UK: Variorum, 1994.

———, *A History of Islamic Legal Theories: An Introduction to Sunnī Usūl al-Fiqh*, Cambridge: Cambridge University Press, 1997.

———, *Authority, Continuity, and Change in Islamic Law*, Cambridge: Cambridge University Press, 2001.

Halliday, Fred, *Islam and the Myth of Confrontation: Religion and Politics in the Middle East*, New York: I.B. Tauris, 2003.

Hamidi, Khalil Ahmad, *Āftāb-i Tāza*, Lahore: Idāra-i Ma'ārif-i Islāmī, 1993.

Haq, Mohammad Enamul, *A History of Sufis in Bengal*, Dacca: Asiatic Society of Bangladesh, 1975.

Hardy, Peter, *Historians of Medieval India: Studies in Indo-Muslim Historical Writing*, London: Luzac, 1960.

———, 'Force and Violence in Indo-Persian Writing on History and Government in Medieval India', *Islamic Society and Culture: Essays in Honour of Professor Aziz Ahmad*, edited by Milton Israel and N.K. Wagle, Delhi: Manohar, 1983, pp. 165–208.

———, 'Didactical Historical Writing in Indian Islam', in *Islam in Asia*, vol. 1, edited by Yohanan Friedmann, Boulder, Colo: Westview Press, 1984.

Hasan, Hadi, *Mughal Poetry: Its Cultural and Historical Value*, Madras: Islamic Literary Society, 1952.

Hasan, Mohibbul, *Babur: Founder of the Mughal Empire in India*, Delhi: Manohar Publications, 1985.

Hasan, S. Nurul, '*Ṣaḥīfa-i Na't-i Muḥammadī* of Zia-ud-Din Barani', *Medieval India Quarterly*, 1, 3–4, 1950, pp. 100–6.

Hasrat, Bikrama Jit, *Dara Shikoh: Life and Works*, Calcutta: Vishwabharati, 1953.

Hourani, G.F., *Reason and Tradition in Islamic Ethics*, Cambridge: Cambridge University Press, 1985.

Hovannisian, Richard G. and George Sabagh, ed., *The Persian Presence in the Islamic World*, Cambridge: Cambridge University Press, 1998.

Husain, S. Azizuddin, 'Political Ideas of Mir Saiyid Ali Hamadani', *Hamdard Islamicus*, vol. 13, no. 4, 1992.

Husaini, Syeda Bilqis Fatema, *A Critical Study of Indo-Persian Literature 1414–1526*, New Delhi: CAAL/School of Languages, Jawaharlal Nehru University, 1988.

Ikran, S.M., *Rūd-i Kauṣar* (Urdu), reprint, Delhi: Adabī Dunyā, n.d.

Islam, Riazul, 'Akbar's Intellectual Contacts with Iran', Milton Israel and N.K. Wagle, eds, *Islamic Culture and Society: Essays in Honour of Aziz Ahmad*, Delhi: Manohar Publications, 1983, pp. 351–73.

Islam, Zafarul, 'Nature of Landed Property in Mughal India: Views of an Eighteenth Century Jurist', *Proceedings of the Indian History Congress*, 36th Session, Aligarh, 1975, pp. 301–9.

Israel, Milton and N.K. Wagle, eds, *Islamic Society and Culture*, Delhi: Manohar Publications, 1983.

Ivanow, Wladimir, *Descriptive Catalogue of the Persian Manuscripts in the Collection of the Asiatic Society of Bengal*, vol. I, Calcutta: Asiatic Society of Bengal, 1924.

Jafar Sharif, *Qanun-i Islam*, English transl. by G.A. Harklots, reprint, London, 1972.

Jalal, Ayesha, *Self and Sovereignty: Individual and Community in South Asian Islam since 1850*, London: Routledge, 2000.

Jalbani, G.N., *Teachings of Shah Waliullah*, Lahore: Sh. Muhammad Ashraf, 1967.

Jalibi, Jamil, *Tārīkh-i Adab-i Urdu*, vols I and II, 5th edn., Delhi: Educational Publishing House, 1993.

Karamustafa, Ahmet T., *God's Unruly Friends: Dervish Groups in the Islamic Later Middle Period, 1200–1550*, Salt Lake City: University of Utah Press, 1994.

Karimuddin, *Maulānā Mawdūdī ke Ghalaṯ Naẕariyāt: az rū'ye Qur'ān, Ḥadīṣ, Sunnat-i Anbiyā' aur 'aql-i 'āmm*, Multān: Jāved Academy, 1976.

Khalidi, Tarif, *Arabic Historical Thought in the Classical Period*, Cambridge: Cambridge University Press, 1994.

Khan, I.A., 'The Turko-Mongol Theory of Kingship', *Medieval India: A Miscellany*, vol., II, Bombay: Asia Publishing House, 1972, pp. 8–18.

———, 'Shaikh Abd ul-Quddus Gangohi: A Reapprisal of His Relations with the Political Authorities,*Medieval India: A Miscellany*, IV, 1977.

Khan, Muhammad Ishaq, 'The Impact of Islam on Kashmir in the Sultanate Period (1320–1586)', *Indian Economic and Social History Review*, 23, 2, 1986.

———, *Kashmir's Transition to Islam: The Role of the Muslim Rishis (Fifteenth to Eighteenth Centuries)*, Delhi: Manohar Publications, 1994.

Khan, Mumtaz Ali, *Some Important Persian Prose Writings of the Thirteenth Century A.D. in India*, Aligarh: Department of Persian, Aligarh Muslim University, 1970.

Khatun, Rehana, *Aḥwāl-i 'Aṣār-i Sirāj al-Dīn 'Alī Khān 'Ārzū*, Delhi: Persian Department, University of Delhi, 1987.

King, Christopher R., *One Language, Two Scripts: The Hindi Movement in Nineteenth Century North India*, Delhi: Oxford University Press, 1994.

Kirmani, Waris, *Dreams Forgotten: An Anthology of Indo-Persian Poetry*, Aligarh: Department of Persian, Aligarh Muslim University, 1984.

Koprulu, Fuäd, 'Babur-Literary Works', *Encyclopedia of Islam*, New Edition, vol. I, Part-2, pp. 848–85.

Kumar, Sunil, 'The Value of '*Ādāb al-Mulūk* as a Historical Source: An Insight into the Ideals and Expectations of Islamic Society in the Middle Period (AD 945–1500)', *The Indian Economic and Social History Review*, vol. 22, no. 3, July-September 1985, pp. 307–27.

———, 'The Emergence of the Delhi Sultanate', Ph.D. dissertation, Duke University, 1992.

———, *The Present in Delhi's Past*, Delhi: Three Essays, 2002.

Lambton, A.K.S., *Theory and Practice in Medieval Persian Government*, London: Variorium, 1980.

———, *State and Government in Medieval Islam: An Introduction to the Study of Islamic Political Theory: The Jurists*, London: Oxford University Press, 1981.

Latif, Syed Muhammad, *Lahore: Its History, Architectural Remains and Antiquities*, Lahore: New Imperial Press, 1892; reprint, Lahore: Oriental Publishers, 1981.

Lawrence, Bruce B., *Defenders of God: The Fundamentalist Revolt Against the Modern Age*, Columbia, SC: University of South Carolina Press, 1995.

———, *Shattering the Myth: Islam beyond Violence*, Princeton: Princeton University Press, 1998.

———, 'An Indo-Persian Perspective on the Significance of Early Sufi Masters', in Leonard Lewisohn, ed., *Classical Persian Sufism from its Origins to Rumi*, London: Khanqahi Nimatullahi Publications, 1993, pp. 19–32.

Lelyveld, David., *Aligarh's First Generation: Muslim Solidarity and English Education in Northern India, 1875–1900*, Princeton: Princeton University Press, 1997.

Lewis, Bernard, *The Assasins: A Radical Sect in Islam*, London: Weidenfeld & Nicolson, 1967.

———, *The Political Language of Islam*, Chicago: University of Chicago Press, 1988.

———, 'Roots of Muslim Rage', *Atlantic Monthly*, September 1990.

———, *What Went Wrong: Western Impact and Middle Eastern Response*, New York: Oxford University Press, 2002.

———, *The Crisis of Islam: Holy War and Unholy Terror*, New York: Modern Library, 2003.

Lloyd, William & Alexander Gerard, *Narrative of Journey from Cawnpore to the Boorendoo Pass . . .*, vol. I, London: J. Madden, 1841.

Maclean, Derryl N., 'Real Man and the False Man at the Court of Akbar: The *Majālis* of Shaykh Mustafa Gujarati' in David Gilmartin and Bruce B. Lawrence, eds, *Beyond Turk and Hindu: Rethinking Religious Identities in Islamicate India*, Gainesville Fl: University of Florida Press, 2000.

Madani, Husain Ahmad, *Muttaḥida Qaumiyat aur Islām*, New Delhi: Qaumī Ektā Trust, 1972.

———, *Pakistan Kyā Hai?*, parts 1 and 2, Delhi: *Jam'īyāt-i 'Ulamā'-i Hind*, 1946.

Madelung, Wilfred, *Religious Trends in Early Islamic Iran*, London: Weidenfeld & Nicolson, 1967.

Mahmud, S.F. (general editor), *Tārīkh-i Adabiyāt-i Musalmānān-i Pākistān-o-Hind, Vol. 4, Fārsī Adab II*, edited by Maqbul Badakhshani; *Volume 5, Fārsī Adab III*, edited by S.F. Mahmud, S.W.H. Abidi and A. Ghani, Lahore: Punjab University, 1971 and 1972.

Malik, Jamal, *Colonialization of Islam: Dissolution of Traditional Institutions in Pakistan*, New Delhi: Manohar, 1996.

Manz, Beatrice Forbes, *The Rise and Rule of Tamerlane*, Cambridge: Cambridge University Press, 1989.

Marlow, Louise. *Hierarchy and Egalitarianism in Islamic Thought in the Classical Period*, Cambridge: Cambridge University Press, 1997.

Masud, M. Khalid, 'The Doctrine of *Siyāsa* in Islamic Law', *Recht van de Islam*, vol. 18, 2001, pp. 1–29.

Mawdudi, Sayyid Abu'l Ala, *Islāmī Riyāsat*, edited by Khurshid Ahmad, Lahore: Islamic Publications, 1962.

Mazumdar, B.P., *Socio-Economic History of Northern India, 1030–1194*, Calcutta: Firma Mukhopadhyaya, 1960.

Metcalf, Barbara D., ed., *Moral Conduct and Authority: The Place of Adab in South Asian Islam*, Berkeley: University of California Press, 1984.

———, 'Presidential Address: Too Little and Too Much: Reflections on Muslims in the History of India', *Journal of Asian Studies*, vol. 54, no. 4, November 1995, pp. 951–67.

———, *Islamic Revival in British India: Deoband, 1860–1900*, Princeton: Princeton University Press, 1982. Also paperback edition, Delhi: Oxford University Press, 2002.

Minault, Gail, *The Khilafat Movement: Religious Symbolism and Political Mobilization in India*, New York: Columbia University Press, 1982.

Mirza, Muhammad Wahid, *Amir Khusrau*, Allahabad: Hindustani Academy, 1949.

———, *The Life and Works of Amir Khusrau*, reprint, Delhi: Idārah-i Adabiyāt-i Dellī, 1974.

Mitchell, Richard P., *The Society of the Muslim Brothers*, London: Oxford University Press, 1969.

Momin, Muhiuddin, *The Chancellery and Persian Epistolography under the Mughals: From Babur to Shah Jahan (1526–1658)*, Calcutta: Iran Society, 1971.

Mottahedeh, R.P., 'The *Shu'ūbiyah* Controversy and the Social History of Early Islamic Iran', *International Journal of Middle Eastern Studies*, vol. 7, 1976, pp. 161–82.

———, 'Mawlā', *Encyclopedia of Islam*, vol. VI, New Edition, Leiden: E.J. Brill, 1991.

Mujeeb, M., *The Indian Muslims*, repr. Delhi: Munshiram Manoharlal, 1995.

Mujtabai, F., *Aspects of Hindu-Muslim Cultural Relations*, Delhi: National Book Bureau, 1978.

Munzavi, Ahmad, *Fihrist-i Nuskhahā-i Khaṭṭī-ye Fārsī*, vol. II, part 2, Islamabad: Markaz-i Taḥqīqāt-i Fārsī-i Iran-o-Pakistan, 1984.

Nadwi, Najib Ashraf, *Muqaddima-i Ruq'āt-i 'Ālamgīrī* (An Introduction to the Letters of Alamgir), Azamgarh: Dār al-Muṣannifīn, 1981.

Nadwi, Abdus Salam, *'Hukamā'-i Islām*, vol. II, Azamgarh: Dār al-Muṣannifīn, 1954.

Nadwi, Abul Hasanat, *Hindustān Kī Qadīm Darsgāheiñ*, Azamgarh: Dār al-Muṣannifīn, 1971.

Nadwi, Saiyid Abu'l Hasan Ali, *Insānī Dunyā par Musalmānoñ ke 'Urūj-o-Zawāl kā Aṡar*, Karachi: Majlis-i Nashrīyāt-i Islām, 1974.

Nadwi, Saiyid Sulaiman, 'Khilāfat aur Hindustān', in *Maqālāt-i Sulaimān*, Azamgarh: Dār al-Muṣannifīn, 1966, pp. 112–84.

Najjar, Fauzi M., '*Siyasa* in Islamic Political Philosophy', Michael E. Marmura, ed., *Islamic Theology and Philosophy*, Albany: Suny Press, 1984.

Nandi, R.N., 'Client, Ritual and Conflict in the Early Brahmanical Order', *Indian Historical Review*, vol. 6, nos 1–2, 1979–1980, pp. 164–78.

Narayanan, Vasudha, 'Religious Vocabulary and Regional Identity: A Study of the Tamil *Cirappuranam*', *Beyond Turk and Hindu: Rethinking Religious Identities in Islamicate South Asia*, Gainesville, Fl: University Press of Florida, 2000, pp. 74–97.

Nasr, S.V.R., *The Vanguard of the Islamic Revolution: The Jama'at-i Islami of Pakistan*, Berkeley: University of California Press, 1994.

———, *Mawdudi and the Making of Islamic Revivalism*, New York: Oxford University Press, 1996.

Nizami, Azra, *Socio-religious Outlook of Abu'l Faẓl*, London: Asia Publishing House, 1972.

Nizami, K.A., 'Fakir', *The Encyclopaedia of Islam*, new edition, Leiden: Brill, 2, pp. 757–78.

———, *'Hayāt-i Shaikh 'Abd al-Haqq Muḥaddis̤ Dihlawī*, Delhi: Nadwat al-Muṣannifīn, 1953.

———, *Salāṯīn-i Dihlī ke Maẕhabī Rujḥnāt*, Delhi: Nadwat-al-Muṣannifīn, 1958.

———, *Studies in Medieval Indian History and Culture*, Allahabad: Kitāb Maḥal, 1966.

———, *Some Aspects of Religion and Politics in India during the 13th Century*, reprint, Delhi: Idārah-i Adabiyāt-i Dellī, 1974.

———, *Tārīkhi Mashā'ikh-i Chisht*, vol. v, Delhi: Idārah-i Adabiyāt-i Dellī, 1984.

———, *Akbar and Religion*, Delhi: Idārah-i Adabiyāt-i Dellī, 1989.

Numani Shibli, *Shi'r al-'Ajam, III*, Reprint, Azamgarh: Dār al-Muṣannifīn, 1991.

Numani, Manzur Ahmad, *Shaikh Maḥammad bin 'Abd al-Wahhāb ke Khilāf, Propaganda aur Hindustān ke 'Ulama'-i Haqq par Uske As̤arāt*, Lucknow: Kutubkhāna al-Furqān, 1978.

Petievich, Carla, *Assemly of Rivals: Delhi, Lucknow, and the Urdu Ghazal*, Delhi: Manohar, 1992.

Phukan, Shantanu, 'Through a Persian Prism: Hindi and *Padmāvat* in the Mughal Imagination', Ph.D. dissertation, University of Chicago, 2000.

Prashad, Durga, *Makhzan-i Akhlāq*, Sandila: Maṭba' Quin Press, 1899.

Pritchett, Frances, 'A Long History of Urdu Literary Culture, Part 2: Histories, Performances, and Masters', Sheldon Pollock, ed., *Literary Cultures in History: Reconstructions from South Asia*, Berkeley: University of California Press, 2003, pp. 864–911.

Qadri, Fozail Ahmad, *Tārīkh-i Mashrab-i Shattār*, Aligarh: Educational Book House, 1996.

Qanungo, Kalika Ranjan, *Dara Shukoh*, vol. I, Biography, Calcutta: S.C. Sarkar & Sons Ltd., 1952.

Rafiqui, A.Q., *History of Sufism in Kashmir*, Delhi: Munshiram Manoharlal, n.d.

Rahman, Fazlur, *Islam*, London: Weidenfeld & Nicolson, 1966.

———, *Islam and Modernity: Transformation of an Intellectual Tradition*, Chicago: University of Chicago Press, 1982.

———, *Revival and Reform in Islam: A Study of Islamic Fundamentalism*, Oxford: One World, 2000.

Rai, Alok, *Hindi Nationalism*, Hyderabad: Orient Longman, 2001.

Rai, Amrit, *A House Divided: The Origin and Development of Hindi/Hindvi*, Delhi: Oxford University Press, 1984.

Rashid, A., *Society and Culture in Medieval India*, Calcutta: Firma Mukhopadhyay, 1969.

Razia Akbar, *Sharḥ-i Aḥwāl-o-Āṣār-i Bābā Fighānī Shīrāzī*, Hyderabad: Shālīmār Publications, 1974.

Richards, J.F., 'Norms of Comportment among Imperial Mughal Officers', *Moral Conduct and Authority: The Place of Adab in South Asian Islam*, edited by Barbara D. Metcalf, Berkeley: University of California Press, 1984, pp. 255–89.

———, *The Mughal Empire: The New Cambridge History of India*, 1.5, Cambridge: Cambridge University Press, 1993.

———, 'The Formulation of Imperial Authority under Akbar and Jahangir', M. Alam and S. Subrahmanyam , eds, *The Mughal State, 1526–1750*, Delhi: Oxford University Press, 1998, 126–67.

Rieu, C., *Catalogue of the Persian Manuscripts in the British Museum, III*, London: 1883.

Rizvi, S.A.A., *A History of Sufism in India*. 2 vols, Delhi: Munshiram Manoharlal, 1978.

———, *A Socio-Intellectual History of the Isna Ashari Shi'is in India*, 2 vols, Canberra: Ma'rifat Publications, Delhi: Munshiram Manoharlal, 1986.

———, *The Muslim Revivalist Movements in India During the Sixteenth and Seventeenth Centuries*, Agra: University of Agra, 1965.

———, *Religious and Intellectual History of the Muslims in Akbar's*

*Reign, 1556–1605, with Special Reference to Abul Fazl*, Delhi: Munshiram Manoharlal, 1975.

Robinson, Francis, *Islam and Muslim History in South Asia*, Delhi: Oxford University Press, 2000.

———, *The 'Ulama of Farangi Mahall and Islamic Culture in South Asia*, Delhi: Permanent Black, 2001.

Rosenthal, E.I.J., *Political Thought in Medieval Islam: An Introductory Outline*, Cambridge: Cambridge University Press, 1958.

Roy, Olivier, *The Failure of Political Islam*, Cambridge: Harvard University Press, 1994.

Rudolph, Susanne H. and James Piscatori, eds, *Transnational Religions and Fading States*, Boulder, Colo.: Westview Press, 1997.

Rypka, Jan, *History of Iranian Literature*, English transl. by P. van Popta-Hope, Dordrecht (Holland): D. Reidel Publishing Company, 1968.

Sabahuddin Abdur Rahman, Syed, *Amir Khusrau as Genius*, Delhi: Idārah-i Adabiyāt-i Dellī, 1982.

Safa, Zabihulla, *Tārīkh-i Adabiyāt-i Iran*, pt. I, Tehran: Intishārāt-i Firdausī, 1956/1335 *sh*.

———, *Mukhtaṣar dar Tārīkh-i Taḥawwul-i Naẓm-i Fārsī*, Tehran: Kitāb-furūshī-ye Ibn-i Sīna, 1959/1338 *sh*.

Salik, Abdul Majid, *Muslim Ṡaqāfat Hindustān Meiñ*, Lahore: Majlis-i Taraqqī-ye Adab, 1957.

Sanyal, Usha, *Devotional Islam and Politics in British India: Ahmad Riza Khan Barelwi and His Movement, 1870–1920*, Delhi: Oxford University Press, 1996.

Sarkar, Jadunath, *History of Aurangzeb*, vol. IV, Calcutta: M.C. Sarkar and Sons, 1919.

Sayili, Aydin, *The Observatory in Islam and its place in the General History of the Observatory*, Ankara: Türk Tārīh Kurumu Basimevī, 1960, revised edn, North Stratford: Ayer Co. Publishers, 1981.

Schacht, Joseph, *An Introduction to Islamic Law*, Oxford: Oxford University Press, 1964.

Schimmel, Annemarie, *Islamic Literatures of India*, vol. 7, part 5 of *A History of Indian Literature*, edited by Jan Gonda, Wiesbaden: Otto Harrassowitz, 1973.

———, *Mystical Dimensions of Islam*, Chapel Hill, NC: University of North Carolina Press, 1975.

Sen, Dinesh Chandra, *History of Bengali Language and Literature*, Calcutta: University of Calcutta, 1954.

———, *Folk Literature of Bengal*, Calcutta: University of Calcutta, 1920; reprint, Delhi: Oriental Reprints, 1982.

Shackle, Christopher, 'Beyond Turk and Hindu: Crossing the Boundaries in Indo-Muslim Romance', *Beyond Turk and Hindu: Rethinking Religious Identities in Islamicate South Asia*, Gainesville, Fl: University Press of Florida, 2000, pp. 55–73.

Sharif, M.M., ed., *A History of Muslim Philosophy*, vol. I, Weisbaden: Otto Harrassowitz, 1963.

Sharma, R.S., *Social Change in Early Medieval India*, Delhi: Peoples Publishing House, 1969.

Sharma, Sri Ram, *The Religions Policy of the Mughal Emperors*, revised edn., London: Asia Publishing House, 1972.

Sherwani, H.K., *Muhammad Quli Qutb Shah: Founder of Haiderabad*, Bombay: Asia Publishing House, 1967.

———, and Joshi, P.M. eds, *History of Medieval Deccan*, vol. I, Hyderabad: Publication Bureau, Government of Andhra Pradesh, 1973.

Siddiqi, Abdul Majid, *Tārīkh-i Golconda*, Hyderabad: Idārah-i Adabiyāt, 1964.

Siddiqi, Muhammad Shakil Ahmad, *Amīr 'Ḥasan Sijzī Dihlawī: Ḥayāt aur Adabī Khidmāt*, Lucknow: Nāmī Press, 1979.

Siddiqi, Muhammad Suleman, *The Bahmani Sufis*, Delhi: Idārah-i Adabiyāt-i Dellī, 1989.

Singha, Radhika, *A Despotism of Law: Crime and Justice in Early Colonial India*, Delhi: Oxford University Press, 1998.

Sivan, Emmanuel, *Radical Islam: Medieval Theology and Modern Politics*, enlarged edition, New Haven: Yale University Press, 1990.

Stewart, Tony K., 'Alternative Structures: Satya *Pīr* on the Frontiers of Bengal', *Beyond Turk and Hindu: Rethinking Religious Identities in Islamicate South Asia*, Gainesville, Fl: University Press of Florida, 2000, pp. 21–54.

Stroumsa, Sara, *Freethinkers of Medieval Islam: Ibn al-Rāwandī, Abū Bakr al-Rāzī and Their Impact on Islamic Thought*, Leiden: E.J. Brill, 1999.

Tayyib, Muhammad, *'Ulama-i Deoband ka Dīnī Rukh aur Maslakī Mizāj*, Deoband: Shu'ba-i Nashr-o-Ishā'at, Dār ul-Ulūm, 1995.

ter Haar, J.G., *Follower and Heir of the Prophet: Shaykh Ahmad Sirhindi (1564–1624) as a Mystic*, Leiden: Het Oosters Instituut, 1992.

Thapar, Romila, *Somanatha: The Many Voices of a History*, Delhi: Penguin Books, 2004.

Titus, Murray T., *Indian Islam*, London: Oxford University Press, 1930; revised edn., *Islam in India and Pakistan: A Religious History of Islam in India*, Calcutta: YMCA Publishing House, 1959, and Karachi: Royal Book Co., 1990.

Trimingham, J.S., *The Sufi Orders of Islam*, London: Oxford University Press, 1971.

Troll, Christian W., *Sayyid Ahmad Khan: A Reinterpretation of Muslim Theology*, Delhi: Vikas Publishing House, 1978.

Umar, Muhammad, *Islam in Northern India During the Eighteenth Century*, Delhi: Munshiram Manoharlal, 1993.

van der Veer, Peter, *Religious Nationalism: Hindus and Muslims in India*, Berkeley: University of California Press, 1994.

Vassie, Roderic, ' 'Abd al-Rahman Chishti and the *Bhagvadgita*: "Unity of Religion Theory in Practice" ', Leonard Lewisohn, ed., *The Heritage of Sufism*, vol. 2, Oxford: One World, 1999.

———, 'Persian Interpretations of the *Bhagvadgita* in the Mughal Period, with Special Reference to the Version of Abd al-Rahman Chishti', unpublished thesis, School of Oriental and African Studies, London, 1988.

Vatikiotis, P.G., *The Fatimid Theory of State*, 2nd edn., Lahore, 1981.

von Grunebaum, E. Gustave, *Modern Islam: The Search for Cultural Identity*, Berkeley: University of California Press, 1962.

Wagoner, Phillip B., 'Harihara Bukka and the Sultan: The Delhi Sultanate in the Political Imagination of Vijayanagar', *Beyond Turk and Hindu: Rethinking Religious Identities in Islamicate South Asia*, Gainesville, Fl: University Press of Florida, 2000, pp. 300–26.

Walzer, Richard, *Greek into Arabic*, Oxford: Bruno Cassirer, 1962.

Watt, W. Montgomery, *Muslim Intellectual: A Study of Al-Ghazali*, Edinburgh: Edinburgh University Press, 1963.

Wickens, G.M., 'Akhlaq-i Naseri', *Encyclopedia Iranica*, vol. I, London: Routledge & Kegan Paul, 1964.

Yadav, B.N.S., *Society and Culture in Nortern India in the Twelfth Century*, Allahabad, Central Book Depot, 1973.

Yarshater Ehsan, 'Persian Poetry in the Timurid and Safavid Periods', P. Jackson and L. Lockhart, eds, *The Cambridge History of Iran*, vol. 6, Cambridge: Cambridge University Press, 1986, pp. 965–94.

———, 'The Indian or Safavid Style: Progress or Decline', in Ehsan Yarshater, ed., *Persian Literature*, New York: Bibliotheca Persica, 1988, pp. 249–87.

———, 'Persian Presence in the Islamic World', Richard G. Hovannisian and Georges Sabagh, eds, *The Persian Presence in the Islamic World*, Cambridge: Cambridge University Press, 1998, pp. 4–125.

Yazdani, G., *Bidar: Its History and Monuments*, London: Oxford University Press, 1947.

Zaman, Muhammad Qasim, *The Ulama in Contemporary Islam: Custodians of Change*, Princeton: Princeton University Press, 2002.

Zeigler, Norman P., 'Some Notes on Rajput Loyalties during the Mughal Period', in M. Alam and S. Subrahmanyam, eds, *The Mughal State, 1526–1750*, Delhi: Oxford University Press, 1998, pp. 168–210.

Zilli, Ishtiaq Ahmad, 'Chishtis and the State: A Case Study of the Relations of Shaikh Nizamuddin with the Khaljis', I.H. Siddiqui, ed., *Islamic Heritage in South Asian Subcontinent*, Jaipur: Publication Scheme, 2000, pp. 46–59.

———, 'Development of *Inshā* Literature to the End of Akbar's Reign', M. Alam, F.N. Delvoye, and M. Gaborieau, eds, *The Making of Indo-Persian Culture: Indian and French Studies*, Delhi: Manohar Publications, 2000, pp. 309–49.

———, 'The Production of Early *Malfuzat*: Fact and Fiction', paper presented at a conference at CEIA, EHESS, Paris, March 2001.

———, 'Early Chishtis and the State', Anup Taneja, ed., *Sufi Cults and the Evolution of Medieval Indian Culture*, Delhi: Indian Council of Historical Research, 2003, pp. 54–108.

Zulfiquar, Ghulam Husain, *Urdu Shā'irī kā Siyāsī aur Samājī Pasmanẓar*, Lahore: University of Punjab, 1966.

# Index